# THE SALLIE HOUSE HAUNTING

## ABOUT THE AUTHOR

Debra and Tony Pickman live with their three sons in Atchison, Kansas. Since their experience of living in the Sallie House, they have become paranormal researchers. Debra and Tony have been featured speakers at various paranormal conferences throughout the Midwest. Visit the Sallie House website (www.thesalliehouse.com) to learn more about their research and investigation into paranormal events.

# THE SALLIE HOUSE HAUNTING

A TRUE STORY

DEBRA PICKMAN

Llewellyn Publications
Woodbury, Minnesota

First Edition
Ninth Printing, 2021

Book design by Donna Burch
Cover © Konradlew, Ruslan Nassyrov, and Maxim Filipchuk
Cover photograph © Debra Pickman
Cover design by Lisa Novak
Editing by Lucy Vilankulu
Interior photographs provided by the author



**Library of Congress Cataloging-in-Publication Data**
The Library of Congress has already cataloged an earlier printing under LCCN: 2010502665



Llewellyn Publications
A Division of Llewellyn Worldwide Ltd.
2143 Wooddale Drive
Woodbury, MN 55125-2989
www.llewellyn.com

Printed in the United States of America

This book is dedicated to my husband, who has not only been an integral contributor in writing this book, but who has also, through the worst of days, toughed it out as the object of a little spirit girl's attention and fascination. I thank him for bearing the brunt of all the physical injuries and afflictions up to and beyond my diary notes which are reflected within these pages.

*To confront one's deepest fears is to show true courage.*

# CONTENTS

# ACKNOWLEDGMENTS

To my sister Karen. Without her suggestion to keep a journal, many of the details in these pages would have been lost.

To those friends and family who believed us, emotionally supported us, and stood by us through the tormenting ridicule of others.

A special thanks to Shannyn Hall for her consistent endeavors in helping with editing and pre-production requirements.

To all the field representatives, psychics, and support personnel whose commitment, compassion, and courage made it all a little easier for us to bear.

And last but not least, a special acknowledgement to psychic Barbara Connor, who reached out to help and guide us when no one else would, and also to our friend Peter James, who through his gentle nature brought us closer to understanding the world we could not see.

# PREFACE

This work is meant to satisfy the curiosity of those who want to know the details of this haunting, and who want to gain a better understanding of the experiences and the processes that were used to reach the conclusions that have been publically presented. This book is for those who research the paranormal through their own investigative work and experiences. It will challenge what we have been told for years, and confront what we think we know about spirits and the activity they supposedly engage in.

In these pages I offer information about who I am and what has made me the person I am today. It will help identify significant traits needed to properly assess a situation and reasonably draw conclusions from the experiences my husband and I went through while living in the house.

From my youth it seems that I've always known that there is more than meets the eye—more than God has shown us, and more than science has taught us. I am not now, nor have I ever been, exceptionally religious or spiritually attuned. I grew up with a fairly strong Catholic background until the age of sixteen when certain circumstances in my life drove me away from the Church. I have since had a major conflict with the teachings of the Bible. I prefer the scientific approach to explaining life and the world around us. I am a "show me proof" type of person and choose to put more credibility in the scientific explanation.

When I was about nine years old, my sister, a few neighbor kids, and I came across a Ouija board. We sat out in the front of our house and tried our best to contact the spirit world. To our dismay, nothing came through. Since then, I have come to learn more about the disadvantages and damage that can result from using Ouija boards, and have not touched one since.

I also remember a teen slumber party where we attempted a séance. Despite our best (unguided) attempts, we achieved no communication with the spirit world. Had any of us known what we were doing at the time, we might have opened up doors, with dangerous results.

As an adult, I have tried not to allow my interest in the supernatural to become an obsession, at least not in a sense that it takes me away from reality and the important things in my life. Except for those childish experiments, I have never been so driven for answers that I have employed any unorthodox method to attain them. I have never used witchcraft, ritual, voodoo, or pagan rites. I have never called on any power other than my own abilities to research when seeking answers. I believe there is a higher power, and that he or she has a plan for us all. In time, we each will know what we need to know and at the time we need to know it.

Although many lose sight of reality, it is extremely important to remain grounded and keep focused in anything you do.

When I was younger my father spent many hours teaching me fundamentals that, in the long run and coupled with common sense, made me the logical and analytical person I am today. Many of the simple examples he used were packed with a tremendous amount of knowledge that I did not appreciate until my later years. One of the most important tools he taught me was to look at things from different perspectives: That no matter what I saw, someone else could see things differently. I needed to see things from all vantage points in order to see a situation clearly.

When we realized our house was haunted, I needed answers and began searching for them at the local library, only to find nothing that had any bearing to our case. The decision to write this book came after months (and countless hours) of research, frustration, and confusion.

Although this book is not based solely on scientific methods, I do hope it will serve others as a basis for comparison with their own studies and investigations. In my search for information and a haunting similar to ours, I found old, limited information often based on secondhand accounts. There is definitely a need to investigate, document, and analyze these events as they occur. In light of the recent wave of paranormal television shows, the public is offered a look into the paranormal world from the safety of their living rooms. I hope more individuals and families will be inclined to share their experiences and call in knowledgeable investigators to help them.

One of my greatest concerns is the reliability of information presented on TV shows, books, documentaries, and haunted tours; I have witnessed firsthand how facts can be twisted. Our own story and the events we lived through have been altered for entertainment or higher ratings. Those taking this creative liberty do not realize that this can confuse, frustrate, and even harm those who rely on this information to help them deal with their own experiences.

The only thing most of these entertainment venues provide is a new level of interest in the paranormal from the general public. In recent years, there has also been an explosion of paranormal information via the internet; our own site dedicated to the Sallie House provides historical resources and information to help distinguish fact from fiction. There is more help for people in need than ever before—they just need to weed through it.

There have been very few brave enough to write of their experiences and take the chance of being ridiculed. Some run from their paranormal experiences; few embrace them and strive to learn from them, and this may explain why there are so few books written with detailed accounts. Years ago, Tony and I were those people, worried about what the neighbors would say. Today we are no longer victims of an extreme haunting; rather we are investigators seeking understanding and a way to provide evidence and help to others.

I truly believe this book is one of a kind and will be enjoyed by paranormal enthusiasts looking for factual information, as well as those looking to experience a true haunting through firsthand experiences.

So, for those with the insatiable interest for "factual" ghost encounters and those who desire to learn about the paranormal through their own experiences, and those of others, I write this for you, without fear of what others may think of me.

# INTRODUCTION

The story of Sallie, the infamous Heartland Ghost, attracts endless rumors and theories of murder, cover-ups, racism, and abuse—all the makings of a horror movie. But this is no movie. This is our life.

The facts surrounding the house, its occupants, and neighbors according to news articles, deeds, obituaries, and other legal documentation are not as innocent as they may have seemed to be. Tony and I had numerous paranormal experiences and he was repeatedly attacked by what many have deemed the spirit of a little girl. Why bother now? The house and its entities demand to be acknowledged for what we now know was more than just attention, and the purpose of our story is to make facts and information available to those who need it.

Our story begins in 1993. We were a young married couple with a baby on the way, renting a turn-of-the-century home that belonged to the family of a doctor back in 1872. Even though there has been much televised attention to the house, this is the first opportunity we've had to share our ordeal, feelings, historical research, and my personal journal entries unedited by the creative efforts of those who would so easily change the facts. This is our story, our life, and even though we moved from the house in 1994, the nightmare still haunts us today and occasionally still leaves its mark.

You, the reader, can walk beside me as I relive the experiences and delve into not only our own evidence, but also that of independent research teams—shocking photos and first-hand experiences that were collected while we searched for reasons and answers as to why this little girl, Sallie, made her presence known to us.

I've made every effort to include direct quotes from the personal journal I kept during our time in that house. It has brought back the turbulent emotions that remain fixed in my memory. When possible I've included dates, times, places, and the names of people present during each occurrence. Although these individuals can be contacted to verify the testimony, I have chosen not to disclose their full identity and in some cases have changed their names for privacy. Out of consideration I refer to family and friends by first name only. Since we live in a small Midwestern town, their privacy is very important to me.

As I describe the strange events that I and others have witnessed, I will discuss how we exhausted every reasonable and logical explanation and theory, and tried to use plain common sense to explain each phenomenon. It is my hope that presenting our efforts will demonstrate the significant attempts we made to search for physical proof of tampering before we drew any conclusions or made any final determinations. I felt my skeptical nature, coupled with our exhaustive efforts, were thorough just the same.

My account is based almost entirely on firsthand experience, and the emotion and reactions tied to that experience. I remember all too well the thoughts that went through my mind when I was alone during an occurrence. Over the duration of our experiences, I have found that the more I think about a particular paranormal event (whether scary or not), the more my fear takes over. Instinctively, I begin to think that whatever happened just couldn't have happened; therefore, it didn't. As hours and perhaps days pass with no further phenomenon, I grow comfortable and shrug off the experience in question...until I witness something else and the process begins again.

If you have an open mind you are more apt to grow comfortable with the idea that anything is possible. Once all logical factors have been ruled out again and again, you are left with one conclusion, a truly unsettling one—supernatural and/or unnatural forces exist.

With the knowledge of how I have reacted in certain situations, I feel comfortable in stating that most people in a similar situation would react and think in a similar manner. This is what my intuition is based on when it comes to identifying whether someone is being honest when describing experiences to me, especially if they are the sole witness to the paranormal phenomenon.

Lastly, and perhaps a significant point of interest, is that the name of this ghost can be spelled two ways: Sallie and Sally. Having only been aware of the later spelling, it was used in my journal and on the drawing Tony did of the little female spirit he saw in the kitchen. Through our research it was realized there was another spelling reflecting a different time period. The ending of "ie" has since been adopted throughout the rest of this book and in all subsequent references.

ONE

# BEFORE IT ALL BEGAN

When I was young, I was a believer in the paranormal and longed for my own experience. In fact, one might say that I have always wanted a ghost of my own and waited years for the opportunity for intelligent communication. I knew there had to be an easy way to do it and given the chance, I was sure I could learn from the experience. In 1993, I was given that remarkable opportunity. I have since come to realize through my own personal experiences in the "Sallie House" that although ghosts do communicate with us, they often use methods we are unaccustomed to. The communications frequently come to us in a manner we are unaware of, therefore rendering us unable to hear, see, or understand that it is there.

My interest in the paranormal may have been a factor in the distance between me and my immediate family. I have always seen things differently and have always been the black sheep. With a desire to step out of the chaos of a dysfunctional situation and control my own life, I left home at the age of sixteen. Over the span of thirteen years, I had lived in several states and ended three marriages. My travels led me to Kansas, where I met Tony. We have been happily married for seventeen years.

Tony came from a religious family and is the second to youngest of eight children. The year we met, I was at the end of a deteriorating marriage and Tony was getting over an equally bad relationship. We frequented the same bar and had secretly watched each other for months before speaking a single word to one another. Each time I saw him in the room I hoped to meet him formally; eventually we did and then spent the evening talking into the wee hours like we were old friends.

Afterwards, not a day passed we did not call or see each other. After a short courtship and several dates, I, my two cats, a dog, and a house full of furniture moved in with him. Spending hours cuddled up on the couch, we talked about so much—childhood memories and our families, religion, dreams, fears, goals, and most importantly, the future we planned to share together. Within a very short period of time there was a level of comfort, familiarity, and security that ignited the solid loving bond we continue to share today. We were married in November of 1992.

It soon became very clear that Tony and I were on opposite ends of the spectrum where the paranormal was concerned. The hope that one day I would have my own experience excited me, whereas any aspect of the paranormal made Tony cringe. There was one conversation, however, that shed a little light on his adamant feelings about ghosts. He described a night when he was young, when he was terribly frightened by the appearance of a male ghost peering out at him from his bedroom closet. Through the rest of his childhood and his adult years, he has avoided both the room and the closet.

We soon discovered I was pregnant, which was a surprise to me, since I had not been able to conceive in my previous marriages. I found it hard to believe and it took time for the reality to set in. Tony, on the other hand, was ecstatic. So, instead of our plans of a February wedding, we were married at the courthouse in November, 1992. As luck would have it, both of our cars were in the shop and we still laugh over the fact that we spent our honeymoon at a local hotel and had to borrow his parents' car to get there. Although we have endured many obstacles in our relationship, we have continued on a destined path. Where I am deficient, he provides; where he faults, I fill in. We've been blessed with both love and friendship.

Here begins our story of life in Sallie's house. Three months pregnant and newly married, my life had finally taken direction. Our first rental home together was quite small and my pregnancy emphasized the need for a larger home. In planning for a family, we were looking for a two specific amenities: a large yard for children and pets to run and play and a much bigger kitchen. We knew that finding our ideal house was not going to be easy. In a small town, you all but have to know someone to get a decent place to rent. In fact, we checked out several dumps before we got a lead from Tony's brother on a small rental house conveniently close, vacant and in need of renters.

This run-down but quaint-looking house stood nestled between two houses just two blocks from the Missouri river. From the outside, it was plain to see it needed a few layers of paint and some attention given to the fences and gardens. I remember wondering why it was the only house on the block that was so low— you had to step down a few steps to enter the front door.

Records for the house and nearby structures revealed that it was the oldest one on the block. The landlord, a local police officer, had purchased the house a month before. He had not been able to do much work on the outside of the house, but had given the inside a much needed face-lift.

We had our first look at the place in mid-December. The feeling in the house was comforting and calm. It had plenty of room for our family and seemed perfect. With the help of family and friends, we moved in on New Year's Eve, 1992. The owner had freshly painted the interior a light peach with a crisp white trim. The colors radiated a level of calm as we entered the house, but looking back, I have often wondered if there was something intangible that drew us to the house.

Although four months pregnant, I enjoyed setting up our first home together. From its exterior, the brick house looked deceptively small.

Inside it was rather spacious, boasting three good-sized bedrooms, one-and-a-half baths upstairs, and a spacious and open floor plan. In our excitement, it didn't take us long to set up house. Little did we know that we were not the only ones living there. Had we known about the other occupants, Tony would never have allowed us to move in.

TWO

# IN THE HOUSE

Although it is difficult to say when it all started, the activity seemed to begin just a few weeks after we moved in. The following is taken from my journal but recalls events that occurred before we realized paranormal activity was happening in our home. Times and dates are approximate in these early entries, since we had no way to pinpoint more detailed information.

## JANUARY-FEBRUARY 1993

We had approximately thirty days of normal life in our home. It was our first Valentine's Day in our new home and after work, I was met at the door by Tony, who had made me a large beautiful heart with a beautiful mushy poem in the center. He had made an incredible Italian dinner to celebrate settling into our new home and the reality that we were having a baby. Little did we know that this wonderful evening would be the last of our ordinary days together.

During a normal evening routine, we would often snuggle on the couch and watch TV. Several evenings in a row, we began to notice that the overhead ceiling light would slowly dim to a soft glow, remaining dim for four to five minutes, and then return to at full wattage. This seemed to happen only at night when we were alone. It was as if someone was using a dimmer switch, which we did not have. This happened sporadically over a period of many weeks and sometimes several times within the same evening.

Tony had checked the switch and changed the bulbs and fuses. At one point we even had an electrician look into the problem to determine if there was a reasonable electrical issue. There was none found. Then one night, when the lights dimmed again inexplicably, Tony joked, "We must have a ghost." We both snickered at the comment and strangely enough, it was the last time the lights dimmed. Had it been a way to get our attention or to be noticed?

Tony and I noticed other strange things happening in the house; subtle little things which we never gave much thought to at the time. I kept a mental note of them and finally wrote them down many weeks later. At the time, we had no reason to suspect a ghost, and we had no reason to keep a written record of events, much less make an effort to uncover trickery or anything else that would have explained the strange occurrences.

When we moved, we brought three cats and a dog with us, all of whom seemed to have paranormal experiences of their own while we lived in the house. The two youngest cats were naturally mischievous—the third was demure and always looking for a quiet place to snooze or hide. Sasha, the dog, was a purebred Samoyed with a very mild temperament who absolutely adored playing with children and animals of any size. Perceptive and protective by nature, she would initially bark at anyone she didn't know.

We had not yet purchased baby furniture for the nursery and so it remained empty for quite some time. The white walls cried out for a theme and decorative touches, but we lacked ideas and inspiration, feeling that it would all come together in due time. One of the first days in the house, Sasha followed Tony upstairs and the two of them stood in the hallway while Tony stared into the room, trying to generate ideas. Tony eventually gave up and walked away, but was drawn back by the dog's incessant barking.

He found Sasha standing outside the nursery, still growling and baring her teeth as if she were being threatened. Looking into the empty room and seeing nothing to warrant such a reaction, Tony tried to calm her by walking into the nursery himself and coaxing her to follow. She wouldn't budge. For a few minutes longer, she continued to show distinct signs of aggressive and defensive behavior.

This strange behavior took place several more times and in the same place. After about a week, however, the threat she sensed was no longer a concern and she had no problem going into or near the room. Tony thought that Sasha might have sensed an unfamiliar animal outside.

A dog will generally consider any stranger a threat until they have become more familiar with the person or until their humans show acceptance of the visitor. After observing no negative reaction from us when the ghost was present (we didn't realize it was a ghost then), Sasha must have concluded it was a friend and stopped being aggressive.

Another typical indicator of a paranormal presence are cold spots or sudden drops in temperature. These cold areas aren't just a few degrees cooler than what is considered to be normal; they can actually be up to forty degrees colder. I think I was the first to notice cold spots.

At no time while we lived at the house did it have central air-conditioning and at the time we could only afford one air conditioner, which we placed in the front window of the master bedroom. Yet I often felt cool air flow past me on the stairs, specifically on the side of the outer wall.

When I first felt it, I thought that the cold was probably from a draft under the door of the air-conditioned bedroom since the bedroom door was just above me and to the right as I walked upstairs. I knew warm air rises and cool air settles, so this theory could not explain the coldness I occasionally felt on my upper body once I reached the top of the stairs.

Over the course of a few weeks, I talked with people who, at one time or another, had been in the house and gone upstairs. I was amazed to find out no one else had experienced the cold feeling except for my brother-in-law's wife.

## MARCH–MAY 1993

During the last trimester of pregnancy, I often found it very uncomfortable to sleep in our water bed. To make matters worse, our only air-conditioner stopped working in mid-May. The heat and humidity was unbearable upstairs, so Tony and I often slept on the couch with the doors and windows open.

One particularly hot night, about 3:30 a.m., when everything in the house and neighborhood was quiet and peaceful, I was abruptly awaken from a sound sleep by what sounded like bloodcurdling screams, then several loud, quick thumps coming down the stairs. Practically in a state of unconsciousness, my only thought was that someone had gotten into the house and was there to do harm. Before I was able to sit up or have any coherent thoughts, something heavy struck my body and face. Stricken with immediate and absolute terror, I screamed at the top of my lungs.

This, of course, woke Tony, who let out an alarming scream equal to mine! As I screamed for the second time, he took a breath. I screamed; he screamed. This went on for several minutes until Tony realized he had no idea what we were screaming about.

Tony tried to calm and quiet me. Wide-eyed and panicked, I sat stiff and motionless in his arms. We both shifted our eyes around the room in an attempt to figure out what had alarmed me so, but saw no telltale signs of anything out of order. Ten minutes later, I had regained composure, but laughed at how ridiculous we must have looked and sounded.

I also noticed my cats' strange behavior. They seemed panicked, their hair was standing on end, and they were slinking around the room as if awaiting an ambush. They were hissing at each other and bolting about, frantically trying to find a hiding place. I had never seen them in this frenzied state.

As I told Tony what had happened, it was as if a light bulb turned on in my head and I realized that the scream I had heard could have come from one of the cats, as well as the distinct and heavy thumping I heard on the stairs and the blows to my body. The question was, what had they encountered that had sent them into such a frenzy? Tony and I decided to take a look.

I remember wondering, as I mounted the stairs, if the neighbor's cat, Marmalade, had somehow gotten into the house. It would not have explained the severe reaction of my cats; they had seen Marmalade many times before.

Oddly enough, as I got to the top of the stairs, I felt a wonderful coolness throughout the whole upper half of the house. We could logically assume that the cool air we felt upstairs was not a result of the night air; it simply was not that cool outside or in the lower level of the house.

When we came back down, we found the cats were still in a panicked and nervous state. No, this abnormal behavior certainly was not the result of running into a neighbor cat. Never had I ever seen such a prolonged response in an animal, especially in a cat. In retrospect, I can't help but wonder if this event had been the first time one or all of the cats had met up with Sallie. Their panic certainly enhanced our own fear and although we may never know what really happened that night, we will never forget how hard we laughed.

## JUNE–JULY 1993

Ghost hunters believe that spirits have the ability to toy with electrical appliances. Knowing nothing about this theory, we were surprised and baffled by activity involving an electric stove top timer.

On June 18, a week before my son was born, I had been cooking in the kitchen and had just put a cake into the second-hand oven we had recently purchased. I set the digital timer for twelve minutes. Less than a minute later, as I was wiping the counter next to the stove, I noticed the timer showed just over four minutes. I looked at my watch and made a mental note on when to take the cake out. Seconds later, my eyes caught sight of the oven timer again, which now read fourteen minutes. I decided to purchase an egg timer on my next trip to the store and didn't give it another thought until the next day.

I had been sitting alone in the living room and suddenly heard an odd buzzing sound coming from the kitchen. I got up and found the oven timer buzzing. I stood there in puzzlement, just staring at it for a while. After about a minute, the timer stopped buzzing and I stood there thinking how strange it was for the thing to stop itself. This model was one where it was up to you to turn off the alarm.

The next day, for no particular reason, the buzzer again went off. The first few times, I hurried into the kitchen and shut it off to stop the annoying buzz. However, the buzzing became so frequent that I simply gave up.

There were also times when the timer went off while we had visitors. At one such time our confused guest said, "No one's been in the kitchen for hours." I nodded my head, and in exasperation told of how it had been going on for days. Someone suggested that we disconnect it and Tony agreed that we probably would. It was the last time the timer went off by itself and after that it kept correct time and worked perfectly fine.

I have often wondered if the buzzing frequencies had been some sort of signal from Sallie, such as a game or an attempt to communicate with us about the timing of something that happened in her lifetime. Perhaps it was something different altogether. Perhaps she was just excited, because on June 26, 1993, our son Taylor Jacob was born.

My doctor insisted on seven days of bed rest after we left the hospital, but I got bored and was anxious to finish decorating the nursery.

On June 28, I pleaded with Tony, who reluctantly gave in and allowed me to start painting.

We had tried for months to choose a theme that would be perfect for the room, but had found it very difficult. Then after the baby was born, for reasons unknown to us, we decided on an even representation of pale pink and baby blue. We had made these choices before knowing about Sallie and afterwards wondered if there wasn't some sort of influence upon that decision.

One day while painting, I hurried to the other room to answer the phone. Fifteen minutes into the conversation, I wandered back to the nursery and a few feet into the room the phone went completely silent. I stood there dumbfounded, wondering if something had happened on the other end of the line. I pressed the "talk" button, which acted as an on/off button, but still nothing.

I rushed towards the door of the room, thinking I might be able to reach another phone before totally losing the connection. As I stepped over the threshold and into the hall, I heard Karen's voice saying, "Hello, hello, are you still there?" It had been at least a minute, if not more, of dead silence.

Not wanting to lose the long distance call again, I remained in the hallway for some time before eventually forgetting and wandering back into the nursery. The same scenario played out again. Afterwards, I recreated the situation several more times and for longer durations of dead silence. Each time the result was the same. We had never had any problem with that phone before (or since), which lead me to believe that something in the nursery was causing interference.

After ruling out battery trouble, we wondered if there was something within the structure of the house and within the walls of the nursery, but we had been on the phone in that room often without any trouble. Once we realized we were being haunted, we learned that spirits give off an intense amount of energy that can create electrical interference.

This interference was not only related to the area in the nursery. It happened on many other occasions in other areas of the house: upstairs and down, in good weather and bad, with local and long distance calls. There seemed to be no real pattern to the disturbances. They sometimes happened so frequently within a single conversation, it was impossible to finish a sentence and I was forced to end the call prematurely. Then one day, the problem ceased completely.

When we first brought Taylor home from the hospital, he had typical newborn confusion. He slept more in the day and awoke often for his feedings in the night. Even though his sleeping habits were naturally a bit backward at first, he began to adapt to a normal regimen. This didn't last long, however, and for weeks we couldn't sleep because he would wake up almost immediately after we laid him in the crib. Tony and I had become so worn out from those sleepless nights that we felt like zombies going through our daily routines.

We asked family and friends for advice, we read books and magazine articles and they all said the same things—that's life with a newborn, it will wear off in a couple of days, try this, try that. We kept waiting for it to wear off, but something just didn't seem right. We ran through all the possibilities we had been alerted to—his cradle wasn't in the path of a cold draft, he wasn't too hot or too cold, his tummy was full, his diaper was clean, and we were pretty sure it wasn't gas or colic because he never sounded that distressed.

We explained Taylor's sleep habits to my sister in New York, who had become a mom herself eighteen months earlier. After offering suggestions to no avail, she offered to fly down. We gratefully accepted the offer.

The day before her arrival, Tony helped me out by doing some of the vacuuming. He had been in the nursery, which was still quite bare except for a changing table and crib. The crib was equipped with the usual blankets, quilts, bumper pads, pillows, toys, and stuffed animals. I had also attached a wind-up musical teddy bear mobile to the side of the crib. While Tony vacuumed, the baby and I were in the only air-conditioned room, across the hall.

Suddenly, Tony came bursting into the room. He said that while he was vacuuming, the teddy bear mobile started playing and turning. I told him about how the new baby monitor worked; one of its special features was if the baby cried for more than a minute, or any other loud noise was generated for the same amount of time, the monitor would play a lullaby in a attempt to soothe the baby back to sleep. I assured him the vacuum had probably set off monitor.

With great conviction, he informed me that it hadn't been because of the vacuum. It was obvious that I had upset him, and he abruptly closed the bedroom door and returned to vacuum the nursery. Soon he was back at the bedroom door, demanding that I take a look. Thinking this was some sort of game he was playing and not being in the mood for one, I told him no. He flatly announced that he was done vacuuming the room.

When we talked about the incident that night, I realized what he had been trying to describe to me earlier was not the loud music of the monitor, but the music of the mobile. I also realized that Tony had actually seen the mobile turning. He adamantly explained to me that the mobile had rotated several times while playing its tune. He had not set it off by bumping the crib because he was nowhere near the crib when he saw the movement. We couldn't come up with an explanation, and by the end of the night we had put it out of our minds.

By now, Taylor was three weeks old. When my sister arrived, she offered to be his caregiver at night to allow us time to catch up on some desperately needed sleep. This worked well. While Karen slept on the couch downstairs, Taylor slept in the cradle near her.

After her first night, I felt so refreshed that we decided to drive to a store in Kansas City to pick up a baby's dresser that matched the crib. When we got back home, Tony and his youngest brother, George, unloaded the dresser from the truck and set it in place in the nursery. Moments later they heard the gentle music of the mobile and watched the carousel turn as the music played. Both agreed that neither of them had wound it up and they came downstairs to tell us what had happened.

I wondered whether Tony had told George about the experience from the previous night and they had conspired to play on it for my sake. I shrugged it off, not wanting to make a big deal about it. As Tony and I got ready for bed later that night, he told me that the mobile coming on by itself had made him and his brother very uneasy.

## THREE

# TEDDY BEARS

Karen's visit was truly a godsend. By taking over the baby's night-time feedings, she allowed Tony and me to get two full nights of peaceful, uninterrupted sleep. We had forgotten what it was like and how rejuvenating it could be. Nevertheless, we really missed having Taylor in our room at night and we didn't want Karen to feel like we were taking advantage of her offer to help out, so on the third night we took back our precious baby and his night-time feedings.

Something was odd, though. Prior to Karen's arrival, Taylor would wake every sixty to ninety minutes. Since her arrival, he had slept for several four-hour chunks of time throughout the night. I didn't give this much thought then, but several weeks later I wondered why the baby had been waking up so often before her arrival and why he had been suddenly able to sleep for long hours while in her care.

Before we realized how quickly the week had gone by, it was July 25 and Karen's last full day with us. Her week-long visit had been uneventful and I'm sure quite boring, since the extent of our nightly entertainment was to rent movies and snack on bite-sized shredded wheat. We never could have anticipated the excitement that was in store for us later that day.

For most of the day we visited at my in-laws' house. We spent time videotaping the baby as well as other relatives of Tony's who had stopped in throughout the day. As we began packing up the baby's things in order to return home, Tony's sister in-law Jan stopped by. She seemed very anxious about something. Eventually she told us that she had dropped by our house just before stopping in at Tony's parents.

A few weeks earlier she had told me about a highchair she no longer needed and I had opted to take it. She had just come from dropping it off at our house. Curious about how we had decorated the nursery, she had gone up to take a peek. Tony and I didn't have a problem with that, but she seemed to feel a nagging guilt about it. In order to relieve her guilty conscience she had sought us out to tell us she had been in the house. I remember telling her that it was no big deal, but she remained nervous and somewhat agitated.

Twenty minutes later, we collected our things and headed across town. We arrived home around 10:00 p.m. Because Taylor was sleeping so soundly, we carried him inside in his carseat and let him sleep. We had barely unpacked the car and the baby's stuff when Tony went upstairs to use the bathroom. When he came back down, he found me in the kitchen and asked why I had moved the stuffed animals in Taylor's room to the floor. Putting the final touches on the nursery that morning, I had displayed several of them in different areas of the room. I hadn't put any of them on the floor. I asked him what he meant.

Looking at me strangely, he explained that all the stuffed animals were sitting on the floor in the middle of the nursery. A little perturbed, I asked, "Well, how did they get there?" My sister came into the kitchen and decided to join us as we went upstairs to look.

Days earlier, I had put a scruffy-looking teddy bear on a small wicker chair just inside and to the left of the nursery room door. I had placed a few teddy bears on a shelf above the crib, several others inside the crib, and a large one on the far side of the room. There were a few other soft or musical stuffed animals laid or hung around the room.

When we got to the room, it was just as Tony had described. All the stuffed animals had been neatly placed in a circle with their backs to each other on the floor in the middle of the room.

We were sure that someone had played a trick on us. We rarely locked the front door. Tony's brother George, or anyone else for that matter, could have gotten in the house to set this up. Perhaps when Jan was in the house she had moved the bears, but I couldn't help wondering why she would have. The more we thought about it, the more unlikely it sounded. If she had wanted to play a trick on us, why would she have gone to the effort to find us and tell us she had been at the house? Besides, it was not in Jan's nature to play tricks like this.

Trying to be logical about the situation, we thought briefly about whether the wind or the cats might have knocked the bears to the floor. But all the windows were closed, and neither of these explanations would account for how the bears all came to be so neatly positioned on the floor.

The three of us stood there for the longest time, just shifting our eyes around the room, and eyeing each other. I checked the bears for any sort of magnet or anomaly within the soft cushioning of the stuffing or anything else that might not have been easily apparent. I thought I might find transparent strings or fishing lines attached to them, but found none.

After exhausting our list of logical possibilities for the strange occurrences, we decided to call Jeanie since she had been the last person in the house. As I dialed the number, I wondered if the toys were already on the floor when she had come into the room to look around. If so, she probably thought we had put them there and didn't think to mention the strangeness of it. I also knew Jan always asked a lot of questions. No matter what the subject, she always had to know why, where, when, and so on. If the bears had been on the floor when she was here, she would have asked about them.

When I got her on the phone, I thanked her for the high chair and chatted for a few minutes, not knowing how to bring up my question. I finally just came right out and said, "Hey Jan, I've got a really odd question for you."

"Yeah?"

"When you were here at the house tonight, did you notice anything weird in the nursery?"

"No, everything seemed to be in perfect order," she said. "Why'd you ask about something weird in the nursery?"

Before explaining the situation, I decided to rephrase my original question. I wanted to be sure that the answer she gave was in no way influenced by what I would tell her. "You didn't by any chance move any of the stuffed animals in the nursery to the floor, did you?"

Calmly, but sounding a little concerned, she said, "No, I didn't touch a thing. Why? Is something wrong?"

I gave her the short version about finding the toys on the floor, but did not say how methodically placed they were. Sounding quite shocked and distressed, she said, "Oh my God," and then called out to her husband.

"I wasn't going to say anything," she started, calling urgently again to her husband. She explained that she had felt really odd while in the house. She had felt that something was very wrong when she had come in. She said that when she'd gone up the stairs, she'd felt a strange cold sensation, and that she'd felt very strongly that something wasn't quite right. When she went into the nursery, she'd felt an overwhelming unease that wouldn't let go of her. She left the room, hurried down the stairs, and out the front door. "It was just really strange; I can't explain it," she said.

At that point, she'd intended to stop by to talk with us at Tony's parents' house, but with all that was going on, she didn't feel the timing was right and let it go. Instead, she profoundly apologized for what she felt was an unannounced intrusion into our house. My heart raced as I relayed Jan's words to Karen and Tony.

If Jan hadn't moved the toys, there were only two explanations. Either someone other than Jan had been in our house between the time Jan left it and the time we got back from my in-laws (about thirty minutes), or the second possibility was one that none of us really wanted to acknowledge. Before any of us spoke the words, Janasked, "Do you think you have a ghost?" She had said the words aloud, and they brought all our stray thoughts to an abrupt halt.

Although I can't remember how I answered her, we soon ended the call. I was left with a disturbing thought, one that up to this point I had been able to push away: perhaps we did have a ghost. I wasn't quite sure how to handle it. Part of me continued to think of the possibilities that having a ghost in the house would bring. The other part clung to the thought that this only happened to other people.

Although the three of us stood in the nursery pondering what seemed to be the last alternate explanation, we returned to the possibility that someone else had gotten into the house while we were gone and set the stage for our return. Tony and his brother George were always playing pranks on each other, so rather than entertain the thought of a ghost any longer, we concluded that it must have been a practical joke. We put the stuffed animals back in their places and Tony turned out the light. We stood for a moment in the hallway, looking back into the room, trying for one last time to assure ourselves that everything was fine.

We descended the stairs. When we reached the bottom of the stairs, Karen glanced back up. When her eyes reached the top of the stairs she noted in a loud, monotone voice, "The light in the nursery is back on." She turned to Tony who had just passed the threshold of the living room and asked, "I thought you turned out the light?"

"I did," he replied. His head tilted quizzically to one side and his eyes were wide.

Seconds later, we were all standing at the bottom of the stairs again, wide-eyed and scared to go back up. Again, we took turns looking at each other, as if waiting for one of us to say, "Ha ha, got ya," but no one did. We each knew we had only been an arm's length from each other. The situation had just become very frightening.

We went back up the stairs, packed closely to each other like a small herd of sheep. We snuck up there as if we might have a chance to catch someone in the act.

We emerged at the top, peered into the room, then stood there motionless for what seem a dreadfully long time staring into what should have been a tranquil room. On the floor in the middle of the room, face up on the floor, lay the small scruffy teddy bear.

We agreed that for the rest of the evening we would stay as close together as possible. This would not only rule out any one of us as the culprit, it would also give us a certain sense of security.

When we had last left the room, I had set the bear back on the little wicker chair just inside and to the left of the doorway. As we stood there, a chilling feeling went through us. Then, still huddled closely and moving as one, we entered the room. Together we checked every square inch of that bear for a magnet, a string or anything else that might explain this trickery. We found nothing.

Now my thoughts got scarier. Had someone been hiding upstairs all along, waiting until he could sneak into the room and set something up? We checked the entire floor and turned up nothing.

Without saying it out loud to each other, we knew we had each been thinking the same thing. Quietly I said, "Since it's playing with the toys, maybe it's a child ghost."

Karen must have been thinking along the same lines. "Maybe it's a nurturing woman who's trying to entertain a baby."

We stood there shifting our eyes slowly at each other, looking for the slightest sign of betrayal. I could tell that each of us in the silence was fighting with the knowledge within. We were the only three in the house and one of us *had* to be making these things happen.

Tony put the bear back on its little wicker chair and I turned out the light. After that, we all headed back down the stairs. As we descended, I feared that as soon I got to the bottom and turned around,

I'd catch a glimpse of activity. But when I got there and looked behind me nothing seemed to be wrong. The others did the same. However, the room remained just as dark as when we had left it.

During the next twenty minutes, we sat in the living room and tried hard not to discuss the recent happenings. Every few minutes one of us would get up and sneak quietly over to the bottom of the stairs, in full view of the others, to see if the light had come back on. Each time, the nursery remained dark.

About 10:50 p.m., I announced that I had to use the bathroom. I could tell that Tony and Karen were shocked that I would think about venturing upstairs, because they asked in synchronicity, "You're going up there alone?"

Pretending to be brave, I said, "Yeah. Why?" They gave each other a look of disbelief.

"We'll wait at the bottom of the stairs for you, okay?"

Whether standing at the bottom of the stairs was their way of keeping an eye on me or out for me, it was okay, because in all truth I was terrified.

If one of them had gone up with me, the other would have been left alone downstairs, and at that point none of us felt comfortable being too far from the others. We discussed this like a covert operation. If both of them followed me upstairs, they would be standing in the hallway just outside the nursery. Both were certain that they didn't want to be in that position. It was agreed that since they could see the doorway to the nursery from the bottom of the stairs, they could also monitor my whereabouts and assure themselves that I wasn't sneaking into the baby's room.

I crept up the stairs while Tony and Karen observed my progress from below. Although scared myself, I decided that as soon as I could see into the nursery, I would peek in and assess the area. I knew I could do this a few steps before actually reaching the upper landing. Not really wanting to, but feeling compelled to do so, I quickly glanced into the room that was dimly lit by the light we had left on in the hall. What

I saw sent a stroke of terror through me and in a low voice I said, "*The bear is on the floor again.*" Karen and Tony came bolting up the stairs to where I still stood staring motionless into the room. Karen said, "Oh, my God, not again." The same bear—which had been, for days, comfortable in the cozy little wicker chair near the doorway—was once again lying in the middle of the floor face up. It was positioned exactly as it had been the last time we found it there.

By this time, our adrenaline was peaking, our blood was racing frantically, and our minds were floundering in a desperate attempt to explain the situation. Again, we carefully inspected the bear, the room, and the surrounding area. We found nothing; no strings tied here or there, no magnets hidden under the carpet or in the bear. We knew that no one had gotten in or out of the house since we last checked the upstairs. I briefly entertained the idea that we had imagined it all, but we knew it was preposterous to assume that all three of us could have imagined the same exact thing.

We stood there just looking at the bear in the middle of the floor. We understood, more solemnly than ever before, that we had likely been witness to the playful antics of a ghost. Speechless, we all stood together, searching each other for some sign of what the others were feeling and desperately trying to fight the crazy thoughts that had begun to creep in. Ghosts do horrible things; they are mischievous, unpredictable, and sometimes just plain nasty. What horrible things would this one do? Would it choose one of us to pick on? Who would it be? When would it start?

Perhaps we didn't run because we still thought that there had to be some logical explanation for what was happening. Perhaps it was simply our curiosity or our unwillingness to be forced out of our own home. Then again, if this turned out to be a trick, we didn't want to be seen running from the house like scared rabbits. We stayed put.

FOUR

# JOSEPH'S VISIT

After the incident with the teddy bear, we decided that we needed someone with an objective point of view—not only someone intelligent and analytical to help us see what we were plainly missing, but someone who could console and calm us. We were sure there had to be a logical explanation for what had happened. We made our way downstairs and waited while Tony called his brother, Joseph. Tony had a hard time persuading him to come over. He explained the strange happenings that had occurred since our earlier phone call to his wife and all but pleaded for him to come over, even if just for a few minutes. Very cautiously Joseph asked, "Really? This isn't a joke, right? You're serious?" Tony assured him we were very serious and in desperate need of his help. When the conversation ended, Joseph had agreed to come over and offer whatever help he could.

The three of us waited for what seemed like forever. None of us knew what to think or say, so we said nothing. Joseph lived just a few minutes away and arrived shortly after 11:20 p.m. I can vividly remember the look of apprehension on his face as we tried to explain what had happened. Later that night he told us, "The only thing that stopped me from thinking that you were all crazy was the fact that I know all of you too well."

After telling Joseph our stories, we led him up to the nursery where the teddy bear still lay on the floor. He suggested that we put the bear back on its chair, turn out the light, and leave the room just as we had done before. We followed his instructions and headed down the stairs. We each took up a spot on the couch, Joseph being the last to sit down. I'm sure he'd taken the time to sneak a look back up the stairs to be sure there was no funny business on our part.

Although we tried to engage in small talk to pass the time while we waited, the conversation returned to the strange things that had already happened. Several times during the conversation, we would all get up and go to the nursery to check for activity. Each time, we found things just the way we'd left them. We began to feel very foolish.

Finding things unchanged on the third trip to the nursery, Joseph suggested putting the items in the same positions as we had found them. "Maybe then something will happen," he said loudly. I know he was trying hard to give us all the benefit of his doubt. We arranged all the teddy bears as we had originally found them and once again headed down the stairs. Joseph continued asking us questions we had already asked ourselves several times. Could the cats have done it? Had anyone else been in the house? Could a breeze or a gust of wind through an open window topple the toys into their positions? And the biggest question of all: had any of us been out of each other's sight?

He was trying to make sense of it all and at the same time trying to catch us off guard, but he came up just as empty-handed as we had. Eventually, he ran out of reasonable explanations for what we had witnessed. Joseph seemed to be quite puzzled about the whole situation, and was probably convinced that it was all a big joke at his expense. After twenty more minutes or so, we all went back upstairs to again find things just as we had left them.

To give our ghost a little more time to "show off" I stood in the middle of the baby's room and hesitantly spoke into the air. "It's OK, you can play now." It was a desperate attempt to get the action we were hoping for so we could confirm the fact that we weren't all crazy. I felt ridiculous and I know I must have looked the part as well. We returned to the first floor and the couch. Suddenly Tony pointed to a stuffed beanbag teddy bear he had given to me as a Christmas gift the year before. It weighed about a pound and stood about twelve inches high. Normally it sat next to the television, facing the room. Now it was facing the wall.

Tony asked, "Who turned it to the wall?"

Of course, all conversation immediately stopped, and in thin, disbelieving voices we each took turns saying, "I didn't." My heart jumped into my throat, my body throbbed with a new surge of adrenaline, and all the nerves that had finally settled down since Joseph's arrival were once again standing at attention. Joseph was the only one who remained calm and skeptical. He asked for our assurance that none of us had moved it and questioned whether it hadn't been that way earlier.

Karen was quick to tell him, "The last time we were all downstairs, I remember looking at it and it was facing forward." As she continued to speak, the bear in question never left her sight because she glared at it from the corner of her eye, almost daring it to move again. "The bear was facing forward. I swear!" she said with the strength of her conviction.

The three of us just sat there, unable to move or speak for several minutes. During this silence Joseph went over and picked up the bear, and then broke the silence. Surprised, he said, "Boy, it's heavy!" Then he put it back down, making sure it was facing forward. Although he didn't want to admit to the possibility of a ghost, he did acknowledge that there was definitely something weird going on in the house. What it was he didn't know, but he could tell from how shaken the three of us appeared, that we were genuinely upset and in need of some answers.

Joseph offered to talk to his boss' sister, Barbara, who was coming to town. She was a well-known psychic who had grown up in town but currently lived in California. "I'll get back to you tomorrow," he said, as he closed the front door, leaving us in complete silence.

Not knowing what to do next, we sat quietly. Our eyes roamed the room, watching for some sort of movement. Restless and wanting to talk to someone, Tony phoned his mother and told her what had happened. She suggested that we pack up a few things and spend the night with her. Tony told her that if anything more happened, it would be our first move.

None of us felt right about imposing on her with four unexpected guests for the night, and I didn't want the added hassle of packing all the things we would need to take with us. "There's nothing wrong," we thought. "We're strong, nothing really bad has happened. We are perfectly fine because all of this might just be in our heads."

Although we were willing to stay in the house, we had to figure out new sleeping arrangements. Karen did not want to sleep alone on the couch as she had been doing. Without thinking, I blurted out, "Perhaps Tony or I could sleep downstairs with you." Tony's instant response was, "Don't think you're going to leave me upstairs alone!" We laughed. The laughter helped eased the tension, but none of us wanted to be alone. Eventually we decided that the safest, most comforting place to sleep would be behind locked doors in the master bedroom.

To this day, each of us laughs at how stupid and childish our reasoning had become by that point of the evening. It's funny that we thought a locked door would stop a ghost. There was really nothing that would stop it from coming into the room with us.

It was now 1:35 a.m. When we had gathered up all that we needed for the night and headed upstairs, we were almost too apprehensive to look into the nursery. At first we thought everything was just as we had left it. However, hanging from a cloth handle on the nursery room doorknob, had been a tiny stuffed heart with the print of a small teddy bear. Tony didn't have to utter a word as he pointed to it; we all knew there was something wrong as we looked at his face. The heart had been turned around so that the bear print faced the door. Although we were not quite sure at what point it had been turned around, Karen remembered admiring it just before we had left for our visit to Tony's parents earlier that afternoon.

It's remarkably hard to put into words all the feelings I had at that moment. Although the stuffed heart being turned around may seem insignificant, it was just enough to set off what little nerves I had left. One minute I was cool, calm, and seemingly in control; the next my heart was again in my throat. As suddenly as the realization hit us we all tried to scream, but all that would come out were faint screeches. Terror-stricken, we ran into the master bedroom and slammed the door shut behind us.

I had collected many plush bears over the years, and it was common to see them in every room of the house. The master bedroom was no different. Once inside the room, I caught sight of them and stood motionless as a dreadful thought came to mind: would the stuffed animals indulge in more playful activity? I barely extended my finger to point to the very large teddy bear on the top of the highboy. I quietly whispered, "The bears; there're lots of them in here." I looked at the bears and determined that none of them had been moved. We each made a mental note for later comparison.

Huddling in the bedroom and feeling ridiculous, we soon realized we had not brought up the television, VCR, or movies. This meant another trip downstairs. We figured two people could bring up what was needed in one trip, and Tony and Karen headed down to the first floor.

While collecting the equipment we needed, Tony and Karen surveyed their surroundings for anything peculiar. Paranoid by this time, they took particular notice of the bean bag teddy bear sitting next to the television. Karen remembered the video camera she had brought with her from New York and set it up to film what she could of the living room. She hoped she might capture something on film during the night.

Ready to return to the second floor, Karen carried the VCR and the movies. Tony, about two feet behind her, carried the television and cords. Karen had taken approximately four steps past the corner of the doorway and was still able to see Tony. He was on the other side of the living room doorway, battling with the cumbersome load in his arms, when he spotted a quick movement out of the corner of his right eye.

Something had moved right where the television had been. Tony saw that the bean bag bear, which had been facing forward the whole time they were downstairs, was now facing the wall. In the blink of an eye, the bear had spun around. When it did, Tony just happened to catch a glimpse of the movement.

Realizing what happened, he let out a horrified, "Oh, shit!" Karen asked, "What?" Tony was unable to move or speak, and when Karen looked, she noticed the position of the bear herself and screamed, "Oh my God!" They bolted up the stairs and burst into the bedroom, both very much out of breath. After regaining what little composure they had left, they told me what had happened. Then Karen suddenly blurted out in exasperation, "I forgot to turn the video camera on!" We were a little disheartened but knew none of us were going to brave another trip outside that room.

After recapping the terrifying events of the evening, we simply sat there: three adults scared half out of our wits, one sleeping infant, a large dog, and three cats, all in a small upstairs bedroom. I put the baby down in his cradle and the rest of us sat close on the bed, waiting for our nerves to calm and our heartbeats to return to normal. Karen and I arranged the cushions on the floor with a sheet and blanket while Tony set up the TV and VCR. Ironically, we had rented two horror movies. Lucky for us, the third rental was a comedy, which we unanimously voted to watch! Eventually, we fell asleep.

FIVE

# THE MORNING AFTER

The next morning, Tony left for work about 6:45. Around 8:00 a.m., Taylor, Karen, and I woke up. We puttered around upstairs, getting ready for the day, and didn't see anything amiss. We talked about how foolish we had been the night before and laughed about how ridiculous we'd acted. It was embarrassing to think about how we had run around in such a panic.

Karen got dressed and went downstairs to pack the rest of her things for the flight home. After the activities of the previous night, I was rather shocked when she went downstairs alone, but since she had an early flight back to Buffalo, it left us very little time to get out the door and be on our way. Our experiences from the night before seemed like a distant dream. Daylight is an amazing boost for bravery.

Since she had forgotten to turn on the video camera, Karen felt confident nothing had been recorded. She began to pack up the recorder without reviewing the tape. Just as she was about to dismantle it, she noticed that the viewfinder had been pulled into an upright position. Although this was not the position she had left it in, she thought maybe Tony had played with it before leaving for work and didn't give it much thought.

Curious to see if he had recorded anything, she put her eye to the viewfinder. She was puzzled by her immediate ability to see a portion of the room she was in. She knew that when you could see through the viewfinder, it meant that the camera was in an energy saving stand-by mode that lasted only a few minutes before the camera shut itself off. In other words, someone or something had interacted with the camera only a few minutes before she'd peered into the viewfinder. Thinking the camera had possibly malfunctioned, and not wanting to draw unwarranted conclusions, she packed it up without saying a word.

En route to the airport, Karen pulled out the camera to film some interesting sights. Kansas and Missouri had had so much rain prior to her arrival that it flooded our whole area, including much of the road to the airport. While filming, she told me what she had noted before leaving the house. During the drive, we tested the automatic shutoff. It seemed to work perfectly, taking the normal three minutes to shut down. We did the math—Tony had left for work more than an hour before Karen or I got up, which meant he couldn't have caused the camera's "ready" mode. When I asked Tony about it later, he said he hadn't touched the camera.

Although we talked as we drove the rest of the way to the airport, we avoided any talk of ghosts. As Karen started to board her plane, I said with pleading eyes and voice, "Hope you had a good time." We both laughed as she responded, "It sure turned out to be an interesting visit!" The sound of her laughter and the happy look on her face assured me that she had enjoyed herself despite the last twenty-four hours of hair-raising experiences.

On the long drive home my mind wandered over the many odd things that had happened during Karen's last night. Before I knew it I was parking the car in front of our house. I really didn't feel nervous or scared as I opened up the front door. I was, however, anxious to see if anything would happen while I was there alone. I decided to make every effort to go about my normal activities as naturally as possible.

As I walked through the house, I could feel my muscles tighten with each step. I scrutinized each room, trying to note where and how various items were placed. I felt like a soldier walking around in an unfamiliar jungle: eyes focused forward, neck stiff, and mind acutely tuned to my surroundings. I paid especially close attention to what I could see in my peripheral vision.

Although I was quite eager for something to happen, I was also very apprehensive. I had always hoped for the experience of turning around to suddenly see a ghostly figure standing or floating behind me, unable to make itself disappear before I caught sight of it. But now that it was actually a possibility, I wasn't sure how I would react. Would I be able to handle it calmly or would I jump out of my skin?

As the hours went by with nothing ghost-like happening, I began to suspect that ghosts were active only during darkness. The uneasy feelings and elevated stress diminished, and before long my sense of curiosity began to surface. The events of the previous night seemed like a movie, something that hadn't really happened. To validate that we really did have paranormal activity, I needed to experience it again. Feeling much calmer, more collected, and clear-headed than the night before, I began to think about how much I had wanted such an experience. The opportunity to experiment with spirit communication was at my finger tips, and I was actually getting excited about it.

Tony was often late getting home from work because he'd stop at his parents' house for a visit. On this day, however, he was unusually late and I began to worry. Had the events of the previous night gotten to him? Had he decided not to come home at all? When he finally showed up, he was barely into the living room before he began telling me what his mother had just told him.

After Tony's phone call to her the previous night, her curiosity had gotten the best of her. While I was taking Karen to the airport, Tony's mother, whom I've always called "Mom," contacted a long-time acquaintance who happened to be the mother of the house's previous tenant. Mom had asked if the woman had ever experienced anything odd while living in the house. This woman volunteered to call her daughter who was currently living in another state. Later in the day, the woman returned Tony's mom's call with some interesting information.

Her daughter reported that she would often smell something odd or foul in the house. She also said that her young son had slept in the corner bedroom, which was now the nursery. She went on to say that she was always picking up his toys and reprimanding him for not putting them away. The boy would often retort, "But, Mama, I didn't play with those toys." The mother had always chalked it up to the typical fibs of a child not wanting to be responsible for picking up his toys.

She added that her daughter had had the bedroom with the walk-in closet. She hadn't remembered anything strange about the room, with one exception. She remembered her little girl had not only grown attached to an imaginary playmate named Sallie, but would entertain herself for hours playing with her in the closet. Remarkably, the little girl had not spoken of Sallie since moving away.

We found the information quite interesting. "Perhaps we have a little girl ghost by the name of Sallie?" I wondered out loud. We both just looked at each other, silently wondering if this was a possibility.

Tony's brother Joseph called. His boss, Annie, had called her sister Barbara and briefly relayed our experiences. Barbara, without having met or talked to us, said she felt we had the spirit of a young girl between five and thirteen years old. She also felt the little spirit not only liked the house and felt comfortable there, but was protecting a baby.

Barbara also explained that the movement of the stuffed animals was probably this little spirit playing with them as if they were her own toys. Barbara had asked Annie whether or not our baby could see this spirit. Even though Annie did not know much about the situation and couldn't answer the question, Barbara had felt confident that Taylor probably could. She had explained to Annie that controlled testing using infrared cameras has shown that young children can see spirits whereas adults—even those sitting right next to the children—cannot. Annie couldn't answer the next question Barbara had asked, either: "Has the baby been waking up a lot during the night?"

The idea that Barbara had known to ask this question indicated she had been able to focus on what had been taking place in our home and she was trying to verify what her psychic abilities had been picking up. As a new mom uncertain of my motherly instincts, I had often blamed myself concerning Taylor's night time sleeping habits; I just knew I must be doing something wrong. Not wanting others to think of me as a failure or a bad mother incapable of taking care of Taylor, I had told no one of the baby's sleeping trouble except my sister. For Barbara to have hit on such a major issue from as far away as California, not to mention by way of a fourth party, was truly astonishing—and it eased the thoughts that it had somehow been my fault.

I held the phone tightly to my ear, listening to the information Barbara had provided. While doing so, I began to draw even more parallels. For instance, I found it uncanny that Barbara had described our spirit as a young girl, the same conclusion I had come to. The idea that she believed the spirit was "playing" with the stuffed animals again paralleled my thoughts. "It's okay, you can play now," I'd said in the nursery.

Barbara suggested we tell the ghost that although she was welcome to stay with us, she would have to behave; she could play with the toys, but she had to put them back when she was done. We were also instructed to make it clear that this was our house and if she wanted to stay with us, she would have to follow our rules.

Joseph said Barbara would welcome a phone call from us and I wrote down the number. Just before ending the conversation, Larry told me the most bone-chilling thing I had ever heard: Barbara had casually mentioned a name which was persistent and overwhelming in her mind. The name was Sallie. I managed to say good-bye before hanging up the phone, but my heart had momentarily stopped as I felt the weight of what that name meant. The imaginary friend named Sallie, which the previous tenant's daughter had played with, was actually a ghost.

I took a couple of deep breaths to calm my thumping heart. Seeing the worry on Tony's face, I recapped everything Joseph had told me. Afterward, we fell silent. We were dazed by the information that his mother and Barbara just revealed to us.

The probability that we had a ghost had just increased greatly. It was like finding out that the adoption went through and there was a new baby waiting for you. Now how would we deal with it? To be perfectly honest, denial would have been a lot easier. I still wasn't sure I was ready to accept the existence of a ghost in our home; I knew Tony wasn't.

I brought up what I felt were obvious concerns and questions. How will we communicate with her? How old is she? When is her birthday? Had she ever lived in the house? Did she die in the house? Why had she chosen to make herself known while my sister was visiting? Was night her only active time? Most importantly, was the baby in any danger ?

We found ourselves wondering about Taylor seeing Sallie. Did she scare him with her antics or did he like her gentle playfulness? This brought to mind Taylor's disturbed sleeping patterns. Was Sallie responsible for this? When we first brought Taylor home, he slept the entire first day. As a result, he was up every hour through the night. We chalked it up to the fact that he was simply trying to make the adjustment from the womb and would soon realize daytime was for being awake and nighttime was for sleeping. Everything we had read had described this transitional phase and said that it would only last a few days. Taylor's adjustment period was going on three weeks.

During my sister's visit, Taylor seemed to sleep just fine. Had Sallie decided not to wake the baby while he slept near my sister? Had Karen's visit and her being a stranger in the house made Sallie uneasy? Still, the question of why she had been waking him in the first place kept coming back. Had Sallie just wanted to play with him, or was there a more important reason for her actions?

Before long, I found myself worrying about Sudden Infant Death Syndrome (SIDS), and I wondered if our son had fallen victim to SIDS several times; perhaps Sallie's waking him had actually been her way of reminding him to breathe. If this were true, we were greatly indebted to her. Of course, we had no way of knowing the answers to our questions and decided to move forward one day at a time.

Around 10:30 p.m., realizing we had talked through the entire evening, Tony and I decided to go to bed. Having just walked upstairs, Tony reached to turn out the hall light. His hand was on the light switch, but he hadn't flipped it and I noticed his blank stare. He was absolutely motionless. I asked him what was wrong and with one of those you've-got-to-be-kidding expressions, he said, "Do you see anything odd?"

I gave him a questioning look as he extended his right arm and pointed to the wall of the stairwell. There, where we had hung a variety of family pictures, I noticed the odd thing that had captured his attention. The photo of Tony and me, although perfectly straight and centered, had been turned upside down. "What do you think it means?" he asked. I shrugged, not wanting to scare him with what was really on my mind, and said, "Maybe she likes us."

"Good night Sallie," I added as I entered the bedroom. Tony did a great job of ignoring what he'd seen along with the fear hammering at his heart. He turned out the light and came to bed.

## SIX

# SCRATCHES AND REPRIMANDS

### JULY 27, 1994

Although we were shaken up by this new development and the idea that more unexplainable things could happen at any moment, the remainder of the night passed without incident.

The next day was uneventful until about 5:00 p.m., when Tony's younger brother George stopped in to visit with the baby—something he did daily since he lived just next door. George, who was just as terrified of ghosts and ghost stories as Tony, showed more interest than I'd expected. His curiosity had been piqued and he wanted to know more.

Tony took him up to the nursery and described how the stuffed animals had been arranged the night before my sister left. George studied the room and its contents, looking for tell-tale signs of trickery. Then with a very serious look on his face, he asked Tony if he had been joking about the whole thing. Perhaps he figured if he caught Tony alone, their brotherly bond would bring out the truth. Tony denied that we'd made up any of it and after a while they returned to the living room.

Arriving downstairs and eager for an ally, Tony showed George the beanbag teddy bear which had been moved. George still wasn't convinced that we were being haunted.

Earlier in the day, I had taken pictures of Taylor and had left our 35mm camera sitting on the dining room table. Being somewhat bored with George's behavior, Tony picked up the camera, aimed it at the beanbag bear, and said, "Sallie, if you're in here, smile and say cheese." George, focusing on the bear, had been standing just off to the side as Tony clicked the shutter button. George shouted, "It moved! The God-damned thing moved!"

Although I'm sure he wasn't ready for the truth, he got what he had been looking for. He had just been witness to paranormal activity occurring right before his eyes. In fact, he reported that he actually saw the bear do an about-face in roughly the same instant that Tony snapped the photograph. As George shouted, Tony quickly snapped off another shot. Tony and George were struck with terror when they realized what they had witnessed.

Their first instinct was to run upstairs where I had been with the baby, and although Tony's legs were in complete agreement, George's failed him. As Tony reached the bottom of the stairs, he heard George say, "Man, I can't move." Tony, not really wanting to slow down, looked at George, whose face was now colorless. He had difficulty breathing, and Tony could see him gasping for air.

George tried to walk, but he looked as if something or someone had a firm hold on him and was forcing him backward. He later described the feelings. "I felt a sudden and noticeable coldness go right through my entire body." He also described that no matter how hard he tried to control or force his muscles, he just couldn't move forward. Whether this was Sallie's doing or his terrified state of mind, we will never know.

After what probably seemed like a lifetime to George, he was able to regain some control over his motor reflexes and sprint up the stairs just behind Tony. Gasping for breath, they burst into the upstairs bedroom where I'd been watching TV. Since I had been unable to hear anything outside the room due to the air-conditioner running, I had no idea what brought them barreling into the room. At first I thought they were hysterical with laughter. I thought they had run to me for cover and protection after pulling a prank on a friend who was now coming after them for retaliation. I gave them a disapproving look, wondering what crazy thing they had just done. Then I noticed George's pale face and realized it wasn't amusement I was seeing—it was terror.

Between short breaths, Tony tried to fill me in. For quite a while, George didn't say a word. He just stared at the floor, shaking his head from side to side. He paced back and forth like a caged animal, saying, "I can't believe it. Oh my God, I actually saw it move. Oh my God. Oh God. Oh shit. Oh God."

Thinking he might be in a state of shock, I had him relay his experience. Then we all talked about what happened. Each time Tony or George retold a portion of their experience, they tensed up all over again. The guys decided we should all leave the house immediately. Being at my un-laws' house would help calm their nerves.

George wasted no time getting downstairs and out the front door. He obviously didn't want to be in the house any longer than he had to. As he paced in front of the house, waiting for us, Tony and I dashed around, gathering the baby and some necessities. We rushed down to the living room, where I placed Taylor's car seat on the sofa and set off to gather a few more things. Tony placed the baby in the car seat and began to buckle him in. Taylor, who had been perfectly content, was now crying and seemed unusually upset. All I can think is that he somehow sensed our anxiety.

Having grabbed what I needed, I stood next to Tony as he tucked in the baby and began to snap the buckle in place. I was packing the diaper bag I had placed on the couch just to the right of the car seat. Tony sat just to the left of the car seat. He was facing Taylor as he leaned in closer to give him the pacifier, hoping it would soothe his distressed cries.

Suddenly, and with a painful grimace, Tony jumped to his feet and quickly flung his arm around to feel for something on his lower back. "Ow! Damn it!" Almost the same instant Tony jumped up, I felt a cold and slightly electrical charge of energy go right through me. It seemed to have entered my back and exited through my torso, right in the direction where Tony had been sitting.

Being more concerned with Tony and why he jumped from obvious pain, I did not take the time to really acknowledge the sensation I'd just had. "What's wrong?" I asked. He scowled, "Oh, probably nothing, but I think something just bit me." We initially thought some sort of bug must have gotten under his shirt, and since we were in such desperate haste to leave, we didn't take the time to inspect his lower back until later.

We were finally out the door and headed to my in-laws with George and the baby in the back seat. I thought of the strange cold sensation I'd had just as Tony had been bitten. I relayed the information to the men and silence fell as we each tried to understand what it could have been. As soon as we arrived at my in-laws', Tony and George conveyed what had happened. The whole time they were telling the story, George paced back and forth in the room out of nervousness.

The story having been told, I remembered the pain in Tony's back. I pulled him aside to lift his shirt and inspect the area. To my surprise, I found three bleeding scratch marks, each about five or six inches long, running down the center of his lower back. My eyes grew wide with shock as I said, "Oh my God!"

I gently let the shirt fall back down into place, turned away, and thought, I don't want to see this. Subconsciously, I must have thought that if I didn't look at it, I wouldn't have to acknowledge it.

I lifted his shirt again, hoping the scratches would be gone and I could chalk this experience up to my imagination, but they weren't. For a fleeting moment I thought Tony had done it, but he would not have been able to reach far enough around his back to scratch himself.

Besides, I had full view of both his hands as he tried to quiet the baby and while we drove to his parents' house.

The thought that Sallie might have done this sent chills down my spine and throughout my body. My heart raced. Then anger set in. To think this little piss-pot ghost would dare hurt someone I loved, in my own house, made me furious. A few minutes later, the anger turned to curiosity, and I wondered how a ghost could do something like that. I was stunned by the possibility that ghosts could make physical contact. I had never heard of such a thing, and it led me to even more troubling thoughts. Why would she have done this horrible thing to Tony? What were we supposed to do about this situation? What could we expect next? Were we in danger? Was the baby in danger?

It took several minutes for me to calm down. Thinking more clearly, I documented the scratches with a photograph but soon realized that a photo would not offer proof that a ghost had actually been responsible for the marks.

## INTERVENTION

Realizing we needed a little more help, I finally called Barbara. Although I really didn't want to bother her during her vacation, I felt this was significant enough to warrant a call. I picked up the phone and dialed the number, not giving any thought to what I was going to say when she answered.

We had never met or spoken before, so I introduced myself, trying to maintain a calm, controlled voice. I didn't want her to think I was in a panic over something trivial or that I was simply some sort of nut. We had a few minutes of idle ghost conversation, which soon turned into a barrage of questions from me. "How do we know when she's in the house? Can she reach things much taller than her?" I was thinking about the upside-down picture on the stairwell. "Yes, she can," Barbara said. "She can go anywhere. She can be crawling on the ceiling, or hovering over your bed. She can do anything she wants to."

"Why is she here?"

"She likes the baby. She's like a little angel and wants to protect him."

"Why is she doing the things she's doing?"

"To let you know she's there. If she just floated through the door, you wouldn't know she was there. But if she opens the door, you know she is in the room. She wants your attention; she wants to be noticed."

Barbara reiterated many of the things that had already been relayed to us through Joseph. "You should talk to her and acknowledge her. Tell her she can stay if she wants to, if that's okay with you, but be firm in letting her know she has to follow your rules. Tell her she can play with the toys, but she has to put them back when she's done. You have to let her know that there are rules, she has to obey them, and if she doesn't, she'll be punished."

My immediate thought was, "Okay, now we're getting a bit ridiculous." We were actually discussing punishing a ghost for bad behavior? Before I could get a word in edgewise to ask how we were supposed to punish her, Barbara was on to other things. Eventually, she had given me so much information and so many suggestions on how to handle the ghost that I felt completely overwhelmed. I knew I wouldn't be able to remember all she was telling me, but I did understand the main idea: We should handle Sallie like we would any other little girl.

Barbara also told me that she got a lot of good feelings from her. "She's a happy little girl and she is there because of the baby. She would probably move pieces of furniture or tug frantically at your shirt to get your attention if the baby was in trouble. I don't get the feeling she'll intentionally harm anyone." There it was, the big topic, the main reason for my phone call. I finally offered "Well, she certainly did tonight." I could tell Barbara was a bit surprised by the news, but she listened intently as I told her about the scratches.

Calmly, Barbara assured me that she didn't think Sallie did it intentionally or maliciously, but most likely Sallie had misinterpreted

Tony's emotions, which had been very intense at the time. "She probably thought Tony was going to hurt the baby, and was just trying to protect him." Almost as if she were talking to herself she said, "This makes me mad! This is no good. This makes me real mad."

The rest of the conversation was more instructive. Barbara gave me suggestions about how to handle the situation. "You need to go home and have a serious talk with her," Barbara reiterated. "Call her into the room and tell her you are mad."

"How do I do that, and how do I know she'll come?"

"You call to her just like you would call any other child in the house. You tell her, "Sallie, if that's what you call her, we are angry and need to have a talk with you, so you get in here right now! And don't worry, she'll come. Give her a few minutes to come to where you are. Then tell her you are very angry, and that what she did was very wrong, you and Tony are that baby's parents, you need to take care of his physical needs, and she is NOT to interfere." Barbara spoke with such harsh conviction and force that I felt myself cowering. "Tell her if she hurts anyone again, she will be punished."

I thought, okay, here we go, I'm going to come out of this next question looking like a fool. "How do we punish her?" Barbara responded matter-of-factly, "You might send her to her room and tell her to stay there for a while. You could tell her she can't play with a particular toy or object. If talking to her doesn't work, there are other ways to get rid of her." With a little hesitation, she added, "If you want to."

"How?" I asked.

Barbara enlightened me once more. "You could have the house blessed by a priest. There is also an incantation you can say while going into each of the rooms, or you could have her exorcized. I can help you with these if you want."

Not wanting to be too hasty, and knowing I would have felt bad throwing a young spirit out of a place where she seemed to be so comfortable, I told Barbara we would first try to talk to her and see how it went.

My final question was whether or not she could be wrong about the spirit in our house being that of a pleasant little girl. She told me she didn't think so, but in order to get a better reading of the situation, she would have to come to the house. At the time, I wasn't really sure what she meant. Had she simply been making a comment about her abilities and that they were somewhat limited due to her not being closer to the entity she was trying to pick up on? Or was she coyly asking for permission to come to the house for business purposes?

We had been told that Barbara made a good portion of her living by going to peoples' homes and giving readings on the spiritual nature of what she found there. We had also been informed that there was a costly charge attached to this type of service, one we surely couldn't afford. I didn't offer her an invitation. In fact, I simply treated her statement as if it were another piece of information. I graciously thanked her for her help and told her we would be in touch if we needed more assistance. "Good luck," she said.

After hanging up, I let out a big sigh—not in relief because I felt better about our situation, because I really didn't feel that at all. I was just so overwhelmed with the information I had accumulated in the conversation with Barbara that I was relieved it was over and I wouldn't have to take in any more.

For the next few hours, my in-laws, Tony, George, and I talked about some of the things that Barbara had brought up. Eventually it was time to go home and Tony and I were able to discuss things in more detail. It had been hard to talk about things the way we wanted to at my in-laws' house because we both knew that their religious beliefs would dominate our discussion, and their lack of acceptance would obliterate any plausible theories and scenarios we might offer.

What we discussed most was how we were supposed to confront Sallie when we returned home. Although Tony was being forced to accept the idea of a ghost living and interacting with us in our own home, he didn't accept it easily or take it well. In fact, he didn't want any part of it. "You'll have to be the one to do the talking, because I just can't," he said. Then he informed me that a ghost is something that is supposed to be dead, and that the idea of holding a conversation with something that is supposed to be dead was just too weird for him. Thinking that perhaps he would eventually grow accustomed to talking to our ghost, I said "That's fine."

## REPRIMANDS

We got to the house a few minutes later. I was a little nervous and uncomfortable with the idea of doing what needed to be done, and I wasn't sure I'd be able to do it right. As we approached the front door, I couldn't help wondering if the things I would tell Sallie would just piss her off. I certainly didn't want to send this little ghost off on some crazed binge of retaliation, and who knew what she was capable of in a fit of anger?

We cautiously opened the front door, peering in to see what, if anything, had moved or taken place during our absence. As we stepped over the threshold, I could feel my heart rate increase tenfold. However, as we looked around, nothing seemed to be amiss. We put the baby, still in his car carrier, on the end of the couch near the front door (the same spot where Tony had been sitting when he got scratched). After taking a minute to figure out how I was going to go about this one-sided conversation, I called out in a controlled voice. "Sallie, we are very angry and need to talk with you, so you better get in here right now." I hoped I hadn't been too harsh, but then I remembered something Barbara had said. "She needs to feel loved and know she's cared about, just like any young child does." Barbara had also expressed the idea that children need and desire the strong upper hand of a parent.

A few minutes later, Tony and I looked at each other and shrugged our shoulders, wondering whether she was in the room with us, let alone the house. How would we have known? On the other hand, what if she was in the room, waiting for us to talk to her? If she was, I certainly didn't want to lose her attention, so I continued with my half-planned lecture. I started out by firmly telling her that what she had done to Tony was bad and we wouldn't stand for that kind of behavior. I explained that Taylor was our baby, not hers, and she could play with him nicely, but she was not to interfere with what we needed to do for him. I also informed her we were his mommy and daddy, we loved him very much, and we would never do anything to hurt him.

I kept looking around the room for some sign of her presence, but found none. Usually when a person talks to someone, eye contact is made. I felt really odd not knowing where to look as I continued speaking to her. I also felt strange about reprimanding someone who was probably floating above me or, worse, not there at all. After a short pause, I informed her that the house she lived in was now ours and even though she may have been there first, it was still ours, which meant we were the bosses. "If you want to stay, it's okay with us, but you will have to follow our rules." Then I listed the rules she would have to follow: no hurting people, no playing with the pictures on the wall, no waking the baby, and after she played with the toys, she would have to put them back so no one would trip over them and get hurt.

As I talked, Tony began to notice a few odd things, especially the behavior of our cats. He had been watching them for several minutes and finally caught my eye to get me to notice them, too. Usually they roamed around whatever room we were in, contemplating trouble they could get into or searching for something to play with. However, this time all three of them were sitting on the floor of the dining room about ten feet in front of us. Silence fell as we observed the back and forth movements of their heads. Their movements were perfectly synchronized with each other as they watched something in the air above. They looked as if they were following each volley of the ball in a tennis game. Apparently the cats were watching something we just couldn't see. Perhaps this meant that Sallie was in the room.

A few minutes passed, and not wanting to lose my audience of one, I resumed my talk while Tony kept an eye on the curious movements of the cats. He noticed that their attention was now focused on the ceiling fan above us. Again, he gently nudged me and motioned for me to look. From the fan hung two separate balls on chains. One ball was brass and controlled the light, and the other was wooden and controlled the fan speed. What had caught Tony's attention was the fact that the wooden one was steadily swinging in a six-inch circle.

Tony and I glanced at each other. We had not turned the ceiling fan on when we got home, nor was there a draft from an open window or door because all were closed. On top of that, we had never seen the wooden ball on our fan or on anyone else's fan swing in that way. We must both have been wondering if the ball on the ceiling fan in the dining room was swinging too, because suddenly we both looked over at it. When we found no movement there, we looked back to the one above our heads.

Over the next ten minutes, we noticed more strangeness. The little wooden ball would occasionally come to a complete stop—not as if naturally slowing down, but stopping somewhat abruptly. For a couple of seconds, it would remain perfectly motionless. Then, for no apparent reason, it would start swinging again in the opposite direction.

Watching the ball, I continued to talk to Sallie and, as I did so, noticed a strange coincidence. Each time the ball stopped swinging, the baby would wake up and stare ahead with what seemed to be great concentration. Within seconds, he would fall back to sleep. Looking back at the wooden ball, we would find it swinging once again. It didn't take us long to conclude the cats—and the baby—had been observing Sallie's antics.

Her initial flight above and about the room had entranced the cat's attention until her efforts were directed to the balls on the ceiling fan and then to the baby. We concluded Sallie was making her presence known. Just like normal children do when you're trying to talk to them and their attention leaps toward something more interesting. She was moving around. It also seemed as if she was trying to show us she could wake the baby whenever she wanted to.

I was concluding my talk with Sallie when the phone rang. I informed Sallie that after I answered the phone, we would finish our talk. The caller was Barbara. She talked about how interested she was in what was going on at our house and that she really wanted to be sure her interpretation had been accurate. She asked if she could come to the house. At the time, I didn't sense that her interest was mercenary; she simply wanted to settle her own mind and confirm what she had said to us. While she continued to talk, I told Tony of her request. Since both of us were at a loss as to how we should deal with our little ghost, we thanked her and extended an invitation.

She said she would be in Kansas City the next day for a radio interview and asked if the following evening would be a good time for her visit. Without consulting Tony, I agreed. Before hanging up, I asked if I should say anything to Sallie about the visit. She said, "That might be a good idea."

Although I was ecstatic about Barbara's visit, I reminded Sallie of what we had talked about before the phone call. In a much more pleasant tone of voice, I told her about my conversation with Barbara, a very special person who was able to see and hear spirits, and that Barbara would be coming for a visit in two days to try and help us all get along and be happy.

While talking, my mind wandered and I realized how nice it would be to have some sort of two-way communication with our little ghost. But how? Perhaps if Sallie liked crayons, she would use them to write to us. Not expecting an answer, I asked, "Hey Sallie, would you like me to leave some crayons and paper for you to draw on? You know, if you drew a picture or wrote something to us, we would be very proud of it, and we would hang it on the refrigerator for everyone to see." Then, as if I had really gotten a response from her, I said with a great deal of enthusiasm, "Yes, that sounds like a really good idea, doesn't it?" I could tell by the look on Tony's face as he watched and listened to me he thought I'd gone nuts. Not wanting any more looks of disapproval, I told Sallie we loved her and we were really happy to have her in our family.

Later at night, I went upstairs and found some blank yellow paper and a brand new box of crayons. I had put the paper and the crayons on a clipboard and was standing in the nursery with thought that maybe I should write her a note. I picked a red crayon, and on one of the blank sheets of paper wrote, "Hi, Sallie. How old are you?" I placed the crayons and the clipboard on the floor in the northeast corner of the nursery. "Sallie, here are your crayons and paper. Maybe you could draw me a picture." Then I told her "good night" and left the room.

We took the film to be developed, anxious to see the images Tony had photographed when George saw the bear spin around. Two days later, I brought them home. Tony and I looked through them and were amazed to find that the camera seemed to have picked up something odd in that particular shot.

You could barely make out what object was in the center of the viewfinder because it was very blurred. However, it was blurred only in the center and along the lower edge of the picture; everything on the other outer edges was clear and in perfect focus. Looking at it, it was easy to see that the fuzzy area resembled a person's head and shoulders. It was as if someone's unseen or transparent head was very close to the camera when the picture was taken, and consequently that area in the picture was out of focus.

We tried to come up with logical explanations for the strange photo. My first thought concerned Tony's unsteadiness when taking pictures. In the past, it had often left us with many blurred photos. However, in this specific instance, instead of the whole photo being blurred, only the center was blurry. There wasn't anything wrong with the camera lens, because the photos before and after showed no anomalies.

After exhausting all logical possibilities, we decided that the blur must have been Sallie. When Tony spoke the words, "Smile and say cheese," just before he snapped the shutter, she had been standing right in front of the camera.

Maybe Sallie enjoyed the attention of having her picture taken. Excited about the possibility of getting a better picture of her should she pose for us again, I remembered some of the many things I had read about ghosts—in particular, ghost photography. Apparently, they showed up better when infrared or Polaroid film was used. Tony and I racked our brains trying to think of who might have a Polaroid camera that we could borrow for use during Barbara's visit the next day.

SEVEN

# EARLY RESEARCH

The next day was July 28, and I noticed nothing out of the ordinary that morning. Shortly after Tony left for work, George stopped by with a college friend who was quite interested in ghostly subjects. George told me he had spoken to a few people since his last visit and had gotten some vague information about a little boy who'd died in front of the house some time ago. No one he'd talked to had mentioned anything about a little girl.

His friend asked me about the history of the house and the previous tenants. Although I didn't have any answers, I mentioned my plan to do some research that afternoon to see what I could find out. He offered to assist me and I took him up on the offer. He was familiar with the research facilities at the library and I was not. We agreed to meet after lunch.

I arrived at the library shortly before 10:00 a.m., thinking I might get a head start on George's friend, but he was sitting at the large table in the center of the research room and was already surrounded by several layers of books, printouts, ledgers, and other reference material. I sat down across from him, surprised by his enthusiasm, and asked,

"Okay, where do I start?" He gave me a summary of historical properties called the Kansas Historic Resources Inventory Reconnaissance Form.

The records had interesting information on many old homes in the area. The legal description of 508 North 2nd Street was referred to as the North 8 1/2' of lot 9 and all of lot 10 of block 70 in Old Atchison. The house had been purchased by Kate Finney; she'd built a home on that land in 1872. The Finneys were a fairly prominent family who owned several other lots of land within and around block 70, including lots 8 through 12. The records also established that members of the Finney family had occupied the home well into the twentieth century, when it became rental property owned by Dr. C. C. Finney. The property remained in the family until 1946. I was stunned to learn that our house was 127 years old.

I also tried to acquire reliable information on the property from before the Finney ownership. Eventually I found a record stating that the land had previously been part of a much larger land holding. The owner of the larger tract was Samuel Pomeroy, who bought the land from the Atchison Town County on April 17, 1857. After this transaction, the land moved into the hands of two brothers, Theodore and Thaddeus Hyatt, on April 5, 1859. Within seven years, a feud between the brothers led to a legal event which resulted in the Hyatt partition in 1866.

Much of the information dating before the Pomeroy ownership was indecipherable, due to the illegible handwriting of the person who recorded the information. Atchison had two floods in 1858 in which many of the historical records had been destroyed. As far as I could make out, the land was at some time owned by a flower company. A person better versed in the legal records of the time would surely be able to make better sense of what I was trying to decipher.

The records referenced three generations of Finneys. Michael Cromen Finney married Kate Kathrens, producing James, Charles, and Agnes. James was a single man until at least 1881. In 1899, Kate Finney purchased the land just to the north of our house (Lot 11, and the South 1' of lot 12). Kate and her children lived in the 508 house until Charles married. Kate gave or sold the land to Charles and he built the house at 510 North 2nd Street in 1905. The third generation of the Finney family also had a Charles H. Finney born to Charles C. Finney and Louise Marie Zibold Finney, and he also became a doctor. Charles C. Finney eventually owned and/or controlled all the family property well into the late 1940s. Through more research, we learned that in March of 1946, Charles C. Finney deeded lots 9 and 10 to his son Charles H. Finney for "one dollar and other considerations."

The Record of Historical Properties mentioned that Agnes Finney True (the daughter of Michael and Kate Finney) and a Catherine Boyes (or Bayes) and Joanna Barnes were involved in the land transactions concerning the Finney lots 9 and 10. There were no clear records to show how Catherine and Joanna fit into the family at the time.

When I continued my research on the deeds several months later, I noticed many conflicting records. The property changed hands several times until 1958, when it was mortgaged to Billie Joan Butler and Ethel Anderson, both single women, and remained so until 1991. In November 1992, just over a month before we moved in, the house was sold to Les Smith.

Having already tied a variety of names to the house, my next objective was to see if any girl child bearing one of those last names had ever died while residing in the house. However, with all the ambiguous records I thought that maybe there were other names that I should consider.

Weeks later, I was researching telephone directory publications preserved by the local library from the beginning of the town's phone service. Instead of searching the directory for a particular name, I had to scan each page for the 508 North 2nd Street address and then note the family name listed with it. Working page by page through eighty-seven directories was very meticulous work. Although there were a few books missing, compiling the results did support my theory that the property was used as a rental.

With my list of names from the deeds and phone records, I headed to the four binders of computer-generated cemetery records. I was relieved that the listings were alphabetically listed by last name. Even though the information wasn't always complete, it made available information such as the full name of the person who had died, what cemetery they were buried in, their gender, the years in which the person lived, the date they died, and sometimes how old the person was at death as well as the cause of death.

I was sure that the information we had gathered, along with the cemetery records, would pay off and we would find the child who was haunting our house. I was looking for a girl between the ages of four and seventeen. As I flipped through the pages, however, I was disheartened. A majority of the listings of young children were boys, and none of the children had a last name that corresponded to anything on my list. This suggested that no child had died in the house.

All I could think was that we couldn't stop here. There had to be something of significance I was missing. Feeling empty-handed, I again enlisted the help of a friend and we began searching newspaper articles and obituaries, as well as church records of births and deaths. Not only were the older records handwritten and worn, but church records, possibly the most informative records available, were in Latin. We looked at microfilm and photos, and pulled even more books and files from their shelves. Eventually we broadened our parameters to include young females with a date of death between the late 1800s and the mid to late 1900s.

We found fifteen possibilities and initial cross referencing ruled out five of them. We ended up with six Sallys or Sallies, as well as three others who had died within the specified dates but without notation of their ages, first names, or gender.

Of those ten individuals, six died between 1927 and 1943, which ruled out the information that Barbara had shared with us before.

There was a child named Sallie Isabell Hall who died in 1905, and three others that died in the late 1800s: Sally M. Foster died Feburary 1865, Sally White died Feburary 12, 1891, and another child, noted as being four years old (no first name listed) died in 1894 in the town of Lancaster. We ruled out Lancaster, leaving us three individuals with the name Sally or Sallie.

Out of those three, we realized one possible connection to one of the surnames. The Hall family was a black family that lived around the corner and up the block from the Finney house. Although we had no proof, we thought this family might have worked as servants for the doctor. Although this information certainly did not validate the name of our ghost, we thought perhaps it would be helpful down the road. In the end, the countless hours of research didn't really help at all. We never found a child with the name Sallie who had ever lived in the house, much less died there.

EIGHT

# BARBARA'S VISIT

The next day was July 29—the day Barbara was due to visit. I began the day with my normal activities, still looking around cautiously at everything as I entered a room. By now, it had become a habit to be on the lookout for anything out of the ordinary. Quite often I had found myself peeking into the nursery for things mysteriously out of place, or for a crayon-written response to the note I had left on the clipboard, but there seemed to be no activity anywhere.

Knowing that Sallie wanted my attention, I began to talk to her as Barbara had suggested. I told her I was happy that she was still with us, and I thought it was nice when she did things to let us know she was around. "When you do things like that, I know you're here in the room with us, and then I can talk with you." I tried to make small talk, one-sided of course, and asked her if she liked it when I talked to her. I also reminded her that Barbara was coming later that day and that she had no reason to be scared. "Barbara's just a friend who's going to try to help all of us."

Barbara was scheduled to do a radio talk show where listeners could call in and ask questions. I thought listening to the show would give me some insight into her psychic ability. During the first half of the show, she talked about psychic phenomena and told about how she had come to know she had abilities.

As a young girl, she had communicated with her brother who had died several years before she was born. One day Barbara's mother heard her humming a tune that her mother had only sung to the infant who had died. This had been a turning point in her family's belief in her abilities. Before then, no one had been able to validate the things she would share "from beyond." Although her brother had died as a baby, he came to her as a young man and grew older as he guided her through her teenage years.

This was the closest encounter I had ever had with a psychic, so I took notes and listened intently. I was disappointed that instead of asking questions about ghosts and spirits, callers asked about things like: Will the bad financial situation I'm in get any better? Will my business venture succeed? Will I come into money? Is the man I'm dating Mr. Right? There was not one paranormal question about life after death or spirit communication. They had missed the point of the interview. Listeners were so self-centered that everything focused on their own personal satisfaction. I couldn't wait to meet Barbara myself because I had so many questions about the spirit world.

Later that afternoon, I visited my neighbor Carol, who had lived in the house north of us for fourteen years. I wanted to ask her a few questions about the people who'd lived in the house before us. I wondered if she'd ever heard about anything weird or unexplainable happenings. I took the baby with me, and the conversation centered on him for quite some time.

I didn't know quite how to approach the subject of our apparent haunting, and I wasn't sure how Carol would respond to it. After unsuccessfully hinting for information, I finally mustered up enough courage to come right out and ask her, "Did you ever hear of anything weird happening in our house?" I could tell that she was puzzled, but curious. I couldn't contain myself any longer; it was inevitable that she would hear about the whole ordeal, so I began telling her of the experiences we'd had.

Now, usually when you tell someone you think you have a ghost in your house, they look at you with disbelief and maybe attempt to humor you. To my surprise, Carol actually showed a great deal of interest. She told me she really didn't know the previous tenants very well and she hadn't heard of anything strange ever happening at the house. At some point we had gotten off the subject and were on to discussing other things, such as how it felt having a new baby in the house. Then she asked me a strange question. "Do you let the baby sleep with the light on?"

Not wanting to offend her, especially if she had done that with her children, I said, "No, he's still sleeping in the cradle we have in our room, and we don't leave the lights on. Why?"

She told me that she and her husband were often up in the wee hours of the night as well as early in the morning, and they had noticed that the light in the nursery always seemed to be on. She also informed me that when we were gone in the evenings, the light was on. I explained to her that because we had often gone in there in the middle of the night for diapers or something, I had put a night light in the nursery and that we had a bad habit of leaving the hallway light on. "That's probably what you have seen." I said.

"No, it's definitely the overhead light because we can see it through the window."

This was confusing. I had never noticed the light on in the middle of the night. I had also never noticed it from the front of the house as we pulled up to park the car. Being very energy conscious, I always turned the lights off before we left the house, except for one of the living room lights.

Carol and I chatted a little while longer before I realized that Tony was due home any minute. I excused myself without mentioning Barbara's impending visit. Carol had been exceptionally receptive to our strange situation, but I still didn't know if she was just trying to be polite or secretly thinking I was wacko. I didn't feel comfortable letting her know we were having a psychic come to the house.

Knowing we were expecting company at six that evening, I picked up the house. Although I knew better, I started again to doubt my own senses. "Maybe we don't have a ghost," I thought. "Nothing really strange happened today and the light coming on was probably just a short in the wiring or something." There were, however, two things that brought me back to the reality at hand. One was the fact Barbara had sensed a certain young presence in the house; the other was the incident where Tony was scratched.

Around 3:30 p.m., Tony came home from work. A short time later, George came over, saying that he wanted to check things out before Barbara got there. It just so happened that he brought his laundry, too. After browsing through the house and examining a few items of interest, he went into the kitchen and put the first load into the washer. When he came back to the dining room where we were we sitting, he pulled out one of the chairs and plopped his cigarettes and lighter down on the table in front of him.

As we talked about Barbara's visit and what might happen with her there, one of us mentioned that it would be nice to record the whole evening on video and Polaroid camera. Should Sallie reveal herself, we wanted to get the best pictures possible. The problem was that none of us owned either type of camera. We racked our brains to think of people we could borrow the equipment from, and were soon on the phone calling family members, friends, and neighbors. We finally found what we needed, and made arrangements to pick it all up a short while later.

After about twenty-five minutes, George realized the washing machine had stopped, so he went into the kitchen to switch his wet load into the dryer. As he passed the bathroom door on the way, he noticed out of the corner of his eye what he thought was a night light in the bathroom. A few days earlier, he had noticed a night light in the nursery and thought I had also placed one in the downstairs bathroom, so he didn't think twice about it. After loading the dryer and passing the bathroom on his way back, he once again glanced into the bathroom and noticed that what he thought was a night light was actually two votive candles sitting on the back of the toilet. When he got back to the dining room he casually asked if either of us had lit them, but we had not.

Several months previously, I'd placed those two candles in the bathroom. Like all the other candles scattered about the house, they were purely decorative and had never been lit. I raced to the bathroom to see if they were still lit. They were, and each candle had a very small pool of wax at the base of its wick, which told me they had not been burning long—perhaps a minute or so.

I tried to think back. There hadn't been a moment during the past ten minutes when one of us had been out of sight from the others long enough to have slipped into the bathroom to light the candles without being noticed. Tony and I had been in the next room within full view of the bathroom doorway and anyone entering it. In addition, Tony and I had not left each other's side during the few minutes George was in the kitchen. George's cigarettes and lighter were still sitting on the dining room table where he had left them. Realizing that no one had the opportunity to light the candles, we decided that the culprit must have been Sallie.

Knowing that my next chore was to scold her, I blew out the candles and took a deep breath. Then in a sharp and angry voice, I called out to her. "Sallie, did you light these candles?" Since I really wasn't expecting a response, I wasted no time in telling her that lighting fires was not a good thing to do, that it was very dangerous, and that a fire could easily get out of control and burn down the house. I explained that if we had no house she would not have a place to stay, either. "So, Sallie," I said in a very strong and chastising voice, "now we have another rule. No playing with fires!"

I returned to the dining room where Tony and George stood snickering. Not just at the idea that I had been yelling at a ghost, but in their disbelief that a ghost had lit the candles. Since thinking of being in the house with an active ghost gave them such an uneasy feeling that for them, laughter was the best response. I have to admit that I was amused, despite the safety issue. Sallie's desire to have her presence known was cute. On the other hand, having an unknown and unsupervised fire in the house really bothered me.

I also found myself baffled. Did she like playing with fire? Was she trying to tell us something? Was she just being ornery, or was this simply a ploy to get noticed? Then I thought about what could have happened if she had actually set the house on fire. What if one of these days she lit a fire while we weren't home or when we weren't close by? To distract myself, I tried focusing my thoughts on George and Tony as they made arrangements for who was going to pick up which camera and who would go to the store for the film.

The guys set off on their errands and returned a little while later. George then went to retrieve the video camera from our neighbors, Don and Carol. Upon his return, we found out that he had for some reason felt compelled to tell the neighbors about who was coming to the house that night and what was going to take place. I was shocked that he had done so.

Two of George's friends, knowing about what was planned for that night, stopped in just to see what was going on. Rodney was one of them, and while we waited for Barbara's arrival, he detailed one of his own ghostly experiences. It had happened when he was young, and although it didn't thrill him, he did come out of it with a curiosity and interest in the subject. George's other friend James was not a believer and probably thought we had made the whole thing up. Given his position on the subject, he was very interested in hearing the line of bull that the psychic was sure to tell us.

I'm sure that Rodney and James also hoped to witness something ghostly during Barbara's visit. Of course, if something did happen, it would be in our best interest to have as many witnesses as possible to support our claim. With that in mind, we agreed to let the two of them stay.

We sat around, waiting impatiently for Barbara's arrival. We talked about breaking into the film so that we could test the Polaroid camera. When Barbara didn't arrive as scheduled, we did just that. We eagerly opened the first package and loaded it into the camera. Since Barbara had once explained that Sallie was protective of the baby, I suggested that we take some photos of Taylor being held by different people.

Tony took the first photo of George holding Taylor on the couch. This picture turned out clear, so we assumed the camera was working fine. Further thinking out our approach, we realized that Sallie was likely comfortable with Tony, me, and George being around the baby, so Taylor was passed to Rodney. When Taylor began to cry and fuss, we took another picture of him. While we waited for the picture to develop, Tony cuddled Taylor in an attempt to comfort him.

A few minutes later, we looked at the photo of Rodney and the baby, and saw an odd whitish fuzzy area between them. Not sure what to make of it, we decided to take another picture. Tony had managed to quiet Taylor, who was now smiling and babbling at him, so I turned toward them and snapped off the next picture. When the picture developed, the same whitish blur showed up between them. Was this Sallie? Before long, we had gone through an entire package of film.

We had several pictures of Taylor alone and in the company of at least one other person. Although it was less apparent in some of the photos, almost every one showed the same fuzzy effect. This effect also showed up when Tony and I were with the baby and in one photo of me alone. It was odd.

In one photograph of Taylor sitting alone on the couch, his left foot is raised off the couch and a small but a very apparent fuzziness can be seen just under it. His focus seems to be on something a little higher than himself and to his left. I couldn't help but wonder if the fuzzy blur under his foot was actually Sallie's presence. Had her hand been under his foot in an attempt to stabilize him from toppling over sideways, as he so often did at this point of his development?

Although it varied in size, density, and orientation within each photo, the blur or fuzzy area consistently showed up in many of the pictures. Although he couldn't see one, Tony wondered if he had gotten a fingerprint smudge on the camera's lens and this is what had appeared as the blurred effect in the developed photos.

Determined to prove his theory, he took the last two pictures of the first roll. One was of Taylor in his baby swing, and the other was a self-portrait taken at arm's length. While those pictures developed, the rest of us again scrutinized the previous pictures. Tony was still convinced that the fuzziness was due to a faulty camera or a bad roll of film, so he opened the second package of film, loaded it into the camera, and took three more pictures.

While those photos were set aside to develop, he looked at the last two from the first roll. Neither photo showed a blur, which discounted both the idea that the film pack was bad and that there was a finger print smudge on the lens of the camera. Although the first two photos of the second roll showed no anomaly, the third picture of the second roll showed a fuzzy blur along Taylor's backside. Out of thirteen photos taken up to this point, eight were marred by a whitish fuzzy blur, five were not. From those eight, we noticed that the blurs were very localized, leaving the rest of the picture in perfect focus. I started to refer to the blur as Sallie.

I remember things like Taylor's disposition and who was near him at the time, and then correlate the intensity of the blur that showed up in a particular picture with what was actually taking place in the picture. It was apparent to me Sallie was more prominently visible when Taylor was upset or when she didn't feel comfortable with the person who was holding him or anywhere near him. Another thing I noticed was the increased density of the blur in the photos of Tony and the baby and of me and the baby. In each of these photos, Taylor was being cuddled in our arms and we were looking at him in a loving way.

He was perfectly content, and there was no reason for Sallie to feel the need to protect him, thus leaving me to conclude that she simply wanted to be included in the family togetherness.

Each of us took a turn at being the photographer, so it was highly unlikely that any one person was to blame for the blur in so many of the other photos. Since some of the pictures within each package of film had turned out perfectly fine, we could assume there was no defect in the film or camera. We felt there was definitely some sort of paranormal energy showing up in the pictures, and we couldn't wait to get Barbara's opinion.

## BARBARA'S ARRIVAL

Barbara arrived about 8:30 p.m., accompanied by her sister. Before they had a chance to sit down, we asked if they had any objection to our documenting the visit with cameras. Barbara thought it was a great idea. We told her of the photos we had taken prior to her arrival and she responded, "I don't want to see them just yet."

I assumed that she wanted as little outside input as possible so she could interpret the situation and energy without external influence. Already extremely skeptical of psychics, I appreciated this approach to avoiding a common pitfall of "cold reading"—a method whereby psychics gain information from photos, facial expressions, voices, and reactions of those they are working with. Tony, however, wasn't yet convinced.

Barbara appeared to be preoccupied as she glanced around the living room, seemingly in a world of her own, getting a feel for whatever or whoever was there with us. It wasn't as if she was actually looking at any "thing" in the room; in fact, as her eyes roved they never seemed to stop or focus on anything in particular or anything we could see. It seemed that she was seeing beyond our physical world, and outside the world of normal expectations. Her body language did not seem to signify a predetermined approach or prepared speech, and she didn't ask a lot of questions that would lead her to cold read responses.

Instead, she roamed between the living and dining rooms for a few minutes, seemingly quite antsy and distracted, and then settled on the couch closest to the front door. She began telling us little things she was feeling and before we realized it, she had connected with the spirit in our house. Later, she told us how she felt when she'd first come into the house; she experienced a really heavy, smothering feeling in her chest, as if she were short of breath. She had tried to communicate to the spirit that she wasn't there to harm her and she didn't have to be scared. Barbara reported that the heaviness lifted and she was finally able to sit down shortly afterward.

Having never been in the same room with a psychic, I continued to take notice of how she "communicated." I wanted to do everything possible to be sure this was the real deal and that we weren't being played for fools to be strung along and set up for some future financial gain. Barbara sat quietly, sometimes closing her eyes or staring straight ahead, mentally trying to foster a trusting relationship and make emotional contact with Sallie. Through the contact, she would then try to understand and relay the feelings that were being conveyed. That in itself was hard to grasp, as the words she replied with were spoken in her own voice, but in the manner and language of a young child.

Then unexpectedly, Barbara asked, "Does anyone have a toothache?" I raised my hand and volunteered that I'd recently had a lot of dental work done; no one else claimed any pain. "No," Barbara said, "a pain, a toothache." She said this while grimacing and holding the left side of her face. She then told us she was trying to distinguish between the feelings of the people in the room and those of the spirit.

She then held out her right hand, rubbing the palm. "Has anyone hurt their hand?" No one claimed that one either. "Okay, okay," Barbara said, apparently better able to determine what feelings were the spirit's, she went on. "She's got a toothache and a bad pain in her hand. She probably died with these pains. They could be connected with how she died." Then abruptly she turned to me and blurted out, "You do a lot of things that bug her!"

I raised my eyebrows. Barbara went on: "You're too bossy! She says you're too bossy." She then went on to ask, "Have you talked to her about rules?" I replied with a most definite, "Yes," and began telling her of the things I'd talked to her about; all the things that Barbara and I had discussed via phone and especially the recent lighting of the candles in the bathroom.

With George fumbling with the video camera and Barbara quite absorbed in communicating, I don't think she heard what I'd said about the candles that Sallie seemed to have set aflame. Had she heard, I would have expected a more significant reaction considering the safety issue that immediately came to mind. Instead, Barbara remained with her head down, trying to focus. During these awkward moments of silence, the rest of us exchanged many a questioning look. Presently, Barbara lifted her head and spoke.

Looking directly at me, "She doesn't like it!" I'm sure I looked exactly what I was thinking, which was who does she think she is anyway? Barbara continued, "I tried to tell her you weren't meaning to be bossy, but that she needed discipline, and you were trying to teach her right from wrong. I don't think she likes it, but then again, what child likes to be disciplined or told no?"

I felt very worried at this point. If she didn't like my bossiness or the rules, what was she capable of doing in anger or defiance? Then Barbara added, in a childlike way, "There are too many rules. She can't remember them all." Hearing those words eased my irritation and anger.

Barbara suggested we help Sallie remember the rules by occasionally repeating them. "When speaking to her, tell her to remember that we don't play with fire, we don't hurt Tony, etc... Keep in mind it is as if you have just adopted a little girl and you need to be patient and understanding but firm. Remember she is very young, and kids of this age often need to be reminded of things." Rodney asked how old Sallie was. "Seven," Barbara said, and in a young, childish tone of voice, she repeated the words, "I'm seven."

The whole process of her communicating with a spirit was truly amazing. None of us really talked much; we nodded in agreement while Barbara talked and we were very aware of what we might be telling Sallie via verbal or non-verbal communication.

Barbara asked if Sallie woke the baby at night. It was not anything she and I had discussed previously, and at this point I let out a big, "Oh, yeah!" I told her of the trouble we had been having with his waking up shortly after we put him down following a diaper change and feeding. "I get the feeling she's been waking him," Barbara said. "You need to be firm in telling her not to. She may have just wanted to play with him or maybe she's been reminding him to breathe. I can't tell."

This comment brought SIDS (Sudden Infant Death Syndrome) to mind. If Taylor was in danger of SIDS, Sallie may have saved him countless times each night. I felt a sense of queasiness followed by a heartfelt thankfulness.

Barbara shared that from her point of view, the stuffed animals and the baby were the only things Sallie had to play with. Barbara thought that the focus on playing with Taylor would stop, or at least lessened, if we were to get her a doll or some toy to call her own.

I had already thought how nice it would be to give Sallie something she could call her own; a doll seemed perfect. Barbara said that if we were to ask Sallie a question and then concentrate, the first thing that came into our mind would probably be Sallie's answer. I tried this, but it didn't seem to work. I was unsure if Sallie was simply being stubborn, if I was unable to concentrate properly, or if she just wasn't in the room when I made these attempts.

I asked Barbara to talk to Sallie and ask if a doll would be all right. "Well, all right," Barbara said in a childlike way, as if Sallie was being made to settle for something less than what she wanted. Barbara said she could tell it wasn't going to be enough; Sallie still wanted to be with the baby. I told Barbara, "Tell Sallie it is okay with me if she spends time with Taylor, but she just had to be careful when playing with him." Barbara responded, "Okay," in an excited, childlike manner.

Looking directly at me, Barbara said, "She's warmer to you because you're the mommy." She said she got the feeling that Sallie had suffered abuse in some way. "Perhaps her father or another man abused her, and that's why she attacked Tony the other night. She's acting as the baby's guardian angel. She's protecting the baby, and men make her uneasy." She reiterated the need to be firm with Sallie, to remind her that we had to be the ones to take care of Taylor's physical needs, and that if she interfered or hurt us, she would be punished. Again I wondered how on earth we would go about punishing someone we couldn't see. How would we actually know if she was taking her punishment at all? But before I could voice these concerns, Barbara was on to another topic.

"I don't think she'll leave the house. She feels safe and secure here." We told Barbara of the research results we had come up with at the library. "Maybe she had been treated by the doctor who had owned the house; maybe she liked him and followed him home. Whatever the reason, she likes it here." At this time, Barbara voiced her only concern, which was how Sallie would deal with our inevitable move. We were only renting the house and would eventually have to move. It was doubtful that she would accept it nicely. We wondered if she would unleash a temper tantrum to show us how unhappy she was about it. Would she throw or break things, set more fires, or do physical harm to someone? The question left an unsettled feeling in the back of my mind because I knew that one day we would have to deal it.

Barbara suggested that when we moved, we should discuss it with Sallie first. Perhaps after we had built a relationship with her, she would be more understanding and trusting of us. If we were up front with her, she might not feel we were abandoning her, and if we felt comfortable with the idea, we could even offer that she move with us. Barbara felt that despite the invitation, Sallie would remain behind.

Throughout the evening, our conversation jumped haphazardly. Barbara tried to tell us of the things Sallie was saying as they became known to her. The topics changed quickly, because young children have a very short attention span.

I told Barbara I had been talking to Sallie a lot during the last couple of days as a way to give her positive reinforcement. I mentioned suggesting that she swing the ball on the ceiling fan as a way of letting us know she was around. At this point I reinforced to Sallie that I liked knowing when she was around because then I knew I could talk to her.

I went on to describe a recent day in the nursery when I had been changing Taylor. He was still too little to roll off the changing table on his own, and I asked Sallie if she would help me by watching him while I stepped out of the room. When I returned, I thanked Sallie and told her she'd done a great job. Barbara excitedly said, "Oh, good, real good. Keep doing things like that." I saw Tony's eyes roll up and back into his head.

She urged me to continue talking and interacting with Sallie in an attempt to gain her trust. Barbara looked at Tony and urged him to do the same, but it was obvious that he was uncomfortable with the idea. She said, "I know you'll feel funny, like you're talking to the air, but you're not. She really is there. People will probably laugh at you, but they don't have to know you do it." Tony agreed with her about the laughing part. I could tell that if he ever talked to her, it would be very rarely.

Barbara asked if Sallie had bothered the two kittens. Before I had a chance to reply, she said, "She likes them. Do they ever cry out?" I told her that up to this point I hadn't noticed any erratic behavior or drastic change in their playfulness, but that I had honestly not been looking for any either.

Next we discussed Sallie's ability to light fires. Barbara told us she didn't need a lighter or matches to do so. She went on to say that Sallie traveled in or with some sort of energy field and that's what she drew on to light the fires. Barbara stressed the fact that if she lit fires, Sallie should be severely reprimanded or punished. "Perhaps send her to her room," Barbara suggested.

I asked Barbara about the cold air I had felt several times on the stairs. "Could Sallie cause this?"

"Yes," she said. "Spirits can bring warm air or cold air with them. Being that it is hot and muggy here, she probably brings cold air." I told her that there was mold growing on odd things in the house, such as the pots and pans, the dog food in the bowl, the magnets on the refrigerator, and some of my Tupperware and small appliances. It was something we noticed shortly after the baby came home and had continued until about two weeks before Barbara's arrival. She said it could be caused by the mix of Sallie's energy and that of the house.

I remembered that several weeks before, the house has been filled with the distinct smell of cooked broccoli, although there had been no broccoli in the house. Tony had not experienced the smell. When I asked Barbara if the broccoli aroma could be from Sallie or signify her presence, she said, "Oh, sure. She could bring you the smells of things she likes." Then she bowed her head in mental communication. "She does like broccoli. She also likes one of the perfumes you wear." I began naming a few of the fragrances I enjoyed, hoping for a confirmation. "She might not know it by name," Barbara said, then paused, "Pearls come to mind." I did have an Avon perfume called Pearls and Lace that was not among those I had already named.

Barbara suggested that we gather some things together and put them out for Sallie to play with. She suggested an old pair of shoes, jewelry, clothes, etc… "But be careful what you give her. For instance, you might not want to give her high heels because you might hear the annoying click-clack of the heels on the floor. Also pick a place for her things—a shelf or box—and put them there. Tell her these things are hers to play with, but she has to put them away when she's done so no one trips over them. She wants something to call her own, she doesn't want to get into trouble playing with your things, she wants to play with something she knows would be safe from Mommy or Daddy saying no. Yes, that's definitely the feeling I get from her. You'll probably want to pick somewhere in the nursery to put her things because that's where she spends most of her time."

My thoughts traveled to the crayons I had left Sallie a few days earlier, and I described where they were. I asked Barbara if she liked the crayons. Barbara bowed her head again, and then said in Sallie's tone of voice, "Yes, I like the crayons. I'm trying to do it." Then, in her own voice, "She's trying to work it up, trying to find a way to do it, to answer you." I had not yet mentioned that I had asked Sallie to draw me a picture or answer the question I'd written for her. I was impressed, and mentioned that three days prior I had written a question asking how old she was.

We discussed the possibility that maybe Sallie was too young to have known how to write and that her inability to read might also be making her response difficult. Perhaps it was too hard to focus enough energy to form the letters. Barbara said, "She might still do it, it might just take her a while."

I thought how interesting it would be if Sallie and I could communicate on a regular basis through writing or pictures. I thought of how much I, and others interested in the paranormal, could learn!

We asked whether Sallie was in the bedroom with us when we slept. Barbara answered with a definite "yes." Then she stressed that the baby should continue to sleep in the same room with us for as long as possible or until we could get Sallie acquainted with what was right and wrong. If Sallie were a physical person, it would naturally be a great concern to leave someone so young alone with a newborn baby. A child spirit was no different, and although Barbara was trying not to alarm us, she wanted us to understand that accidents can and do happen.

Because Sallie was new to the family and perhaps to a newborn baby, we couldn't trust her not to play too roughly with him. Did she know that she shouldn't lift him or push the swing too hard? Barbara

was trying to tell us that Sallie needed to find out where and how she fit in with us before having freedom to be with the baby. I wondered how I would stop her and hoped my presence in the room would deter any questionable or risky activity on her part.

George asked Barbara if Sallie would do things while other people were around or in the house. Barbara responded that Sallie might do so, but would be more comfortable with the family and thus more likely to do things around us. Then, as if jumping into the conversation via Barbara, Barbara spoke in Sallie's childlike voice and said, "I'll show off for your friends if you want."

The idea that Sallie had just voluntarily communicated something to us made us feel as though she was already starting to feel more comfortable. From her statement, I could tell she liked attention—what little girl doesn't?

I asked Barbara if she knew why Sallie had picked the time during my sister's visit to make her presence known to us, and why she did the things she was doing. "Well, if she just floats through doors and walls," Barbara said, "you don't know she's there. She wants to be noticed; she wants your attention and love. Maybe she felt comfortable with your sister, or maybe she wanted someone else to witness her antics and know she was here." I wondered if Sallie saw how much love and attention the new baby was getting from us and Karen, and in jealousy acted out for her own portion of attention. Barbara looked at Tony and said, "You need to make friends with her, too." I could tell Tony was thinking, "Yeah, right. I'm not going to talk to something floating above my head."

We asked about the time in which Sallie lived, and Barbara admitted that she was not very good at determining that sort of thing; she really had no answer for us. Tony started to tell her about a dream he'd had the night before, in which Sallie and a boy named Jonathan were sitting against a tree in the yard. Sallie was calling the boy by name and had her arm stretched out while pointing to something. Tony, being an excellent sketch artist, had drawn what he'd seen in his dream, and he shared the drawing with Barbara. Sallie was wearing a blue dress and had long chestnut hair. The boy was wearing knickers. Barbara said, "That's a very good likeness of her." As we continued to discuss the fashions depicted in the drawing, we concluded that Sallie might have lived in the late 1930s or early 1940s. Barbara made reference to the fact that Tony's dream could have been the manifestation of Sallie's consciousness. In other words, it might have been something Sallie was trying to show him.

To this day, we have not yet been able to figure out who Jonathan was. We have wondered if he was the reason Sallie was so attached to Taylor. Had Jonathan been a younger relative when she was alive, or just a friend? In the end, there was no confirmation from Barbara or Sallie on any of it.

About an hour into the visit, we offered to take Barbara to the nursery, thinking that if Sallie spent most of her time up there, maybe Barbara could get a stronger feeling in that area. She responded eagerly. Her sister opted to stay downstairs, and said she would keep a lookout.

Carrying the baby in my arms, I went up first, followed by Barbara and the rest. George brought the video camera, and Tony had the Polaroid, which he later exchanged for the 35mm camera. Shortly after stepping into the room, I started to feel claustrophobic and it was hard to breathe. It was as if there wasn't enough oxygen for all of us. I had never felt so weird, and in my perplexed state, I turned around to look at Barbara.

Throughout her visit, I had watched her intently in an attempt to understand her and what was being presented. In my skepticism, I was desperately trying to read her movements and mannerisms. I noticed now that Barbara's breath had become labored. She pointed to the northwest corner of the room and said, "That's her corner." She paused, and then, still looking at the corner, said, "She's standing right there." George moved in closer with the camera and Tony took two pictures of the corner while Barbara and I continued to talk.

Near the same corner sat a ten-gallon glass water bottle which had been decorated and was used as the baby's savings bank. Visitors would often empty their pocket change into it. Rodney recalled the first time he had been in the room and doing just that. He remembered walking over to deposit his change and feeling a really strange cold sensation. "Well, that's her spot," Barbara said. George asked if Sallie was still in the room with us. Barbara said firmly, "Oh, yes, she's here."

Barbara was still breathing heavily, and I became concerned for her. I wasn't sure if this was normal for her after climbing the stairs or a side effect of communicating with spirits. Tony asked if she was okay. "Yes, I'm all right," she said, in a preoccupied voice.

I asked her to relay to Sallie that I was happy she'd talked with Barbara. "Yeah," she responded in Sallie's tone of voice. Then Barbara added in a bossy, childlike way, "Too many people! Get out!" Everyone except for Barbara, the baby, and me exited the room and positioned themselves just outside the door in order to keep within earshot of the conversation.

Almost immediately, Barbara's breathing improved. Feeling better, she took a few steps towards the end of the crib again. Pointing to Sallie's corner, she said, "That's where you'll want to put her things." Sallie was happy with the plans for her corner, as Barbara smiled and said in a childish manner, "Oh, good!"

I asked, "Is she happy you came to talk with her?"

"Oh, yeah," she said and went on to explain. "At first, when we all came into the room, I felt a tremendous pressure on my chest; I had to tell myself to 'breathe, breathe'!"

Still standing at the door, Rodney described how weird it was that he'd felt claustrophobic as well. Barbara interjected, "It was Sallie's way of telling us this is her room and 'you all just get out of here'." With a quick jerk of her head, as if she had some sort of neurological tick, she explained that Sallie had just corrected her, saying "*Our* room." We continued to listen to what seemed like Barbara in a one-sided conversation. "Yes, yes ... that's okay." We all thought about what we could only imagine this little girl was saying. I thought it precocious that this little ghost girl had such conviction about what she wanted and believed was hers by right.

Barbara smiled, "She's really happy with this. She's happy I talked to you, and she'll be good, but she forgets." Then, with what was clearly deep adoration, in words that resonate with me to this day, Barbara said, "She's a lovely child, a very pretty little girl."

I told Barbara that at one point during my pregnancy, I had hoped for a girl. Barbara was quick to interject with a scared, childlike voice and said, "Oh, no, no, no, no, no, he's okay." Obviously, Sallie really liked her little brother, Taylor! "She knew when you moved into the house that you were pregnant and having a boy," Barbara said, "and she loves him dearly."

Sallie apparently told Barbara, "I'll be good, I'll be good," but we only heard Barbara say, "Yeah, we know," as if she was tired of listening to Sallie say the same thing over and over. Barbara asked Sallie if there was anything else she wanted to say. "I forget," she said with a childlike air of sadness and shame. As we left the nursery Barbara looked back several times, all the while smiling contentedly, with a sense of closure. "She's fine with this. She's okay now."

As we all descended the stairs, Barbara said, "She runs up and down these stairs a lot." We speculated that Sallie's energy as she ran past me on the stairs may have created the cold sensation I'd felt on so many occasions. "You probably feel it more because she's around you more."

While the rest of us headed downstairs, Tony remained a few steps behind. He now had the 35mm camera, and as he got to the bottom of the stairs, he had a strange feeling that something or someone was behind him. Barbara instructed him to take a picture aiming toward the top of the stairs. The photos on this roll of film weren't developed until almost a week later; when they were, they showed a large gray mass of murky color over the stairs. We shared this image with Barbara via mail weeks later. She felt that the anomaly was Sallie standing on the stairs, hand on the railing, in a stance of protection so that no one but family would enter what she perceived was the private area of our home.

Barbara's sister, who had been alone downstairs, informed us that she had asked Sallie to move something or do something to prove she was there. Barbara said, "She didn't, did she?" and knowing the answer, she went on to say, "Because she was upstairs with us." We all chuckled.

Rodney asked if the spirit's name was really Sallie. Sallie responded (through Barbara, as she had all evening), "That's okay. Yes." We wondered if this was simply the name that the little girl who lived here before us had given her. Maybe Sallie liked the name and chose it for herself. Over the years, we tried to find out who this ghost was. How did she come to be here, what is her connection, and why does she remain? To this day, we have not been able to answer these questions.

At this point, we offered to let Barbara see the photos we had taken just prior to her arrival. We didn't tell Barbara of any theories we had come up with as we looked at the blurs in the instamatic photos. But as she looked at them, she pointed out where Sallie was in almost every one. This confirmed our suspicions about the out-of-focus and blurred areas that had shown up.

At some point, Tony went into the kitchen to get everyone beverages while the rest of us continued talking. Suddenly, the overhead light in the living room went out. For at least two seconds we all sat silently and stared up at the dark fixture. We all knew who was responsible, and in unison, we all said, "Thank you, Sallie." A moment later the overhead light came on, just as the light in the dining room went dark. Then it was back on, and I caught myself smiling. We had just experienced a friendly spirit phenomenon.

Tony came into the dining room with drinks in hand and reported that the kitchen light had also gone out for a split second. The light switches were nowhere near Tony, who had been the only one standing up or out of sight.

We all hoped and asked for additional activity. Although there was nothing more, I know we all felt a sense of wonder at what we had witnessed. Had Sallie wanted attention? Was she just showing off? Or was she simply showing us that she was happy?

I asked Barbara how much energy Sallie expended when she interacted with our environment, thinking back to when she had moved all the bears several times that first night. I was also curious about how much energy might be available to her. Was it a source that she tapped into, or did it come directly from her, with or without limitations?

"They [meaning professionals in the field] have yet to find a way to measure it, so they really don't know," Barbara told us.

Turning the lights off and on was probably easier than other activities because they work on an energy current, seemingly similar to the energy a spirit is able to manipulate. Was Sallie's youthful and inexperienced spirit causing disturbances unintentionally? Could this have been the situation when Tony got scratched as he buckled the baby into the car seat? Had that been an uncontrolled expression of emotion, or did she mean to harm him?

Could a spirit's ability to speak to, or through, a psychic mean that spirits have psychic abilities themselves? I couldn't help but wonder if this was a gift they had in life or something obtained in death. It could explain why we seem to get communication from some spirits but not others. When I came out of my own drifting thoughts, the conversation had shifted.

As Barbara sipped her water, she asked if any of us drank or liked Kool-aid. Most of us said yes, recalling childhood memories. Tony mentioned that he was drinking a fruity kind of drink. Barbara said, "I'm tasting Kool-aid, very, very strongly." Then suddenly, as if someone opened a fresh pack of Kool-aid and passed it under my nose, I smelled the most pungent cherry smell I had ever sensed. Rodney and Barbara's sister agreed. Was it the power of suggestion? The power of suggestion had never before made my senses feel or smell something so vividly.

"She'll bring you the smell of things she likes," Barbara noted, "and she likes Kool-aid. She's trying to tell you something about herself. She brought me the taste and you the smell."

Barbara knew what I was going to ask next, but before the words could come tumbling out, she said, "No. She couldn't drink it, just like if you would set a place for her at the dinner table, she couldn't eat it. Now, she might sit there with you," she paused, "and she's telling me she does." In an almost pitiful little child's voice she added, "I stand there." My heart ached.

When Tony and I ate dinner, Taylor was usually in bed already—Sallie hadn't just been spending time with Taylor, but apparently with me and Tony, too. Had standing by us as we ate made her feel a part of a family again? A feeling of sadness for her existence crept over. It must be hard for her to live her current state and not be able to feel a hug or be cuddled by someone who loved her. Was her only comfort to stand close by and pretend?

I felt such pity for her. Tony must have, too, because together we decided to pull out a chair for her and try to include her more in our daily activities. This was easier said than done, however. We would easily go a whole day, not realizing or remembering she was around. I would often miss the opportunity to invite her to watch *Sesame Street* with Taylor or join us when I read a book; the feelings of sorrow would then creep in.

When we asked her if Sallie was always around, Barbara told us she could come and go at will. "She might grow with Taylor and give him guidance over the years. She might persuade Taylor to make specific choices, such as picking his prom date or picking a job. Sallie might decide to take revenge for Taylor and even tell him some of his future... anything is possible." Hearing these words, I wasn't quite sure whether to rejoice or be fearful.

I gave Barbara a big hug and told her how much we appreciated her time and help. She told us to call anytime, and to keep her posted on the situation, and she would try to help us in any way she could. I felt refreshed as I closed the door behind her, but at the same time drained from all the information we had been given to process. I took a long, deep breath.

NINE

# AFTERMATH AND PHOTOGRAPHS

I really hadn't wanted to see Barbara leave; there were still so many unanswered questions. The evening had been interesting and exciting, but it was like being sent home with your first newborn all over again; I questioned my role and my ability to handle it.

None of us really knew what to say, so we sat in awkward silence, scanning the room to see if Sallie would make her presence known. We asked several questions and when there seemed to be no response we asked her to show off for us, but nothing happened.

Tony was soon on the phone inviting his parents to come watch the video that was taken of the evening, and his brother went to the neighbors' to return the camera and invite them over to watch the film as well. My in-laws arrived first, and at some point we realized that we had not finished using the Polaroid film. So we took a few of Tony's parents.

Nothing odd showed up in the one of Tony's dad, but then he wasn't holding Taylor, either. The one I took of Tony's mom and the baby showed the familiar blur we had seen earlier in the evening on the other photos. Additionally, there was what looked like a strand of multicolored yarn on the lower portion of her blouse. I couldn't imagine where she would have picked it up.

When the photo was completely developed I immediately checked my mother-in-law's blouse and the area in which she had been standing, but the strand of yarn wasn't there. More importantly, the multicolored band really didn't look like a piece of yarn either. Could it have been a band of energy instead? I wondered if it had been another form of Sallie, and if so, why had she shown up differently this time?

George returned with our neighbors Don, Carol, and one of their sons. Carol was holding two baby dolls, a small "talking" doll in light blue pajamas with a pull-string by the neck and a larger, naked doll that was fairly dirty. Carol's children had played with them as children, and after hearing George's account of Barbara's visit, pulled the dolls out of storage. "A peace offering," Don said. Everyone was amused, but I thanked them for being so thoughtful. Tony and George took the dolls directly to the nursery.

Almost immediately they returned with the dolls still in hand and asked if anyone had been upstairs. No one had. When we inquired why they had asked, they reported that one of the teddy bears had been moved again, and there was something written on the paper attached to the clipboard I had left for Sallie.

In my excitement, I couldn't wait to get upstairs and see with my own eyes what they were talking about. I was followed by everyone else. We found that the bear, which had sat on the chair just inside the nursery room door, had been moved to the corner. I said aloud, 'Oh, you really like that teddy bear huh, Sallie?"

At first glance "Sallie's" corner looked the same as it had earlier that day. The red crayon I had used to write "Hello, Sally. How are you?" was on top of the papers and the box of crayons was right next to it.

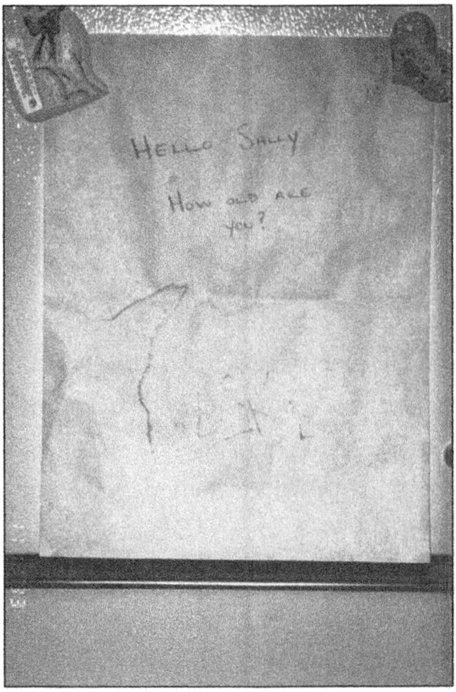


I gathered the two dolls and arranged them in the corner, side by side, nestling them in with the bear she had enjoyed playing with. "Well, here are two baby dolls just for you to play with, too." I looked at the clipboard and box of crayons. Every day I had taken out a new color, clipped a clean paper to the clipboard and written a simple question, leaving the crayon on top of the paper for easy access. I even tried to entice her participation by telling her that I would proudly display her artwork or answer on our refrigerator.

That is when I saw, in distinct child-like handwriting: "7 LIKE." This had been written with a green crayon; not the one that I had left out for her. I was absolutely delighted. She had mustered the energy to perform the task and in doing so she communicated several things to us; she was seven, she was happy, and that she liked the color green.

My head swam with the possibilities! We could write back and forth and she could answer all my questions about the other side. I told Sallie

I was very proud of her and happy that she had answered my questions. Then I told her I would hang the paper up on the refrigerator for everyone to see, just like I had told her I would. Later that night, I did just that.

Every day, for the next several months, I either drew Sallie a picture with the crayons or wrote her a little note asking about her birthday or things she liked, and each time I told her that we loved her. Wondering how literate she was at age seven, I would point to each word as I read it aloud to her, hoping that if she didn't understand what I wrote, perhaps my reading it to her would help her learn.

Months passed with no written answers to my questions, and I began to wonder if I was giving her enough time to answer. After all, it had taken three days the first time. So, I started leaving each note for longer periods of time. After another month with no written communication, I wondered if she was just being stubborn and began to expand my theory.

I remembered a conversation with Barbara concerning spirits being in a plane of existence that was energy based. Had the excitement surrounding the evening with Barbara facilitated a high level of emotional energy, allowing her to perform the chore of writing? It seemed obvious that something she needed for the task was not at her disposal.

I was persistent in my attempt to gain her trust and continued writing to her for several more months. I encouraged her and was hopeful that she would feel compelled to do something in order to please me, but she never again responded directly to any of my questions.

## PHOTOGRAPHS

The day after Barbara's visit, I puttered around the house as usual and while in the nursery I glanced over at the large, naked doll still sitting in the corner. It wasn't very clean, and I thought if I were a little girl, I wouldn't want to play with such a dirty old thing. After a bit of searching, I found a dress and a pair of bloomers and returned to the nursery.

"What do you say we give your baby doll a bath, just like Taylor, and then we can get her dressed," I said out loud. I took a baby wipe, sat down in the corner, and invited Sallie to come help me. I gently cleaned the doll from head to toe with a baby wipe and then held up the dress. "Wouldn't this make her look pretty?" I said as I began to dress her. When I was finished, I held her up. "Oh, doesn't she look so pretty! I think we should take a picture. What do you think, Sallie?" I went to get our camera, then stood in the doorway and took a picture of the dolls in the corner and a few more around the room. I hoped that the camera might catch a glimpse of Sallie's presence.

Later the same day, I finished the roll of film and took it to be developed. The pictures would not be ready for four days. I impatiently waited for Monday to come. All the while the house was quiet; there were no signs of Sallie or any other activity. When Monday came, I went to the store as soon as it opened, collected my photo envelope at the electronics counter, picked up a few additional things along the way, and headed to the front registers to pay for everything.

Impatient, and waiting in what seemed to be a long, slow line, I opened the envelope to take a peek. What I saw took my breath away and I swear my heart dropped to my feet. The first photo in the stack

was the one I had taken of Sallie's baby dolls sitting in the corner. In the center of the picture was an ominous, blue swirl of darkness, somewhat opaque and obscuring most of picture. Although I was utterly horrified, I couldn't take my eyes off of it. I stared dumbfounded for what seemed like forever while my mind raced. Had the developing chemicals ruined the photo and possibly the whole roll, or was this Sallie? If the latter, was that what she looked like when she was angry or mad?

I looked at the photo more closely. In the middle of the thick swirl of color was something similar to the eye of the hurricane; there was no blue color at all, in fact the coloring was perfectly normal. Through this "eye" I could see the baby dolls, teddy bear, and clipboard of papers that we had given to Sallie. Had she encircled the things that were hers to show she was she happy? I tried to keep that possibility in mind, while another part of me just felt a heavy feeling of dread as I focused on the murky blue mass of color all over the photo.

I gathered the courage to look at the next picture. To my horror, it was just as disturbing, and I quickly fanned through the rest of the stack to see if they were all similar; they were not. I managed to regain an awareness of my place in line, and shuffled forward to the second photo.

It was a picture I had taken of Taylor's crib, and it, too, had a large area of dark blue color in the center of it. This splotch of color, however, was smaller and differently shaped. It seemed to take on the general shape of a body or a teddy bear. It had a big head and outstretched arms and legs. It was also somewhat opaque enough to show the crib behind it. Had she been trying to tell me that the baby doll should go in the crib, or was there a more sinister reason for this mass of color over the crib? Was Taylor in danger? Were we in danger?

Although I tried, I could not shake the feeling of utter terror that these photographs gave me. I struggled to regain my composure, just wanting to pay for my things and get to my car. At the same time, I was anxious see the rest of the photos, and almost involuntarily my

hand started shuffling photos from the top of the stack to the bottom. Except for two photos with slight anomalies (much less disturbing than the first two) the rest of the photos looked normal.

The first one had been taken from the master bedroom of the nursery across the hall. The image shows what seems like a cluster of cloudy lights just outside the baby's doorway. Although certainly strange, it was not terrifying.

The other photo was one Tony had taken at the bottom of the stairs the night Barbara had visited and right after we had all come downstairs. If I didn't know better I would have thought the murky anomaly was my Siamese cat running up the stairs at the speed of light. I didn't feel ill at the sight of this one; instead it brought about a sense of curiosity concerning the significant differences in what the camera lens was picking up.

I showed the photos to Tony later that afternoon, and we discussed what the photos might actually be showing or telling us. Each of us interpreted them slightly differently. Where I saw the swirled shadow of a girl in a dress, a large teddy bear, cloudy lights, and a fast cat running up the stairs, Tony saw the large-headed figure with arms and legs, a fast cat running up the stairs, and a hand with a finger pointing upward. He also insisted the dark blue areas on the photos were ink marks from poor developing procedures. I made copies of the photographs and sent them with a letter to Barbara, hoping she might have insight on what was in the photos and why they were so different in each.

With these images burned into my mind, I became paranoid while in the house alone. I wasn't quite sure if we were still dealing with a good little spirit. For many days to come, I was much more on guard and aware of my surroundings, watching everything out of the corner of my eye. After witnessing no activity for a week, I once again questioned if we'd imagined everything (something I would continue to do for months to come). Eventually, the lack of activity allowed me to become more comfortable and at ease again.

One morning, I put Taylor down for his nap in our bedroom and went downstairs to do some chores. I turned the baby monitor on and set it in the window. The green light was illuminated to signal that the unit was working. I checked it frequently, and after some time—expecting sounds of Taylor stirring but hearing none—I walked over to the monitor and found it sitting upside down on the windowsill. No one else had been in the house that day and although I really didn't expect an answer, I asked, "Sallie, did you do that?" There was no reply.

The rest of the afternoon, I noticed several times that the wooden ball on the ceiling fan in the living room would swing around in a circle. Each time I saw it move, I said hello to Sallie and made small talk with her to make her feel welcomed.

That evening while Tony was at work, George came over and we talked about the ongoing experiences. The disturbing photos made us wonder if Sallie might be unhappy with the hand-me-down dolls. To make it up to her, we decided to go shopping for a new one. We decided on a baby doll rather than a Barbie doll, and a boy doll if possible. We hoped that if she had a "baby" of her own, we could redirect her possessive tendencies away from Taylor.

I had made a habit of carrying the camera with me during the day and snapped many photos in the hope of capturing anomalies. In one set of photos, a smoky looking figure stood or floated near the ceiling at the top of the stairs. It appeared to be a male figure dressed in a dark suit or uniform. The shirt was white and he was clearly wearing a brimmed hat. He also seemed to be holding a sword or bayonet. For the most part, however, the multitude of photos I had been taking didn't capture what I was looking for.

The next day, George and I bought a new doll and some wrapping paper (I feel a gift should always be wrapped). I gathered a number of things to create Sallie's own space and a place for her things. I dug out a Cabbage Patch Doll that was special to me, and a fancy old dress. I found a hat, beads, barrettes, a baby bottle, a rattle, and a few other things and placed them all in a large burgundy file box I had bought that morning. I did this in part so that she had a place to contain her treasures, and partly to hide the things from people who might otherwise find them out of place in our son's room.

When Tony came home from work, he was a little put off by what I had done. He seemed to think this ghost thing was getting a little out of hand. He thought it was nuts to buy gifts for a ghost and asked sarcastically, "Do you really think she's going to unwrap them?"

"You never know, she might," I told him. I didn't pay much attention to his remarks and continued what I was doing. I took off all the twist ties securing the doll in its box to make it easier for Sallie and replaced it neatly before wrapping it. On the gift card I wrote, "To Sallie. We all love you and hope you like your new baby doll. Love, Uncle George, Daddy, Mommy, and Taylor."

I took the gift and the burgundy box up to the nursery.

As I entered the room, I quickly noticed that the baby dolls I'd left sitting side by side were now in different positions—the little doll now sat in the lap of the big doll. I remember thinking how cute this was. I sat in Sallie's corner and called her into the room. I went through the box, and showed her the things I was giving her to play with. I explained that the Cabbage Patch Doll had been my special doll and I was giving it to her, "my special little girl." I had quickly grown accustomed to talking to her as if she was right in the room with me.

TEN

# LIVING WITH SPIRIT

## JUST ODD: AUGUST 1993

Life in our home continued quietly for several days; there was nothing odd at all. In fact, it was so quiet, we wondered if our little spirit girl had gone for good. My thoughts recalled all the events that led to our believing we had a ghost and wondered if there was room for an interpretation we had missed. Did we and others read too much into the experiences? Had the psychic played on our naïveté? Had the anomalies in the photos resulted from human error, indirectly leading us to the theory that we had a ghost?

On Thursday, August 5th, there were signs of activity. Peeking into the nursery on a trip to the bathroom, I noticed that the dress I had placed in the cardboard box in Sallie's corner was partially pulled out through the hole that served as the handle. My first thought was that one of the cats had stuck a playful paw inside and had gotten a claw caught on the dress as he pulled his paw from the box. However, with a ghost in the house, I was sure there were other possibilities, too.

Had Sallie tried to get the dress out? I looked at the box and debated whether I should have removed the box's top to allow Sallie easier access, but decided to leave it on for a few more days. I was anxious to see whether she would get what she was after. That night, I encouraged more activity by placing her gift-wrapped box onto the burgundy box. I told her it was a special gift just for her and that she could open it anytime.

Over the next few days, I looked into the nursery more often than usual, expecting Sallie would be just as excited about the special gift as I was. Two days later, it had remained untouched. I began to think that Tony was right—Sallie wasn't going to unwrap it.

Later that afternoon, while I changed the baby's diaper at the changing table in the nursery, I took the opportunity to survey the room. Nothing was out of order. I took Taylor to our bedroom and set him on the bed so I could get dressed myself. Ten minutes later, I needed something from the bathroom and left Taylor in the middle of the bed, as he was still too young to roll over. I peered into the nursery as usual and was shocked at what I saw. The brand new baby doll was out of the box and laying in the center of Taylor's crib.

The package and wrappings, however, had been undisturbed; as far as I could see the gift remained unopened in her corner where I had left it. Amazed by the situation and knowing it deserved a reaction, I looked into the crib and said, "Oh, Sallie, you have a beautiful baby doll!" I went on to tell her we should take a picture and hurried to get the camera. I took two pictures, hoping that she would show up in them, but she didn't.

A few minutes later, I remember standing in the nursery's doorway with Taylor in my arms for several minutes, looking back and forth between the still-wrapped gift on the floor and the new doll in the crib. I couldn't help but re-think the moments before finding the doll in the crib; I had to process every possibility to assure myself that no one else could have been responsible for what I seemed to have experienced.

Someone would have had to sneak into the house, get up the stairs and into the nursery, remove the doll from the box, lay it in the crib, reseal the gift wrapping, return the wrapped box to its original place, and leave the house, all within about ten minutes and without being noticed. I was sure this was not possible.

I took the gift box downstairs, called George, explained what had happened, and asked him to come over. I needed another person to see that the tape on the paper had not been disturbed and to witness the contents of the box. Surely the doll was still in the box; I couldn't fathom how the doll would have gotten out of the box without signs of tampering. When he arrived, I carefully opened the box in front of him. As I did, the only thing that seemed odd was that one of the end flaps of the box had been dog-eared and the flaps had not been closed in the same order as I had done when I took the twist ties off.

I was dumbfounded and stared quietly at the box. It was completely empty except for the cardboard support that once held the doll. I'm sure that George wondered if I was pulling a fast one on him, but I was preoccupied with trying to understand how a spirit could move a physical item through a physical barrier. The box had certainly been opened in some manner, as the flaps showed signs of being opened and closed again. One could only assume that the gift wrapping would have been opened too, but this was not the case. The wrapping paper looked untouched, the tape undisturbed. I tried to carefully take the tape off, but the paper it was attached to tore as expected.

The following day, a stack of freshly washed baby bottles and nipples that had been sitting on the kitchen counter went toppling to the floor as I stood in the dining room a few feet away. I spun around expecting to see one of the cats in a guilty pose or in a panicked exodus from the room, but there was no one.

Sallie had made her presence known the day before, and I wondered if this might have been her way of getting my attention. If so, why the bottles? "Sallie, if you want a bottle for your baby doll, there is one in your box. Come on, I'll show you." When I got to the nursery, I found not only the toy bottle that I had put in there a few days earlier, but also one of the Playtex ones that had been sitting on the counter ten minutes before.

The following Monday, we had plans to finish wallpapering the kitchen and had enlisted the help of Tony's mother. I was rather surprised that she agreed to come by, because being in our house made her uneasy. She had made it clear on several occasions that Tony and I should have gotten rid of Sallie already; she had even threatened that while we were gone someday, she would bring a priest over to do an exorcism. For months, I had taken Sallie's side. She was just a little girl playing games and really wasn't being mean or trying to hurt anyone. I pointed out that Sallie needed to fit in and that until she did so, it was going to be a trying experience for all of us.

When Tony's mom got to the house, George was holding Taylor on the couch. Without even putting her purse down, she went over and took Taylor from him, "You people don't know how to hold a baby." She wasn't being mean—it was just her way, and it gave her an excuse to hold her grandchild.

Soon Taylor fell asleep in her arms, as he always did. She placed him in the downstairs cradle, which stood in the dining room just past the end of the sofa and its end table. On the table stood a box of Kleenex, the portable telephone, and an oil lamp. (With mischievous and unpredictable cats, I had always felt safer with oil lamps rather than open-flame candles during a power outage.)

Tony's mom and I went into the kitchen to start working. After ten minutes, she stepped away to check on the baby. He was still fast asleep, so she returned to hang another piece of wallpaper, and then checked on him again. Finding that he was still sound asleep, she turned and took about three steps towards the kitchen. Suddenly she heard a horribly painful cry come from Taylor, as if someone had pinched or poked him. I heard it from the kitchen and tried to remove the glue from my hands so I could investigate. Peering into the room, I noticed there were no cats dashing out of the room. In fact, there was no one in the room at all, because Tony had gone upstairs a few minutes prior.

I knew my mother-in-law would not have done anything to cause the baby to wake up screaming, but instinctively felt that Sallie might have. I wanted to scold her and warn her from doing it again, but I also knew my mother-in-law was already unsettled about our spirit. If she were to see me interacting with it, it would have been like throwing salt on an open wound. I decided to address the problem, and Sallie, later.

Apparently Tony's mom had come around to my point of view; she rushed over to pick up the screaming baby. While cradling him in her arms, she harshly scolded Sallie. "Sallie, if you hurt this baby again, I'm going to spank your butt!"

Still standing in the kitchen, my first impulse was to laugh. I had never thought I would witness my mother-in-law talking to a ghost, let alone raising her voice to one so sternly. I felt a surge of pride that she had interacted with our spirit. Then I had a strong feeling that Sallie didn't like this old woman scolding her. I had already sensed a surge of jealousy from Sallie each time Tony's mom picked up the baby. I guess in an odd way, I had become tied to Sallie's emotions as well as her thoughts. I almost told Tony's mom, "Oh, great! Now you've just pissed her off."

Hearing the baby, Tony came downstairs, and we explained the situation. Taylor was still quite upset, so Tony took him and stretched out at the far end of our sectional sofa (closest to the front windows and away from the dining room). The baby was much calmer, and thinking he would be safe with Tony holding him, my mother-in-law and I returned to work in the kitchen.

We hadn't stepped out of the living room for more than two minutes when we heard Tony holler, "Debra, you better have a talk with her!" I again stopped what I was doing and headed for the living room to ask why, but when I rounded the corner of the kitchen doorway, I caught sight of the glass globe from the oil lamp lying on the floor in the dining room.

Tony was just getting up off the couch, baby still on his chest, when I walked into the room. He described what he had just seen. "It lifted straight off of the oil lamp base like a slow motion rocket and then floated about three feet above the floor and across the room as if it was being carried. When I hollered your name, it suddenly dropped to the floor. I think she's scared of you, Deb." I remember the look on his face. It was a cross between shock and amazement.

I ruled out any other possible scenarios, realizing that there was no way Tony would have had the time or ability to accomplish putting the glass globe on the floor across the room without his mother or me seeing him and without waking the baby laying on his chest. So, I quickly took on the "mommy" role and scolded Sallie for her behavior. "What you did was wrong and you need to go to your room to think about it for a few minutes." Of course, I had no idea if she really went.

I knew my mother-in-law didn't like Sallie or say nice things about her, and that was one of the reasons Sallie didn't like her. For weeks I had warned her and reminded her about waking the baby, so she knew it was bad and I would get mad if she did. Likely, Sallie felt that if my mother-in-law was responsible for waking the baby, she would get into trouble.

When that didn't work and Tony's mom scolded her, she got more irritated and became actively defiant. Imagine a little girl picking up the oil lamp's glass globe, as if to say, "Na na nana na na, I can do this and you can't stop me." Of course, this was the action that got her into trouble. Inside, I giggled at the scenario.

## WAKE-UP CALL: AUGUST 14TH, 1993

On Friday, August 13th, Tony had worked his usual midnight shift which ended at 7:00 a.m. On his way home he picked up George, who had since moved to another rental property. Without a car, he often needed a ride to work. Since he didn't need to be to work until 9:00 a.m. they turned on the television until they had to leave. Tony lay down at one end of the sofa and George on the other.

About 8:45 a.m., George was awakened by a sudden thump and a heaviness on his chest. Thinking one of the cats had jumped on him, he reached, without opening his eyes, to pick up the cat and toss it to the floor. To his surprise, he didn't grasp the neck of a cat. Instead he opened his eyes to see, sitting on his chest and staring at him almost eye level, the stiff and motionless form of the (now infamous) bean bag teddy bear.

Still holding the bear by its neck, he woke Tony and practically shoved the bear into his face. Scared and almost unable to speak, he muttered, "Look, look." Tony, still in a sleepy stupor and grumbly from being awakened for what seemed no good reason, said, "So what? It's a bear," and laughed.

"It dropped on my chest. She dropped it on me!" George insisted. Tony's eyes widened as his consciousness woke up with reality. He knew that the bear had always sat across the room and had been there when they laid down.

I was just waking and coming downstairs for the day when they told me what had happened. I couldn't help but see the humor in it and I laughed. George was not amused. When I regained my composure, I had George lie on the couch as he had been and I held the bear over his chest. I then dropped it several times from various heights. We were able to determine, by comparing the pressure he felt each time it fell, that it had been dropped from a height of about two feet above him.

It was also a reasonable assumption that George awakened and opened his eyes a second or so after the bear hit his chest. Had it been Tony playing a prank, George would have seen him. If he had tossed it onto George's chest, how ironic that the bear landed upright and facing George when he opened his eyes.

Questions flooded my head. Had Sallie meant to scare George or was she just being playful with him? Did she understand that George needed to get up in time for work and if so, how did she know what time it was? Was the timing of this incident just coincidental?

## KITTEN BEHAVIOR: AUGUST 16, 1993

Although it's usual for a young kitten to dart around and play most of the day, I had noticed our new kitten displaying strange behavior for several days in a row. When it ran through the room it wasn't in a playful manner, but urgent and fearful. There were times I would hear it screech, but when I turned to look none of the other cats was anywhere near it. Whenever it crawled in my lap, it would fall into a deep, exhausted sleep.

The kitten seemed wary of moving freely in the house, and quite often I found it cowering in some remote, out of the way place for no apparent reason. It had also become quite skinny. Giving more thought to the situation, I realized I had not seen it eat with our other two cats. I grew concerned that it wasn't being allowed to eat.

I placed the kitten at the food dish at the next feeding and watched the cats' behaviors. They all seemed happy to see each other and the kitten ate like she'd been starved. Having ruled out my older cats causing the kitten's stressed behavior, I now considered the possibility that Sallie might be harassing the kitten. I spoke to her and told her that she had to stop playing with the kitten until it was older. I explained that it was just a baby like Taylor and it needed a lot of rest. I continued to tell her she wasn't to scare it or hurt it because that just wasn't fair. A few days later, the kitten was back to its usual behavior.

## LIGHTS OUT: AUGUST 20, 1993

Several days later, we had a party at the house for a friend going off to college. Several of the guests got into an extensive discussion about Sallie and through that conversation, others learned of the haunting in our home. Although some were interested, others were disturbed by the information and several of them left.

Later that evening, one of the girls needed to go to the bathroom. She was extremely reluctant to go upstairs by herself, so I volunteered to go with her. As we ascended the stairs, I told Tammy I would wait just outside the door. While doing so, I felt several cool drafts. When the bathroom visit was done, we both stood in the nursery and talked for a bit. Perhaps it was the peacefulness of seeing the baby's room that made her feel comfortable again. George soon came up to join us and the three of us sat quietly on the floor of the room.

All three of us felt the cold draft of Sallie's closeness. We asked her to do something for us, and then waited quietly. Suddenly, Tammy jumped to her feet, scurried out the door, and ran down the stairs. Surprised, I looked at George who explained that he had seen the crayon on the paper move—not roll, but move slightly. In fact he not only saw it, but heard it shift across the paper. I can't say I saw it move, but I did hear a sound that could have been the crayon sliding sideways across the paper and it was apparent that Tammy saw and heard it, too. George and I checked the crayon for attached strings or another reason it moved in the manner it did, but we found nothing.

A few minutes later, Tammy came back upstairs. She explained that she saw the crayon move and it really spooked her. She said the earlier talk about Sallie not liking strangers in the nursery reminded her that her presence in the room might make Sallie mad. Tammy eventually decided that what she had seen wasn't really scary, just startling. Curiosity won out over fear and she felt the need to return. We asked Sallie to do something, but nothing happened.

Soon the others from downstairs had come up—some of them sat on the floor with us, others stood. Most everyone mentioned feeling a cold draft, even those who stood in the hallway, too nervous to come in, but trying to determine if the rest of us were pulling their leg about what we were experiencing.

We asked Sallie to show off, but nothing happened. Everyone was getting rather restless, so I directed my thoughts to forcing her into a reaction. Knowing that she didn't like strangers upstairs, I told her that if she showed off for us once, we would leave her room. I felt bad that I had to bribe her, but I knew chances were good that I'd get a reaction.

I wanted the nonbelievers to witness what we had been telling them about.

After about a minute or so the hallway light suddenly went off. No one had been standing near the light switch. As each person checked the person next to them and the area for signs of trickery, the light in the hall came back on. Two seconds later the light in the nursery went out. Then it came back on.

Our guests saw what they needed to see and although many did not know how to respond, some simply took a deep breath and stated that they had seen enough. A few thanked Sallie and I kept my promise. I shuffled everyone out of the nursery and down the stairs, told her she was a good girl, and turned out the light before leaving the room myself.

## STATIC: AUGUST 25, 1993

I had believed that Sallie wouldn't intentionally bring harm to Taylor. Late in August, I was in the nursery straightening up while Taylor was in the baby swing. Realizing I needed something from downstairs and knowing that the baby was not big enough to squirm his way out of the swing, I felt comfortable leaving him unattended for a few minutes. I also took a big leap of faith and enlisted Sallie to make her feel more useful in the care of the baby. "Sallie, can you watch Taylor for a minute while I run and get something?"

When I got downstairs, I passed by the baby monitor and heard not only the distinct sound of the swing mechanics but also a static-like noise that seemed to coincide with the rhythm of the swing at one of its highest points. I pictured Sallie proudly standing in front of the swing and the baby she'd been asked to care for, each burst of static expressing her excitement.

## INTERFERENCE: SEPTEMBER 2, 1993

About 10:30 p.m., after saying good night to Tony as he left for work, I'd realized I had not yet washed the day's dishes. My favorite TV show was on, so I decided to get as much as I could get done on each commercial break. On one of the first breaks, as I stood in the kitchen, I heard the TV emit an irritating static noise. My first thought was that something was wrong with the television station, but as soon as I walked into the living room the static stopped.

Oddly enough this happened each commercial break. Static and electrical interference seemed to signify Sallie's presence. If it was her, why would the static stop as soon as I returned to the room? Why did she want me in the room with her?

I told Sallie that when I was done in the kitchen, I would sit and read her a book. I watched the end of my show, finished in the kitchen and walked into the living room and over to the children's books. Again, the static on the television stopped as soon as I got into the room.

I wanted to keep my promise, no matter how silly I was going to feel while doing it, and one by one I held a book and asked, "Would you like me to read this one?" or "How about this one, or maybe this one?" When I got to the book about hats (one of Taylor's favorites), the static from the TV suddenly blared loudly. I continued, holding up each of the next five books and asked the same questions, but the static had stopped.

I took joy in the thought that this might be a new form of communication between us, but not wanting to make such a quick assessment of the situation, I decided to test my theory. I began holding the books, one by one, and as I did before and asked the same question, "This one?" Not until I held up the book about the hats did the static come back to the TV. It seemed like a distinct confirmation.

I had always read to Taylor in the rocking chair or the glider, and feeling Sallie would want the same closeness, I said, "Okay, let's go sit in the rocking chair and read it." With my hand, I patted my lap and invited her to sit down while I read. Without a doubt, it felt awkward reading a children's storybook to a ghost child with the same exuberance as I would have read it to my own son. However, I knew if she really was there, she wanted to be cared about as she had seen me care for Taylor. I heard no more static from the TV that night.

## FINGERPRINTS: SEPTEMBER 10, 1993

While hanging pictures in the dining room, Tony noticed something odd about the one of the two taper candles sitting in sconces on the wall. I'd left the original plastic wrap on to help prevent them from collecting dust and looking dingy, and as Tony looked closer, he saw brown burn marks on the plastic at the base of one of the candles. Although the wax below the plastic had experienced enough heat that indentations had been formed in the wax itself, the heat did not break through the plastic.

The configuration of the melted spots was very strange. There were four marks on one side of the candle and a single, larger mark on the other. I began turning the candle over in my hand and my fingers nestled into fairly comfortable places within these small indentations. Could the marks have been left by a set of small fingers and a thumb—the hand of a child?

During the time Tony was out of the house I took the opportunity to talk to Sallie as often as I thought about it. It had become easier to do, especially without Tony around. If I did it in front of him he would get uncomfortable or make fun of me. So, each night as I lay in bed, I asked Sallie if she was still happy. I'd tell her that she had been a good girl or that I loved her, and I'd also tell her of approaching family plans or activities so that she was always aware of them.

I even began inviting her to cuddle up next to me in bed. I wasn't quite sure why I was doing it or if it was the right thing to do. Was I taking it all too far? Or was I helping this little spirit feel the love that she'd likely missed for decades?

I also wondered if what I was doing was actually keeping her from moving on, and this question made me unsure on how to interact with her. My mothering instincts prevailed, and as the days passed I grew more comfortable with our odd little relationship.

## COLD SPOTS: SEPTEMBER 12, 1993

At 1:30 a.m. I was in bed, stretched out on my left side with my left arm stretched across the bed. I suddenly felt a very cold sensation on that arm and on the front of my upper torso. I knew the parts of me that were feeling cold were the same parts someone would touch if cuddled right next to me. The cold feeling did not encompass my whole body, just my front side. It was a coldness I was familiar with; I felt it was Sallie.

## CANDLES: SEPTEMBER 15, 1993

While I was dusting the shelf on the wall in the living room above the couch, one of the candles again caught my eye. The wick was darkened as if it had been lit. Oddly, though, there was no pool of wax near its base. The tip of the candle was still rounded. Additionally, I saw wax drippings from about halfway down the sides of the candle upwards and beyond the tip of the wick. It looked as if it had been melted near the base of the candle and then held so that the wax would drip up the candle and off the wick.

I never lit any of the candles in our house; they were simply for decoration. The open flames of candles sitting low would have been a fire hazard with cats in the house. I could find no reasonable explanation for the condition of the candle. Further inspection verified that there were no foreign marks anywhere on the candle. There were no finger marks like the ones we'd seen the previous month. The base of the candle looked as if it had been warmed by an intense source.

A paranormal investigator visiting the house months later suggested that a hair dryer could have generated this effect. Already curious about this possibility, I had tried to simulate it, with no positive result. The hair dryer did not heat the candle enough to make it drip in a thin stream of wax. Instead, the wax melted in a more unified way along the entire candle. Realizing that in order to get the thin stream effect, we would have to have a more focused heat source, we opted to try a lighter with a smaller flame. This did not work either, because although the flame was small, it didn't heat enough of an area at one time to allow wax to actually flow. When the flame was turned up, the wax still did not drip in the thin stream we had found on our candle. Although I have tried variations of this same experiment with different kinds of candles, heat sources, and angles, we have yet to replicate the condition of the candle.

By mid-September, I had completed my maternity leave and was working a day job three days a week. After dropping the baby off at a sitter, Tony was free to sleep. By early afternoon, he was bored, and I often returned home to find that he'd vacuumed and dusted. On several occasions I got reports of the vacuum being turned off while he was using it, and a few times he told me he'd actually seen the switch on the vacuum being flipped to the off position.

## SALLIE'S WARNING: SEPTEMBER 22, 1993

I had never given much thought to a spirit interacting in a way that would show that they cared about what happened in the human world they watched from the other side. Amazingly enough, Sallie was able to reach out of the darkness to give us firsthand experience, and it about broke my heart.

On this particular morning, I dragged myself out of bed and down to the kitchen, switched a load of laundry from the washer into the dryer, and went to take a shower. About thirty minutes later, I opened the dryer and pulled out what I needed. Running late as usual, I had very little time to properly deal with what remained. I left some of the clothes in the basket in front of the dryer and the rest inside. I went back upstairs, finished getting ready for work, then headed off, leaving Tony and the baby asleep upstairs.

When Tony got up that afternoon, he got a cup of coffee and something to eat and soon realized that most of the clothes in and around the dryer were still damp, so he pushed them all back into the dryer, closed the door and set it to dry. He immediately heard a loud thump thump, thump, thump, thump, but ignored it, thinking somewhere in the load was a pair of tennis shoes.

He played a little with the baby and then decided to tidy up the house. He turned on the stereo in the living room and headed to the front closet for the vacuum. He'd only taken a few steps before the music from the stereo abruptly stopped. He went back to find it had been turned off, and turned it back on. A few steps toward the closet and the music stopped again. Having gone through this many times before he resolved to just leave it off rather than play the ON-OFF game with an ornery little spirit.

Having retrieved the vacuum, he plugged it in and turned it on. It wasn't but a second later and it turned off. He turned it back on and he could make one long sweep forward, it was again turned off. He'd become quite aggravated at this point at what he thought was Sallie being extremely mischievous. He told me later that he must have turned it back on at least six times before getting so mad he yelled out loud, "God damn it, Sallie! Knock it off, already!" At one point he had even watched the toggle switch flip back to the off position of its own accord. Eventually, he was able to finish the downstairs without any further interference. The rest of the afternoon was quiet and uneventful.

At the end of my workday, I came home and together with the baby in the walker we were all in the kitchen while Tony started cooking dinner. He mentioned his experience with the vacuum earlier that day and how noisy the tennis shoes in the last load had been while they dried that afternoon. His comment reminded me that there was laundry to fold and another load to put in, so I decided to switch laundry loads while he was busy with dinner preparations.

Reflecting on his comment, I could not remember having a pair of shoes in the dryer that morning. I opened the dryer and began to pull things out to fold them. I immediately began noticing strange brown spots on everything and began setting the items aside; the whole time trying to process in my head what could have possibly caused all the spots on our clothes. They certainly weren't on anything I had pulled out earlier that morning. In fact, some of the spotted things I was pulling out were things I had come across while searching for my shirt earlier that day, so I knew that whatever got all over the clothes, did so after I had been through the clothes that morning.

I wondered if something had been left in one of the pockets, or if some foreign object such as a pen had been in the dryer and the heat had caused it to explode. The more I thought about it, the more it just didn't make sense. The spots were a dark reddish-brown, not blue or black which would suggest ink. I couldn't help but think that it looked a lot like dried blood, but I couldn't imagine how so much blood could have gotten in the dryer. I shared all these thoughts with Tony as he continued with dinner.

As I leaned slightly forward toward the opening to get another handful of clothes, I noticed that the piece of clothing I was retrieving was splattered with brown spots. I immediately felt light-headed and that I was about to faint. Staring ahead of me, dreading coming face-to-face with what I knew I would find if I went any further, I robotically stepped backwards and began to scream. I don't remember saying a word, I just screamed, "No, no, no!" Then I screamed again. I knew what had happened, and then suddenly Tony knew.

One of my cats had apparently crawled into the dryer to cuddle and sleep among the warm clothes. Tony, not realizing this, had simply thrown the damp clothes back into the dryer on top of her, shut the door, and set it for the usual ninety-minute cycle.

Tony tried to soothe me and quiet my screaming. He knew poor Taylor was terrified at hearing me. He was able to calm me down enough to suggest I take the baby over to my in-laws' while he cleaned up the mess. Honestly, I don't know how I managed to drive there, but I did.

Later that night, I returned home to find that Tony had put my cat in a large tin container amongst her toys and laid it on a soft bed of pillow stuffing and silk material. I knew he felt responsible for what had happened, because he was the one who closed the door, put it on a 90-minute cycle, and ignored the insistent activity that seemingly tried to warn him that something was very, very wrong.

I tried not to make him feel worse in telling him of my conclusions about the whole incident—instead I tried to show him that Sallie was actually trying to be helpful. She was trying to get his attention, trying to warn him. "I'm sure she would do something similar if Taylor were ever in danger, so next time, give some thought as to why she might be doing something so adamantly." He agreed.

I then turned my attention to Sallie and called her into the room. I wanted to let her know that we understood that she had been warning Tony about the cat in the dryer. I told her that I knew she felt badly about it, but it was not her fault.

"It was an accident, honey; we all feel bad about it. Daddy didn't mean to hurt the cat. He simply didn't know she was in the dryer."

While lying in bed that same night, I wondered why Sallie didn't just turn off the dryer. Did it have something to do with the higher electrical current? Was that something she was not able to handle? Was low-level electricity the only thing that she could manipulate? Or were direct life-and-death interventions against the rules for a spirit? I never did ask her about it; I guess I didn't want her to feel guilty or think it was her fault that the cat died.

Several days passed, then a week or more without an inkling of activity. I wondered why. Was she resting, gathering, or regenerating her energy? And if that was the case, how and where did she do that?

Was she, perhaps, sulking and mourning the loss of the cat? There was always the possibility that she had simply moved on and was no longer interested in our home and family.

I secretly hoped that day would never come. I enjoyed the interaction and hoped for meaningful forms of communication to be established between us. I wanted to learn so much, and I just knew this little spirit would give me the opportunity to do so.

ELEVEN

# TONY SEES SALLIE

## OCTOBER 1993

Sallie's behavior was similar to other kids her age. Now that we have three of our own, I see how they clamor for acceptance and attention, especially when you are on the phone or attending to something else. They will do anything to get your attention and it doesn't matter if it is good or bad.

Although there were times when Tony did notice Sallie's activity, he often chose not to acknowledge it or respond to her. She tried desperately to get his attention, and some days she was more rambunctious than others. October 1st was one of those days and she just wouldn't leave him alone.

Throughout the day, it seemed she delighted in turning the TV or stereo back on after he had turned it off, or turning it off after he'd turned it on. She did the same thing with other electrical and kitchen appliances he tried to use that afternoon. Try as he might to ignore her activity and continue his daily routines, she took every opportunity to thwart his efforts. This playfulness continued well into the evening.

About 9:00 that night, I had gone upstairs to get ready for bed while Tony took his dirty glass to the kitchen sink. Before coming up to bed, as he did every night, he briefly stopped in front of the TV to hit the off switch. He had just gotten to the bottom of the stairs when he heard the familiar sound of the TV turning on. When this had happened before, we would only have taken a few steps before it came back on. This night, she let him get much farther.

The second time it happened, he'd taken several steps up the stairs and the third time he had gotten about halfway before the TV came back on. The fourth time, he hit the button and raced up the stairs as fast as possible. Although he'd been through the On-Off game with her many times before, the thought of a ghost hanging out close to him and playing with him was always unnerving.

As if Sallie was making up for lost time and days of inactivity, her antics steadily continued. By the time Tony left for work the next night, we had noticed several instances of activity during the course of the day. The motor on the microwave had been running, with its light on and the timer counting down, when no one was using it. We knew that running the unit without something inside could ruin it, so I would run over and open the door to stop the process and remind Sallie not to play with the microwave.

Sometimes I didn't catch it in time and I would hear the familiar beep signifying that it had just completed a programmed cycle. It became apparent that Sallie was working at manipulating energy and she had found something fun to play with. I felt a real sadness for her. Having to interact with electrical appliances for fun or attention seemed pitiful to me and I hesitated to scold her. I didn't want to take away what may have been her only means of fun, but I also feared that this continued activity might ruin the microwave, or worse yet, cause an electrical problem or even a fire. I decided that something had to be done.

I always felt awkward talking to her in front of Tony, so I waited until after he went to work. I had learned from experience that Sallie did try to accommodate the guidelines we laid out, so I set out to explain my concerns. I showed her that the power level on the microwave could be set to zero. "Setting the level to zero will be safer and the timer you like to play with will still run." I hoped she understood and had the ability to comply. Quickly enough, I got my answer. Over the next couple of days, I heard the unit beep often, and frequently I would run into the kitchen to notice that the timer had been counting down but no interior light was on. No light, no motor.

It truly warmed my heart to know that such real communication could be attained with a spirit. Once again, she had succeeded in following my rules. I made a point of praising her and told her how smart she was to have learned it so quickly. I hoped that doing so would help deepen our relationship.

I had no idea how this interaction and understanding was possible. Sallie was, in my understanding, on the other side—dead. Although I had heard of rapping and tapping to communicate with a ghost, I had not heard or read much on any detailed communication. I was delighted that I was able to experience it first hand and wondered how long it might continue. I also felt that I had a distorted sense of what a ghost actually was. Over the course of several months, I had experimented with Sallie to find out what ghosts might be capable of. In those months she showed me so much more than I could have imagined.

Ghosts and spirits, in my mind, are very different things. A ghost is non-interactive and is often represented by residual haunting. It is simply a repetitive energy that plays over and over like a film; usually at a specific time and place. It's a mere snapshot in time—a memory. Spirit energy on the other hand, seems to show some level of the spirit, or soul, it represents: the feelings, thoughts, and personality of someone once living.

This would lead one to believe that in some form, our soul energy does move on after death. A spirit has some degree of consciousness, which explains why they can interact, respond, and communicate. I wondered if ghosts were aware of their surroundings and if they were aware of how their actions affected the world of the living. I wondered if a ghost could have a true consciousness. My level of excitement rose with each new experience. It seemed I was getting some kind of answers to these questions.

On October 4th, Tony's mom and dad came for dinner. The night before they came, I told Sallie they were coming and reminded her to behave. We were having coffee about 7:30 p.m. when Taylor woke from his nap. Tony had taken him to the end of the couch to change him. As he finished, his mother, anxious to be the first one to hold him, went over to pick him up. She had only taken a few steps away when suddenly the basket and oil lamp were flung from the top of the end table and onto the couch next to Tony.

Tony and I looked at each other, both of us wide-eyed. Although his mom had her back turned toward Tony and the couch as she walked away, she did hear the commotion and quickly turned to find the disheveled array of items lying on the cushions. I had to stop myself from laughing—I wondered if either of them really understood the situation.

I could just feel a gnawing anger and jealously inside that was not my own. I knew Sallie was upset. Had Sallie been sitting right next to Taylor when my mother-in-law plucked him from her? I hollered at Sallie, "Now Sallie, you quit that!"

I spoke to Sallie after everyone had gone. I told her that although it was all right not to like Taylor's grandma, she had to stop doing bad things when grandma was around. Wanting to end on a positive note, I told her, "I still love you, even though sometimes you do bad things."

For several days afterward, we peacefully coexisted. Feeling that Sallie had been doing a good job at following the rules we set, I would occasionally praise her for doing so. It still felt very awkward talking to someone I couldn't see.

Working the third shift, Tony often found himself not getting enough sleep. Generally, he would fall asleep on the couch in the early evening after we had put Taylor to bed. About 10:00 p.m. on October

10th, we were lying on the couch, talking about things in general. We were soon on the subject of Sallie, and he told me that for about a week he had often felt the sensation someone was gently biting on his toes.

I snickered, thinking he was making it up, but he was serious and I listened because it was the first time *he* had brought Sallie up in conversation and verbally acknowledged her interactions with him. Usually he would only make eye contact and gestures to point out the activity he noticed. He went on to tell me he had felt the biting in bed, while watching TV, and at the dinner table. He was positive it was Sallie. She had apparently found another way to seek his attention and a reaction, only she wasn't getting it from him directly.

A few minutes later, I headed upstairs to take a shower and couldn't help thinking it was an awfully cute way for Sallie to play with him. As I reached the top I heard Tony loudly yell, "Ow! Damn it!" I didn't hear anything else, so I entered the bathroom and shut the door. Tony must have been listening for the shower to stop because when I came out, twenty minutes later, he was standing in the hall with a strange look of mixed surprise, anger, and perplexity.

Before I had a chance to ask what the problem was, he unbuttoned his jeans and dropped them to the floor. I started to laugh. Hearing but ignoring my apparent insensitivity, he turned slightly sideways, kept his focus on my face for my reaction, and pointed out an area on the outer part of his upper thigh. "She bit me!" he said in exasperation.

I was still grinning when he glared at me and growled, "It's not funny! Say something to her!" Seeing how serious he was, I regained as much composure as I could and asked, "What do you want me to say to her, 'Bad Sallie, don't bite Daddy?'" I then took a closer look at his leg, "What did you do to piss her off?" He gave me another dirty look but said nothing.

I expected to find marks created to look like teeth. After all, Tony had not been happy with my behavior concerning her presence in our house and wanted her gone. If he could prove to me that she was dangerous it would give me a reason to get rid of her. However, the marks looked genuine.

The area was beet-red. In the center was a distinct set of small teeth marks imprinted on his upper thigh. The reddened area suggested that the trauma had happened very recently. I tried to figure out how the marks got there. Taylor had been sleeping and had no teeth. The bite was not in a place that Tony would have been able to reach himself. Besides, the configuration was unmistakably small and child-sized.

"Perhaps you should acknowledge her once in a while when the balls of the ceiling light start to swing. You know she wants to be accepted by you and you never want to admit that she's there."

"It's hard, Deb. It just isn't right!"

Still finding humor in the situation, but seeing his anguish, I enlisted my self-control and firmly told Sallie that what she did wasn't nice and although it was okay to play with Daddy, she had played too rough and hurt him. With that said, Tony pulled up his pants and walked away looking dejected and frustrated. Although I had given him my honest thoughts, he hadn't wanted to hear what I had to say.

The next day, the teeth marks had disappeared, but a large bruise the size of a baseball was clearly visible. A few days after that, Tony finally came to see the humor in that night and laughed with me as we recalled it. We also talked about his seeing dark shadows throughout the house and out of the corner of his eye. He saw them on light fixtures, within the reflective surface of shiny objects around the house, and on the walls or ceiling. I had not seen them, but over the course of the next few weeks, I began looking for them.

On the 17th, I was talking to my sister in New York. Since her visit, Karen had called at least once a week to check on us and always asked what Sallie was up to. In a letter to me weeks earlier, she had enclosed a package of cherry Kool-aid and a crayon drawing that her own little girl had done for Sallie. I had put them on top of Sallie's box in the nursery and told her who they were from.

During that phone conversation, Karen asked if Sallie had liked the Kool-aid she sent the week prior and she wanted me to relay the message that, "Aunt Karen says 'hi'—remember, she sent you the crayon drawing that her little girl drew for you and the Kool-aid?" A few moments later, as if in response to the question, a doll on the shelf behind the stereo fell to the floor. There were no cats in the room and the doll was not sitting anywhere near the edge of the shelf. I can't be sure it was directly related, but it was one of the few times I ever saw something happen with my own eyes.

The next day was October 30th. About 5:00 p.m., I walked past the downstairs bathroom to find one of the small tea candles on the toilet tank lit. Judging from the pool of wax at the base of the wick, it had been burning for ten to twenty minutes. I scolded Sallie and just as Barbara had suggested in her letter, I told her she was not to light any more fires or she would have to leave because fires could badly hurt Taylor or his Mom or Dad, and burn down the house, which would leave us no place to live.

That same day a friend stopped by for a visit. As he walked toward the dining room and past the stereo, he was startled to hear a quick, sharp noise to his left. On the stereo was a large 8 x 10 framed photograph of Taylor which had been sitting at a slight backward slant on its easel. It had been the only thing in that area that could have made that sound, and it was now lying face down.

## HALLOWEEN: OCTOBER 31, 1993

About 7:15 a.m., Tony had walked just to the left of the butcher block, got the orange juice from the refrigerator on the way to the counter across the room, and then continued to the cupboards on the right side of the stove and at the far side of the room. Although extremely tired when he came off this shift, he always took a few minutes to unwind before coming to bed. He'd gotten a glass out of the cupboard and poured the juice and just as he was about to take a drink, he turned around to face the center of the kitchen and got the shock of his life.

Standing in the middle of the room, just past the butcher-block table, was a little girl with a surprised look in her big blue eyes. He judged her to be about three and a half feet tall. Instantly his heart plummeted to his feet and every muscle froze. In that instant, several things went through his mind. "Who are you, where did you come from, what do you want, and how did you get in my kitchen?" Then he realized he had not heard either of the doors and that she had not walked in with him.

Realization had begun to creep in as he noticed something odd about the way she was dressed. Her hair was neatly fastened on top with a ribbon and a large, fancy bow. She looked to be in her Sunday best, but the style was old-fashioned: white eyelet lace and puffy sleeves. She had sweetly round, cherubic cheeks. She stood there shocked, curious and motionless, staring at him wide-eyed.

For that instant Tony seemed to lose control of his thoughts, muscles, and emotions. The glass slipped from his hand to the floor.

The sound broke the trance he was in and he instinctively looked at the floor in front of him—juice and broken glass lay all over the floor. When he looked back up, the little girl was gone. She had not made a sound as she left the room. It happened in the blink of an eye. Still unable to move, Tony's fear squeezed him more as he began to realize what he had just witnessed. He'd just seen Sallie.

A second wave of terror shot through his body and he stood there unable to move. Thoughts continued to flood his mind: Was she still in the house? What would he see around the next corner or in another room? Had he hallucinated the girl—was there something wrong with his mind? If it was a ghost, why did she choose to show herself to him?

The skeptical side of his mind didn't want to acknowledge what he had seen, but as he replayed the scene in his mind, he realized it was true. Still unable to move, he wondered what to do next. Who would he tell? Who would believe him? Why did he have to turn around and see that? Living people just aren't supposed to see things that are dead!

What seemed to surprise him the most, though, was that she looked so real; just as solid and fleshy as he was. Although he had regained some level of muscle control, those thoughts brought another wave of panic and he sprinted out of the room up the stairs to the bedroom where I was still sleeping.

Hearing the commotion on the stairs, I was already awake when he burst into the room. With big eyes and desperately gasping for breath, he said "I saw her. God damn it, Debra, I saw her!" His legs gave out when he reached the edge of the bed and his knees hit the carpet. The top half of his body slumped in an exhausted state on the bed with his arms stretched out toward me.

Not yet thinking straight, irritated at my sudden awakening, and not understanding what he'd gone through, I gruffly asked, "Who?"

"Just a minute," he said. "I need to catch my breath first." Then, hardly taking that breath, he said, "Sallie." I sat up, suddenly wide awake. I could tell that whatever had happened, it had scared the life out of him. I rubbed his back and arms to let him know I was there. I could feel his heartbeat racing furiously and I waited for more details.

"She was right there," he said gasping for another breath. "Plain as day."

"Where?" I asked.

"In the kitchen." Gasp.

"What did she look like?" I asked.

"Barbara was right." Gasp. "She's cute as hell!"

He tilted his head and raised an eyebrow in a quizzical sort of understanding and realization.

For the next twenty minutes or so, Tony desperately tried to regain his composure. I however, was ecstatic. For every answer he gave me, I asked another two questions. I needed to know every detail. He finally started from the beginning and explained to me exactly what he had seen. Shaking his head in disbelief at the clarity, he said, "She sure wasn't poor when she was alive!" He went on, "She had a real cute little face and I could see her just like I can see you." He continued shaking his head, "She looked just as solid as you or me!"

He told me how she had been standing on the other side of the butcher block and that he couldn't quite tell if she was standing on the floor or floating. "She wasn't eerie or creepy-looking at all. I couldn't see through her. It wasn't anything like I expected it to be. She just stood there."

I remember asking if she had done or said anything. "No, she didn't move. She just stared at me." Then he got a real serious look about him and said, "She doesn't look seven years old and she sure is a cute little thing!" I asked him how long she had stood there in front of him.

"Only a few seconds," he said. "As soon as I dropped the glass, she was gone. I did get a real good look at her, though."

Through all my questioning, Tony kept saying that he needed to draw her; that he had to do it before he forgot what she looked like. "You gotta come with me," he said. "I don't want to be walking around the house alone and run into her again." I threw on a robe and we went downstairs.

While he sketched, I cleaned up the juice and broken glass and then sat near him on the couch in quiet anticipation. His hands were shaky and he condemned his own hurried work, but it only took him a few minutes longer to finish, right down to the blank stare of her eyes.

It looked like the picture of a five-year-old child, maybe even younger and we wondered if Sallie hadn't stretched the truth about her age, as young children often do. Then again, maybe it was her tiny little features that made her look so young and adorable—the face of a cherub or a doll. She looked well-kept and prosperous. The white, frilly dress had a lace-edged yoke that came up to her neck, and her sleeves looked plush and puffy. Her dark hair was pulled up, on top of her head, and secured with a large floppy bow. Those big blue eyes seemed cold as they stared without expression.

After discussing the details of her features, Tony and I agreed that this little girl didn't seem like the kind of child that would do all the things we had been witness to. She didn't look rebellious, ornery, or mischievous. How could this sweet-looking child possibly be mean enough to have scratched Tony, lit fires, or pinched the baby to make him cry out in pain?

I decided to display the drawing like all our other family members' photos and placed it in an antique-looking frame, hoping that by doing so I would help Sallie feel more accepted. I placed it next to Taylor's photo, which sat on the built-in shelves behind the stereo in the living room. To this day, the sketch is displayed in our home.

Questions continued to come up on a regular basis. Was there significance in her having shown herself the morning of Halloween, or was it coincidence? Why did she show herself to Tony, of all people? I had asked her, even pleaded with her, to allow me to see her, but she never did. Then I got to thinking that perhaps she didn't feel the need to show herself to me because I already believed in her.

I wondered if there was a more specific reason for her to show herself to Tony. She knew he could draw well and that he would draw her if he saw her. If that happened, she would have an image like our other family members, and perhaps a place next to them.

## TWELVE

# I AM HERE

### NOVEMBER 1993

With most of my family living in the state of New York or Georgia, it was not often that we were able to spend holidays together. We took care to plan and celebrate Thanksgiving a week early to accommodate my mother coming in from Georgia, and my sister and her family from New York.

At some point, I called Sallie into the room to tell her the news so that she wouldn't be overwhelmed or frightened, like children often are, by people she had never met before. I told her about my sister's little girl, Kori. "She is a very nice little girl, just like you, Sallie. Do you think it would it be all right if she slept in the nursery with you and Taylor?" This question had a two-fold purpose. One, I hoped that it made her feel that we cared about how she felt, and two, it suggested in advance the possibility of Kori staying in the nursery so that she wasn't caught off guard when it happened. In the back of my mind, there was always a concern that upsetting Sallie could put us all in an unsafe situation.

I really didn't expect to receive a response. Over the course of the next few days it was so quiet that I found myself wondering if she was mad. Was she building or reserving energy to show anger while our guests were here? Every night until their arrival, I gently reminded her of the impending visit and how important it was for her to behave.

My next hurdle was whether or not to tell my mother about our ghost. Saying something in advance offered no evidence for our claim, but not being up front about it, however, set her up for the scare of her life.

I called Karen to discuss the possibilities. Karen admitted that if she hadn't witnessed Sallie's antics during her last visit, she would have seriously questioned my credibility and that I should expect that from anyone. I decided that there would be a time during my mother's visit to tell her.

I was also unsure of how my father would react to news of Sallie. When I was younger we got along very well, but in his older years he had become harsh and judgmental. Ironically, the opportunity to address this came sooner than I expected when Dad called one day before the holidays. He sensed uneasiness in the conversation and finally asked what was wrong. At first, I tried to convince him it was nothing, but eventually I told him about our ghost.

"What makes you think you have a ghost?" he asked. I knew his logical mind was preparing to assess the information I was about to give him. I told him as much of the story as I could. He was intrigued and I was grateful for his acceptance and understanding.

The call with Dad had gone so well and I felt so empowered that I called my mother later that afternoon with the sole intent of working the topic of our ghost into the conversation. I waited for a lull in the discussion and then blurted out, "So, let me ask you something. What are your thoughts on ghosts?"

Perplexed, she said, "Why do you ask?" I could already sense how the conversation would go; my mother was not ready for this information. I tried the same approach that had worked with my father, but after everything I shared with her, she just said, "I'd have to see it with my own eyes." I assured her that she might well get that chance during her visit.

A week passed without incident. As the days went by, I began to mourn Sallie's absence. I'm not sure why. I just knew that each day I had looked forward to seeing signs that she was around and figuring out a way to communicate with her. Sometimes I felt that I was the only one in the world that had such an opportunity and I wanted to make the most of it. I wanted so many answers about the existence of ghosts and the Other Side.

On November 9th, Tony brought me a photo of Sallie's corner in the nursery. He asked when it had been taken, but having taken so many photos, I couldn't know for sure. When I took photos in the nursery, I would often ask Sallie if she wanted to be in the picture. I swear that sometimes I could feel her excitement in the air. Although I always hoped for some sort of manifestation of her to show up in the photos, nothing ever did as far as I could tell.

In this particular photo, I could see the box of crayons and the clipboard of papers on the lid of Sallie's toy box, but nothing out of the ordinary. Tony then pointed to the crayon that had caught his eye and asked, "Do you see the shadow behind it?" When I took a second look, it was very clear that the tip of the crayon had a shadow attached to it. That shadow however, was shorter than its subject and was not parallel to the crayon; instead, it went off at a slight angle.

It was so odd that we took turns looking at it through a magnifying glass. We could see no strings or anything else attached to the crayon; it was very apparent that the crayon was standing up by itself. It proved how easily some of the small things a spirit might do could go unnoticed. I had looked at that photo right after it was developed and seen nothing.

November 12th arrived and I picked up Karen and her daughter at the airport. Her husband, Donnie, would arrive two days later. While the kids napped, we prepared the next meal. Much of our conversation centered on Sallie and her more recent activity.

At one point, I walked past the open bathroom door and saw that one of the small decorative candles had been lit. Neither of us was responsible for this and I gruffly scolded Sallie, reminding her of the rules. "No more fires, Sallie! You get one more chance, and if you light any more fires, you will have to leave the house." I didn't send her to her room this time, because I didn't want to send a scolded child up to a room where other little ones were.

Now that I am the mother of three boys, I worry that I may have been a little too harsh with Sallie. My place was to remind her of the rules, as children her age often need this. I should have realized that she was excited about our visitors. In hindsight, I'm sure she just wanted to say "hi," or simply let us know she was there. I imagine a spirit's difficulty in communicating might be similar to autism, which makes it is very hard to convey what you really want to say.

After dinner, as Tony, Karen, and I sat in the living room, we heard noises coming from the kitchen. Most of the sounds I recognized: baby bottles being knocked over, silverware rattling in the drainer, and electrical timers going off. There were no drafts; our windows had been shut. Our dog was outside and I had recently adopted out my two cats, which left no animals in the house. There wasn't an obvious explanation for what was making the noises we heard.

About 8:00 that evening, Karen stood at the sink doing dishes. She heard disturbing scratching noises at the window in front of her. She refrained from looking up for fear that she would see something frightening; too many horror movies can make a person's mind run wild at times like these. The noise continued, and as her mind wandered the sound got creepier. She told herself that a tree branch was scraping the window, but at a certain point she could take it no more and left the room.

The three of us assessed the situation and noted that there was no tree in the yard near the window. There was nothing in the yard tall enough for anyone to stand on or allow an animal to jump on to reach the windowsill in question. The window's ledge was seven or eight feet from the ground.

By 10:00, Kori was tucked into her makeshift bed in the nursery, and an over-stimulated Taylor was being rocked by Tony in the living room. Tony suddenly felt a brisk coldness across his lower legs. With his cowboy boots still on, he knew he wasn't feeling an ordinary draft. Tony hated knowing a ghost was that close. Although he wanted to move, Taylor had just drifted to sleep and he knew if he moved the baby would wake. To his surprise, the cold sensation did not stay long and twenty minutes later he was able to lay Taylor in his crib.

With the children in bed and the house quiet, the three of us sat down to watch a movie. Suddenly there was a commotion in the kitchen. The dog lying at our feet perked his ears and our eyes went wide with surprise. Tony turned down the television and we glanced at each other to see if we had all heard the same thing. We remained motionless for several minutes, awaiting the next sound. For almost half an hour we spoke only in whispers, but the house remained silent. Midnight came and we decided to go to bed. To our surprise Karen claimed the couch and I can remember joking about how fearless she was. The rest of the night was uneventful.

The next day we didn't notice any sign of Sallie and the mood in the house was calm and relaxed. While Tony was at work, Karen and I spent the day playing with our children and catching up with each other. We had dinner after Tony got home. Shortly before 11:00 p.m., I drove to the airport and picked up my mother, who had flown in from Atlanta, Georgia. We all visited for about an hour and then went to bed.

The next day we were all up early and filled the morning with breakfast activities, cooing over the children, and girly chatter in the kitchen. Karen and I almost forgot to be aware of Sallie's activity, but while we were making pies in the afternoon, Mom just happened to be looking at the microwave clock when she suddenly saw it flip to 00:00

and start counting backwards. Never having seen a timer work of its own accord, she asked what was wrong with it.

Karen did not miss a beat. With an almost comical grin and a matter-of-fact tone in her voice, Karen said, "Sallie." Our eyes met, and we knew that the time had come for an interesting conversation. Grins streaked across our faces. I'm sure Mom thought we were pulling a joke on her, but I assured her that she had just witnessed the activity of Sallie.

"I can't believe it," she said. "I just happened to be looking at it."

We said nothing more, for there was nothing either of us could say that would convince her; she would have to process the experience in her own way.

Interestingly, this was the first time someone saw the exact moment the clock reset itself. I noted that the mixer, which had been running at the time of the incident, was on the same circuit and did not have a power disruption. Knowing the clock in the living room was also on the same circuit, I checked it. It was not blinking or otherwise indicating that the power had been interrupted. The power fluctuation had been specific to only one appliance. Mom was rather puzzled by our serious approach to the situation and our tenacity in checking the other electrical items on that electrical circuit. Her silent curiosity was apparent as she shifted her eyes between Karen and me, looking for an indication that we were pulling her leg.

By 1:45 p.m., both children were taking a nap and Tony and Karen were in the living room observing the distinct and patterned movement of the wooden balls on the ceiling fan. Karen was aware of what the movement signified, and the two of them watched it for several minutes before it dawned on them that Mom might be interested in seeing it. By that time, the movement had ceased. The three of us knew that Sallie was letting us know she was around.

That afternoon, we headed to the airport once again to pick up Donnie, returning without any delays. About 3:30, while the children napped and the rest of us fixed dinner, Donnie and Karen fell asleep on the couch. The house had been quiet for a while and I was startled when I turned around to find Karen standing in the doorway, eyes wide. She was holding out the beanbag teddy bear—the same one that had been turned toward the wall by Sallie on several occasions.

"It was on fire!" she said as she entered the room.

"What?" I asked, not quite believing what I had just heard.

"I don't know why I woke up," she continued. "But when I did, it had a six to eight inch flame coming out of its head. Just like on that TV show I called you about a few weeks ago. When I picked it up, it was still shooting a flame and as I got to the kitchen, it went out."

A week earlier, I'd received a call from Karen about an episode of *Unsolved Mysteries*. She explained that the young couple had a ghost and its activities had driven the couple to the point of moving. In the midst of packing, the woman said something derogatory about the ghost, and almost immediately the crown of a bare light bulb shot out a flame two to three feet high. The story had ended with the couple moving and never being bothered again.

Inspecting the bear, I was completely stunned by its appearance, and wondered if Sallie had learned this trick from watching the television. Did we now need to censor what we watched on TV?

I took a closer look at the bear and the strange burns. There was a circular spot the size of a quarter on top of its head and almost the entire side of its face was melted. The circular burn was very strange. It had burned or melted the acrylic fur right down to the base of the fabric. In the center of the circle, however, there was still a dime-sized patch of fur that had been totally unaffected by the fire. I shook my head in disbelief, trying to understand what could have made this sort of mark. I had never seen anything like it.

I handed the bear to my mother, who was trying to make her own sense of the situation. You could see it in her expression—she just knew Karen and I were trying to pull a fast one on her. She was determined to be ready for the big laugh at the end of the joke, but we were not laughing. Had it been a different kind of incident, I might have laughed, but the thought of such a large unsupervised fire in the house was downright alarming.

With this incident, Mom began to accept how real the circumstances might be. Without taking her level of comfort into consideration, I began to severely reprimand the ghost we could not see. Mom stood there, speechless.

## SCOLDING

I scolded Sallie harshly and told her the fire was very bad. I reminded her of the last time she lit a fire and the fact that I had told her "one more fire and you're out of here." I quickly realized that my parenting skills were not up to the task at hand.

I reminded Sallie of all the things we had spoken of concerning the fires and risk of burning down the house, and then I asked her if she wanted me to send her away. I told her that by setting the fire she had destroyed something that was special to me. I then sent her to "her" room to think about what she had done. I was actually buying time because I really wasn't sure what to say next. This was the first time she had set fire to an object other than a candle. It scared me and made me mad. I feared my harsh scolding might make her mad, and wondered what might happen in that situation. Would she light another fire? What item would it be, and would we find it in time? I began to think how very lucky we were that Karen caught sight of this one.

Poor Donnie had been sleeping on the couch when I began hollering and scolding Sallie. He entered the room to find out what the yelling was about. He hadn't seen the fire and when Karen told him, he found it very hard to believe. He wanted to know why she hadn't awakened him so he could see it, too. She told him that her first thoughts were to take the bear to me, douse it, or put it in the sink.

I could tell that in the back of my mother's mind she was still wondering if this had all been planned, but with a dead serious expression she said, "The fires could really get out of hand." I assured her that I understood the danger but that I didn't quite know what to do about it.

"Why don't you just get rid of all the matches and lighters in the house," Mom suggested. Karen and I were extremely amused by her simple solution; she just didn't understand. Had she not realized that we had been trying to deal with this spirit and her activity for several months already? Without being too defensive, I simply said, "If it was that easy, I would have done it a long time before this, Mom."

We informed her that Sallie didn't need matches or a lighter to start a fire. I tried to explain the best I could that Sallie's activity was based on some other type of energy. Mom remained perplexed and rightfully concerned. "Well, what if she were to light a fire while you were out of the house? Or what if no one caught the fire before it got out of hand?"

I explained as well as I could: "Sallie lights fires to get our attention. She seems to do it only when we're home." Looking at the bear again, I showed her the fur on the left side of its face as well as at the very top of its left ear. Although not as severe as the ring on the top of his head, it was clear that both areas had met with a heat source and the fur had been melted or singed down to the cloth itself. When Karen noticed the bear burning, the only flame she saw was confined to a very small area on top of its head.

I went on to explain that because these three burned areas did not connect, we could assume that each area had been burned on separate occasions. Karen saw only one of them, but they could have taken place days, hours, or minutes earlier. What was significant was the fact that they *had* been extinguished. It seemed that when the fires went unnoticed, they were put out. I suggested that this meant that Sallie would probably not let the fire get out of hand. I wasn't always quite as sure as I sounded, though.

Not comfortable with my explanation, Mom asked, "Doesn't it make you nervous thinking about what else she could do? Doesn't it concern you that she might hurt the baby?"Although I know she was just concerned, she continued with a dissatisfied tone that made me feel increasingly defensive. I didn't know what to do. Had she not yet realized the stress, the concern, and the worry we had been living with? Did she not think we had asked the same questions?

I told Mom we had lived with Sallie for quite some time now and it was like living with a pet or anyone else who could not communicate verbally. Through your experiences with them you get to know them and sense what drives them, their desires, moods, capabilities, and generally what you can expect from them.

"Barbara told us that Sallie adores Taylor as if he were her own brother and would never do anything to harm him," I said.

All I really knew was that she wouldn't "intentionally" do anything to harm any of us, but a little girl might not realize how quickly a fire could get out of hand.

Karen and I went outside to talk about how to deal with the situation. I told Karen that I enjoyed Sallie and really didn't want to get rid of her. Karen replied that the safety of our family was more important than my wanting to keep Sallie with us. I agreed, but said I wasn't sure how to go about making her leave, let alone do it without provoking a tantrum. We eventually decided to call Barbara for suggestions.

Barbara was glad to hear from me and after a few polite remarks, I presented the problem. She asked about any recent changes in the house and after hearing what was going on, she offered a few observations. She suggested that Sallie was uneasy because Kori was there and sleeping in Taylor's room. Although she didn't think Sallie would hurt Kori, she was picking up a distinctly jealous vibe. "If possible, find somewhere else for Kori to sleep. Then tell Sallie that she can't throw temper tantrums, and one more fire, she's gotta go. Be very firm with her!" I listened and felt my throat tighten as if I were going to cry.

"I can help you get rid of her if that's what you want, but you have to tell me," Barbara said.

I really didn't think Sallie wanted to be bad. I felt guilty for not recognizing her attempts to be acknowledged, and I really believed she had been trying her best to abide by the rules. I couldn't help thinking that it must be so hard for her to feel ignored, unloved, and disconnected from the only family she had available to her.

I felt even worse when I imagined how much she wanted to be a part of our family, to be noticed and regarded with love like any child. It seemed that the only way she could accomplish this was to do things we were telling her not to do. That led to harsh reprimands and a threat to get rid of her.

She had gone a long time without lighting a fire. Maybe, in wanting to let us know that she was with us, she had forgotten the rules. I had been remiss in helping her remember. Perhaps we all needed a little bit more time to adjust to living with each other.

I told Barbara, "I guess we can give her a little more time. For now, let's just leave things the way they are."

Tony must have been listening in on my conversation from the kitchen and he hollered out, "Ask Barbara, did Sallie die by fire?"

"No," Barbara said. "If she died by fire, she wouldn't light fires. She'd be scared of them." That made sense. Then I asked, "Is she still happy here with us?"

"Yes, I still get very good and happy feelings from her."

Hearing those words made me feel better. For many weeks I had wondered, and although I always felt an air of excitement and happiness in the house, I didn't feel comfortable depending on my gut feelings to interpret Sallie's emotions. For all I knew, they were just my own hopeful emotions and excitement.

I then asked about the letter I'd sent Barbara several weeks before. I had hoped that the lack of response was not intentional but certainly didn't want to make her feel obligated; she had already done so much and asked for nothing in return.

"Yes, I got it and I sent you a response about two weeks ago. Didn't you get it?"

Relieved that her interest was still there and her intentions were still in our favor, I let her know that we never got it. She went on to tell me that she really appreciated the photos, had used them in several of her lectures, and that they had stirred up quite a bit of interest.

She went on to describe what she had written in her letter. She mentioned the strange things showing up in so many of our photographs. "That is Sallie." She explained that the different colors revealed emotions—for example, the murky whitish-gray color signified fear and protectiveness, most apparent in the picture taken of the stairs where Sallie had been standing with her hand on the railing and protecting that area. She apparently did not want anyone up there.

The bluish colors surrounding the baby doll in the nursery photos were a sign of great happiness and love. "She is allowing you to see the love she has for the baby doll." Once again my heart was warmed by the emotion from this seemingly precious little spirit in our house.

I told Barbara that Tony had actually seen Sallie here.

"Oh, good!" she said, "When?"

I detailed the experience for her and joked about feeling slighted in not having seen her for myself.

"Sallie knows you believe in her and she's got nothing to prove to you."

Next, I asked her a question that had recently come up several times. "Could there be more than one spirit in the house?"

Barbara got quiet for a few seconds. "A boy," she said, and then paused, "No, that's the baby." Then she went on. "If there is, Sallie is the dominant one and wouldn't let anything bad happen." Although her response was a relief to me, I wondered if she was just saying that to soothe our fears.

We no sooner said our good-byes when I was inundated with questions from the others, who were anxiously waiting to hear about our options. I had tried to take notes during the conversation and relayed them as best as I could. It was decided that I would go up to talk to Sallie and Karen would go up to check on Kori and be my support.

We each took a camera and headed up the stairs. Karen stopped me and silently indicated that we should take a photo of the stairs. It was the same place Sallie had stood before, forbidding passage to the second floor.

"Sallie," I called out, "Come and sit down with me so we can talk about what you did." Karen continued to take pictures from the doorway and I planted myself on the floor in Sallie's northwest corner of the room.

"Sallie," I said in firm but gentle tone, "what you did was bad and made me very sad because the bear you set on fire was a special gift from Tony." A little firmly, I said, "The fire could have hurt someone in this house, even Taylor, and you could have set the whole house on fire and then none of us would have a place to live." With my voice raised in anger I added, "You have GOT to stop setting fires to things. If there are any more fires, you are out of here! Do you understand me? I won't stand for it anymore! You have one more chance, and that's it. NO! MORE! FIRES!"

I sat quietly for a minute to let the words sink in, then in a more calm and understanding tone, I said, "If you are upset about something, you have to tell me without starting a fire. Now let's talk about why you did start it. Do you remember when I told you that we were going to have company for a few days and that Kori would stay in the nursery? I had hoped that was OK, but now I think that it must have upset you and I am sorry."

Being so focused on the conversation I had forgotten that Karen was a few steps away in the hallway. I was startled and my heart jumped into my throat when she interjected, "Sallie, I'm sorry, too." Trying to regain my composure, I continued. "We'll find somewhere else for Kori to sleep, okay? You have to remember though, that these people are guests in our house and you have to be nice to them." As we left the room, we decided to put Kori's playpen in the upstairs hallway.

The rest of my family's visit went without incident and they all left on November 15. A few days later, after having time to unpack and settle back into her own home, Karen called me on the telephone to ask if I was by chance missing a pot lid. I thought the question was strange and joked about it, but realized that she was serious when she said, "No, really, are you missing a pot lid?" I made my way to the kitchen and checked the cupboards. To my surprise, I was indeed missing a lid to my second smallest Revereware cooking pot. "I guess I am. Why do you ask?"

She reported that when she unpacked her suitcase, she found a lid in it and had since been trying to figure out why and how it got there. "I packed those suitcases myself and I know I didn't put it in there!"

We talked about how unlikely it was that either of the children or any of the adults would have gotten into the suitcases after her final pack. The situation left us extremely bewildered.

Before hanging up, she mentioned the film she'd just sent off to be developed and promised that she would send me copies. About a week later, I got the pictures. They had been taken in the nursery during the last conversation I'd had with Sallie. As we had hoped, something odd did seem to show up in them.

In every photo, a small arc of light had shown up along the baseboard and under the window in Sallie's corner. At first, I thought it was a refraction of light or a reflection of the flash off the glass money jar that sat near me on the floor. Then I realized that in more than one of the photos, I had been sitting between the camera flash and this jar, meaning that the flash could not have generated an arc of light. Another interesting thing was that no matter where Karen had been positioned when she took the pictures, the arc of light showed up in the same exact place each time: the bottom of the north windowsill.

A co-worker stopped by for a visit several days later, on November 19. He and Tony kicked back to relax in front of the TV. Ray was on the floor and Tony sat at the far end of the couch. At some point, Tony noticed the wooden balls on the ceiling fan swinging and silently pointed it out to Ray. Our spirit wanted to be noticed. Through experience, we knew that when this didn't happen, the activity picked up.

Already aware of this information, Ray announced in an abnormally loud voice that he was just going lay his head down and take a short nap. He closed his eyes to simulate falling asleep and immediately something went whizzing by, close and over his head. It had been so close and fast, he heard it and immediately sat up.

Tony had seen what happened, but it happened so fast that he only caught it out of the corner of his eye. He wasn't quite sure what had flown through the air and hit the wall across the room. They both inspected the dent in the wall and found a tiny ceramic vase lying on the floor below it. The vase had been sitting on one of the end tables. Ray realized that Tony couldn't have been responsible for throwing it over his head from where it had been sitting.

Tony was excited when I got home later that day and the conversation with him was interesting. Without me there to see the activity or pick up any emotions from Sallie's perspective, Tony was forced to come up with his own theory.

"I think she was upset because we weren't paying attention to her," he said. "We didn't make a fuss over the balls on the ceiling fan when I noticed them. I think she got mad because we ignored her and threw the vase in a tantrum."

I agreed and was secretly proud of his thoughts and approach.

Several days later, Ray caught up with Tony and asked if he thought our ghost would be able to follow him home. It was a curious question, but we had no answer. Ray then went on to describe several nights of strange activity. One night, an item of clothing moved from one side of Ray's bedroom to the other. The next night, a twenty-four-inch box fan had done the same thing.

The strangest thing, however, was what he described as a large, sopping wet puddle in the middle of his dining room floor. He was unable to find any reason for it. It was not close to an open window, he did not have any indoor animals that might have had an accident in the middle of the night, and there was no visible sign on the ceiling that it had sprung a leak. In fact, it had not rained for almost two weeks.

THIRTEEN

# HOLIDAY FIRE

## DECEMBER 1993

After Sallie's display with the vase, Tony and I had four days without any ghostly activity. We wondered if Sallie had used an excessive amount of energy in throwing the vase. I had heard that spirits can lie dormant while gathering energy to unleash a powerful blow when needed.

Four days turned into several weeks and the longest bout of inactivity we had yet seen. Was she afraid of getting into trouble, or was it the calm before the storm? Was she upset or angry with us for something we were unaware of? Was she gathering strength for retaliation? Not knowing made the lack of activity worse than the activity itself.

This quiet period continued into the holiday season. We were planning a Christmas party for December 18. We were anticipating more than forty-five guests and as the days passed, I became very anxious. I would rather have Sallie act up before the party than during it, because there would be many strangers in attendance. The paranormal situations we had encountered to date would have been difficult to explain to them.

The house remained quiet, however, and the day finally arrived for the traditional Christmas party we had planned: popcorn balls and brown-paper-wrapped gifts exchanged with loved ones, maintaining a sense of family togetherness and creating memories to last.

The night before the party, we blew up hundreds of sixteen-inch red and white balloons. We filled sixty of them with helium and left them to float about the ceiling of the first floor. At some point prior to the arrival of our guests, we were alarmed to hear a series of loud and intrusive thuds. The sound sent my heart racing up into the back of my throat. I wondered what Sallie was doing.

Terrified about what I might find, I ran from the kitchen and into the dining room where the noise seemed to have originated. As I rounded the corner I realized the ruckus had come from several balloons fighting for freedom from the blades of the ceiling fan. Although our hearts still raced, we laughed at how quickly we'd assumed it was activity from Sallie.

As our guests arrived, we took their coats to the master bedroom and allowed people to mingle, and indulge in conversation, laughter, drink, and food. The children were shown to the back bedroom upstairs, which I had equipped with a television, VCR, several holiday movies, and craft supplies to keep them entertained.

We had planned for a relative to make an appearance as Santa. He was running late, and Taylor drifted to sleep before his arrival. Shortly after 8:00, jingle bells were rung outside the children's playroom on the second floor and thumps on the roof simulated reindeer hooves. As the children hurried downstairs to meet him, Santa grabbed the sack full of gifts on the front porch and came in the front door.

He made it around the room with a "Ho, ho, ho, and a Merry Christmas" before sitting down in the rocking chair. It wasn't long before each child had sat on Santa's lap, posed for a picture, and collected a gift bag. I was enjoying the smiles and squeals of the little ones, but as I watched, I was saddened because Taylor had missed it. I felt a strangely compelling twinge of unhappiness and even envy as I thought of Sallie. I had not prepared a gift bag for her, and it seemed I could feel the sorrow of being left out. The sadness was overwhelming.

For the rest of the evening, my thoughts wandered over ways that I could have incorporated Sallie without making the rest of the family feel uncomfortable. In the end, I understood that there had been no way. Not having a gift for her, however, was like denying her very existence, and I wondered if this had upset her.

Santa left and the kids retreated to their party room while the adults began their gift exchange. It was during this time that my father-in-law saw the beanbag teddy bear move.

We ruled out alcohol as an influence because, with his diabetic medications, my father-in-law had stopped drinking years ago. In fact, he had not thought anything of the experience because he was sure a draft from the ceiling fan caused the movement. It wasn't until my mother-in-law mentioned it to us after the party that we realized something had happened.

As it got late, the guests began to leave. Tony retrieved the last of the coats from our bedroom while his brother and niece waited near the bottom of the stairs. Tony had almost reached the top landing when the smoke alarm above his head abruptly began shrieking.

Tony caught sight of his brother at the bottom of the stairs looking up, wide-eyed, and pointing to a handmade mop doll sitting on the fifth step up; it had burst into flames. Tony knew that the doll had not been on fire as he passed it. In the time it took him to reach the top of the staircase, enough smoke had collected at the top of the stairs to set off the alarm.

Tony rushed back down the stairs, snatched up the doll, and ran back upstairs with it. He did this to avoid the remaining guests and the awkward questions that would follow. As he ran, the flame grew larger, and small burning pieces of the doll began to drop off onto the carpet. Trying to keep the flaming doll from burning his arm or setting his shirt on fire, he stomped out the embers falling to the floor as he raced up the stairs. Tony scolded Sallie under his breath, so those who had gathered at the bottom of the stairs couldn't hear him.

He returned his attention to the flaming doll in his hands. The bathroom sink was closest and when he got there, he was also able to see his own injuries; both of his forearms were burned. Not wanting to draw further attention or concern, he didn't speak of it until later.

One of the last people to leave was Aunt Louise, and as we hugged and said our good-byes, she said something surprising. "Sallie probably felt left out because she didn't get anything from Santa."

I could not believe my ears—someone else had said what I had been thinking all night! The next thing I knew, she had offered to bring Santa back so Taylor would have the experience, we would have the photos, and Sallie would have the opportunity for a gift from Santa. It was a wonderful offer and I thanked her for her understanding.

When everyone was gone, I called out to Sallie and demanded her presence. I explained that what she did was very bad and that the fire had caused damage. I explained how the fire had almost gotten out of hand, and the house could have burned to the ground. I told her that what she did scared us as well as everyone else. I told her she was a bad little girl. "You have got to stop this. NO MORE FIRES," I said, and repeated it several times.

Then, feeling horribly saddened by her exclusion in the gift giving, I continued in a slightly more understanding tone of voice. "Santa didn't know you were here, honey, and that's why he didn't have anything for you."

After the scolding, Tony and I sat on the couch revisiting every detail of the experience. After much deliberation, we knew we had to put a stop to the uncontrolled fires and find a better way for her to communicate.

The next day I was in the nursery and noticed something written in green crayon on Sallie's clipboard of papers. Not quite recognizing what it said, I took it to Tony. He could clearly see the letters "G" and "O." Sallie had written to us just as I had suggested she do when she was upset or had something to say. Had I not seen it in time? Is that why she lit the fire?

Throughout the day, I thought about how to handle the fires. I figured that no matter what we threatened her with, the fires would not stop if it was the easiest form of communication she had available to her. I thought that if we couldn't stop the fires, perhaps we could make them a little safer.

I called out to Sallie. "I have an idea and I'd like to talk to you about it. I think you will like it, too. See this fire?" I pointed to the oil lamp I'd already lit several minutes earlier. "I know we said no more fires, but now I am saying that you can put one in here and you won't get in trouble."

Two days after the Christmas party and early in the day on Sunday, December 20, I noticed the musical clown Taylor got as a gift from Tony's parents was playing music as it sat untouched by human hands. No one except the three of us had been in the house all day. I couldn't help but be pleased that Sallie was back to her usual self, and enjoyed her playful antics throughout the house that day.

We expected Santa late in the afternoon and, concerned that Santa's overpowering presence might scare Taylor, we sat in the rocking chair at the far end of the living room. Next to the chair was an end table with a fish tank, a small figurine, a book, and the oil lamp I had given Sallie permission to use.

Santa arrived about 7:30 p.m., ringing a sleigh bell to signal his entrance. "Taylor, look who's here. It's Santa Claus. Hi, Santa Claus." Santa paused at the front door, not wanting to scare the baby, and as he slowly advanced, I stood up and took a few steps toward him. Tony had been taking pictures of the baby and was already in front of us.

A moment later, Aunt Louise became wide-eyed with surprise and fear. Before I could ask what was wrong, she hollered, "There's smoke, there's smoke! My God, Debbie! There's black smoke behind you!" Fear struck at my heart. I didn't immediately think of Sallie's oil lamp until I turned and saw the thick black smoke billowing out from the top of the lamp.

The wick was engulfed in a brilliant bright yellow flame. It was Sallie's way to scream "I'm here, I'm here! See me, Santa, I'm here." I felt a big smile sprawl over my face as my heart filled with delight. Apparently Sallie did understand how to be noticed without the dangers of open and uncontrolled fires.

I told Aunt Louise about the arrangement with Sallie and the lamp. Her look of worry and concern quickly diminished. This allowed Santa's jolly nature to return. "Well hi, Sallie. How are you? Yes, I know you're here." As she talked to Sallie, I walked over to the lamp and said warmly, "That's great that you put a fire in the lamp to let us know you're here. I am so happy and proud of you."

We took a few pictures of Taylor on Santa's lap and Santa even invited Sallie to join him. It was almost comical seeing Santa's arm around Taylor on one knee, and his other arm stretched out as if he was holding someone on the other, empty knee. We were excited to get the photos developed, and hoped to catch a glimpse of Sallie, but we were disappointed. Not only was there no sign of Sallie, but the photos were dark and indistinct. Had her presence in the photos caused them to be so dark? We had not previously or since had any problems with that camera.

Christmas Eve was a few days later. Expected at my in-laws' house at 9:00 a.m. the next morning, we decided to open gifts with Taylor on Christmas Eve. Our tree was so large that we had to move the table over to open gifts. By 8:00 p.m., there were toys and wrappings all over the dining room and Taylor was content. With camera in hand, Tony suggested I help Sallie open her gifts.

I was certainly caught off-guard by this suggestion, because I knew how difficult it was for him to acknowledge Sallie's presence. I had bought her a few inexpensive things: a small stuffed animal, a coloring book, and a little white purse. In addition, I had made a wooden cradle for the baby doll we had given her several months earlier.

"Hey, Sallie, come on over here. We'll open your gifts, okay?" I waited a second and then peeked under the wrapping, saying things like, "I wonder what it is? It sure is funny shaped, isn't it?' I really felt foolish making a big deal about the gift, seemingly sitting there all by myself with Tony surely judging me from across the room, but I continued. I soon had the wrapping off and invited Sallie to have her picture taken with her new cradle. We had no sign though, that she was even in the room.

I dropped the film off for developing on the 26th and I looked at the photos as I stood in line to pay for them. Not only had Sallie been with us Christmas Eve, but some other entity or energy had been present. In three of the photos there were two distinctly different anomalies on either side of me; one was a grayish mass, the other a cloudy-looking blur of lights. These visuals certainly seemed to confirm what Tony had known for a while; there was more than one spirit in our house.

My mind whirled and I remembered what Barbara had said about the murky anomaly and the marbleized grouping of lights that had shown up in earlier photos. "She's upset and protecting her space." I wondered what these two spirits were upset about. Who were they mad at?

More questions flooded my thoughts. Did Sallie bring this other spirit? Was the other one also a child? Did Sallie even know this other spirit? Was there an open door between our worlds for other spirits to come in? Could this mean there were more spirits in our house, and would they be friendly or antagonistic?

Tony's reaction to the photographs and the two separate entities was a profound, "I knew it. Sallie just doesn't look or seem like the type of child who would do some of the things that have been happening around here." I decided right then to write a letter to Barbara and ask if she was able to pick up anything more about our situation.

FOURTEEN

# THE REMOTE

## JANUARY 1994

We rang in the New Year without incident and it wasn't until January 5th that another of the spirits in the house made its presence known. For several hours, Tony and I had been sleeping in the master bedroom. The door, as usual, had been left open. Being a light sleeper, Tony woke to strange thumps that sounded a lot like footfalls on the stairs and in the hallway just outside our door. It was something he had heard for many a night, but had assumed that it was our cats playing outside the room. Because he had not thought it odd, he had not felt the need to mention it to me.

About 1:00 in the morning and frustrated that he had not been able to fall asleep because of the constant noise, he could finally take it no longer. He got out of bed and stood at the top of the stairs waiting for one of the cats to run up. He was planning to catch it and lock it in a room so it would be quiet.

As he stood at the top of the stairs waiting for one of them to come running up, he began to hear the familiar thumping noise; somewhat heavy and evenly spaced. But he saw nothing on the stairs. As the sound got closer to where he stood, he froze with fear and anticipation, his heart pounding in his chest. Every part of his body was paralyzed except for his eyes, which roamed to catch sight of what was to come. The sound passed by him, and he felt a distinct coldness go right through him. He remained frozen, waiting for something to happen, something to move, but it didn't. Then, for a split second, his fear released its grip and he was able to run back to the bedroom to wake me and tell me of the event.

I woke to the abrupt sloshing of the water bed as Tony, alarmed by what had just happened to him, jumped into it hoping for my support and comfort. He was gasping for air and shaking my body in a desperate attempt to wake me. I am a very heavy sleeper, and even when it seems I am awake, I'm usually still incoherent. I hardly remember talking to him and after a few minutes, I drifted back off to sleep. Although I couldn't remember details, I did remember being startled and opening my eyes to find his frantic, wide-eyed face above mine. Not realizing the desperate nature of the situation, I fell back asleep and left him alone with his fear.

Not long after I drifted off, Tony heard a thudding noise. He reached out to grab me and said, "Deb, Deb, it's here in the room with us!" Although I was still in a sleepy stupor, I must have recognized a note of alarm in his voice and without even opening an eye, I told him in a monotone sort of voice that, "it was one of the cats jumping up on the vanity. Just go to sleep." I'm sure Tony thought I was being extremely insensitive, but the plain fact of the matter was I was exhausted and incoherent. In hindsight, I wish I'd been more attentive.

When we woke the next morning, he recapped the nighttime events and an odd dream he'd had afterwards. This was strange, because Tony rarely dreamed and rarely recalled the few dreams he did have. In this one, someone he couldn't see had taken him by the wrists and had been trying to pull him out of bed.

"But there was no one there!' he exclaimed.

"How did it end?" I asked.

He said that he had firmly told whoever it was to let go and it did so almost immediately. He went on to explain, "My legs were still on the bed and my top half was over the edge. When the hold on my arms eased up, I crawled back into bed. But what was weird is that I think I was actually awake when I crawled back into bed."

The dream seemed all too real. Later that day Tony grew curious about a persistent pain on his wrists. When he unbuttoned his shirt sleeves he found red and blistered welts on the inside of each wrist.

When he showed them to me, they looked like second degree burns, but looking closer I could detect that someone's fingers had grasped his wrists and in doing so, had left marks on him. The blisters were in the shape of a child's hand and fingertips.

"Remember that dream I had last night? That is the same place where I was grabbed in my dream." We sat there for a long time, speechless and trying to understand what had happened.

For the rest of the month and until the latter part of January, the house remained rather quiet. On the 29th we got together with Tony's brother George and a few friends: Mark, Samantha, and their little girl Tara; Rodney, his wife Jenny, and their little girl Michelle. The babies were all within six months of each others' age and we often got together in order to compare notes as parents. We had strange experiences throughout the entire evening.

The group started out in the living room while the little ones played on the floor in the middle of the room. The TV volume was low, and there were several different conversations going on. Although no one had entered the kitchen since their arrival, we heard the sound of the microwave timer several times.

Before long, all the conversations centered on Sallie and her activity. Tony and I had pulled out several bizarre photos and numerous other things that we had surmised had been affected by Sallie and or her energy. Later that evening, as the babies napped, we moved our conversation to the dining room table. At one point, we all smelled something burning. After searching the immediate vicinity, we were not able to find the source and continued our discussions.

Mark had been looking at a stack of photos that he held in his hand, slightly tilted backward but still somewhat upright. Suddenly several of them simply jumped up and out of his hand. "Did you see that?" he asked. Unfortunately no one had. "It was like someone hit the top picture and then they jumped off over the back of my hand."

Somewhere around 8:30 p.m., George walked into the kitchen to get a drink. On the way back to the dining room, he had noticed my collection of small spoons from various states. Each had been turned around backward. When he came back into the dining room he asked me why I had them facing the wall.

Samantha jumped up and ran into the kitchen. "No way," she said. "I was just looking at them a little while ago and they were all facing forward." As she rounded the corner to see them, she shrieked, "Oh my God, they are!" Thinking back, none of us could remember anyone having gone around the corner of the kitchen unnoticed; especially long enough to have turned all eighteen of them around so nicely and neatly. Samantha insisted that she had been admiring them only minutes before they were discovered turned backward.

A short time later, one of the guys noticed George's wool jersey jacket, which had been hanging on the back of one of the chairs. It had a rather bad scorch mark above the left pocket. George insisted that it had not been there when he arrived earlier that evening. The burned area was small, about three inches in diameter. As we all inspected it, someone suggested that the unpleasant burning smell we had all smelled earlier might have been his coat.

By 10:00 p.m., everyone had left except Samantha, Mark, and Tara. They frequently stayed later then everyone else, and we had grown accustomed to taking this time to catch up with each other. As their baby slept on the couch, Samantha sat to her left and Mark to her right. Samantha had been holding the baby's pacifier in her lap for quite some time as she watched over her sleeping daughter.

She hadn't moved from the couch for quite a while, but when she reached for the pacifier that should have been in her lap, it wasn't there. The rest of us looked for it everywhere. Samantha eventually stood up and looked on the floor near her feet, as well as under the couch and between the cushions where she had been sitting. After ten minutes of looking, we gave up. "That's okay. I have others at home," Samantha said, seemingly undisturbed.

About half a minute passed when I heard the slight but familiar sound of a NUK pacifier. Having used the NUK brand pacifier for Taylor, I was easily able to identify the distinct sound that a pacifier makes when its handle slaps against the mouthpiece. Samantha looked at her lap. To her surprise the pacifier was back in her lap, just where it had been before she stood up to look for it. "Look, it's right here," she said.

"I don't know how it got there. I just felt something hit my lap and heard that sound. You know the sound it makes. And there it was." We peered at each other from under raised eyebrows. Was Sallie playing a game? As Mark and Samantha packed their things to leave, we laughed about our amusing evening.

## LOST REMOTE: FEBRUARY 1994

The afternoon of February 9th, Tony and I had been watching our TV, a newer 19-inch Sony equipped with a remote. When we reached for the remote it wasn't where we usually placed it. Neither of us had gotten up or left the room, so we searched the couch cushions, floor, and tables. Still, we were unable to find it.

Almost in unison, we said, "It's gotta be somewhere," and with that we expanded our search to the other rooms and in every conceivable place we could think of. Still we found nothing and eventually gave up. By 10:30 that night, Tony had fallen asleep on the couch and I took the opportunity to take a bath upstairs. Before leaving the room, I had noticed Tony's arms were tucked under him as if he was cold, so I covered him with an afghan.

About thirty minutes later, I returned to the living room where Tony was still asleep. I noticed two things. Tony was still lying in the exact same position I had left him in, and across the lower part of his thighs lay the television remote. My first thought was that he had placed it there himself, but I realized that there was simply no way he could have done it without repositioning himself and rumpling the afghan that I had tucked around him earlier.

As I contemplated the situation further, he rolled over and the remote dropped to the floor. Hearing it drop, he was now awake. "So where did you find it?" I asked.

He thought I had played a trick on him and asked, "Where did *you* find it?"

I explained where it was when I came back into the room. Both of us waited and watched for signs that the other had played a practical joke.

"So really, where did you find it?" I asked again.

"Stop playing games with me," he said. "I heard you tell me, 'Here's your remote.'"

At first I smirked, thinking it was an amusing game, but as he sat up with a serious look on his face, I realized something was just not right. I firmly denied his accusation, "No, I did not!"

"What do you mean?" he asked. "I could have sworn it was you. I heard a woman's voice say, 'Tony, here's your remote.'"

"It wasn't me," I assured him. "I've been upstairs in the bathroom and just now came downstairs."

More fully awake now, he said, "Don't play games with me, Deb. I felt you touch my shoulder and say, 'Tony, here's your remote.'"

I dug my heels in. "Okay. I swear to God, Tony, it wasn't me." Tony's face suddenly lost all color and he looked me straight in the eye with a pleading expression.

"Don't tell me that."

Realizing he was upset, I didn't say another word. I simply looked at him with an expression that plainly said, "What else can I say?"

This experience led me to surmise that the other spirit in the house was a woman, and she had finally made her presence known, at least to Tony.

Two days later, Tony and I were getting ready to go out to dinner. Taylor was sleeping in the nursery. Tony was in the upstairs bathroom getting ready in front of the mirror, and I was sitting at my vanity in the master bedroom wearing nothing but my underwear and combing my wet hair. All of a sudden, Tony's voice startled me.

"Did you just walk past the bath..." He stopped in mid-sentence as he realized the answer before he'd finished the question and the look on his face was very puzzled.

He explained seeing the figure of a woman with blonde hair piled up on her head walk toward the craft room. He had caught a glimpse of this figure out of the corner of his eye. "I could have sworn it was you," he said. Then there was that quizzical look again as his thoughts finally caught up with the sight of me sitting there. "But you're not even dressed and she was wearing long sleeves and had her hair up."

I didn't know what to say. All I knew was that the female spirit was positively trying to get Tony's attention. I didn't dare say that out loud, however.

Along with being jealous, I found the situation ironic. First, there was my poor husband who's deepest fear was ghosts and he had seen two in our own house. Secondly, I had always desired to see a ghost and had not yet been given the opportunity. I couldn't help but wonder—if I were a ghost, why would I want to show myself to someone who didn't believe in me or ignored me?

## BINKIES

Over the course of the next few days, it seemed I was always losing the baby's pacifiers. I would put one down, and reach for it a minute later only to find it wasn't there. Once, I set a pacifier on the changing table near Taylor's crib. It was only an arm's length away and I never turned away. Of course, I turned the room upside-down looking for it and came up empty-handed. About twenty minutes later I found it lying in the middle of the crib as plain as day.

"Sallie, it's not nice to hide Taylor's pacifiers, please don't do it anymore." Although the pacifiers disappeared a few more times over the next few days, my request was finally granted and they stopped disappearing.

One afternoon George stopped in to see the baby, but he was napping. As we stood at the front door talking, George mentioned he had something he wanted to try.

"What?" I asked.

"Just something I want to try, to find out who's here...something someone told me about."

"A séance?" I asked.

"Kind of," he said. "But not really. I'll tell you more later."

"When?" I asked eagerly.

"I'll be by after I get off work tonight, okay?"

"'Yeah, I guess so," I said, and he was gone.

When Tony got home from work, I told him of the conversation with George and to expect him later that evening. George worked at the neighborhood grocery store only five minutes away and his shift ended at 10:00, so we expected him to arrive shortly afterward. We went about our daily routine, had dinner, put Taylor down for the night about 9:00, and waited for George. He arrived at 10:45 with a few co-workers. I'll refer to them as Chris and John.

Right after they came into the house, Sallie's oil lamp was inexplicably lit. Was she excited about George's plan? Was she making herself known so that we could try to communicate with her?

As I told Sallie hello, George asked if the lamp had already been lit. "No, it just happened after you walked in the door." Having never before been at the house when something like this happened, the other two individuals grew rather quiet. I'm sure they wondered if it was a trick and how it was done.

As I put out the flame I said, "Let's blow it out and see if she does it again." Then I asked George about his plan.

"You'll see," he said.

By then, I was getting frustrated at his vagueness and concluded that maybe he didn't have a plan—maybe he'd just wanted to bring some friends over. While the rest of us talked about nothing in particular, George wandered around, seemingly in his own little world. At times his face would lose color, he would look like he wanted to cry and then he would announce, "She's here."

Eventually he sat down at the dining room table with us.

Tony sat in a chair with his back facing the living room. I was on his left, John was on my left, and Chris was on John's left. George eventually squeezed in between Tony and Chris and this is the manner in which we sat for the majority of the night. Before long, several of us were feeling cool drafts of air circulating around our backs or faces, or across our arms or legs. No one had gotten up from the table to create even the slightest air movement, so we deduced that we had at least one spirit in the room with us.

We decided to turn out the lights, illuminating the immediate area with a small candle. I went to the bathroom and got one of the votive candles that Sallie had ignited so many times previously, lit the wick and placed it the center of the table. We really weren't trying to create a séance-type atmosphere—it just turned out that way.

We continued with more leisurely conversation before someone said, "Okay. Whoever is here, give us a sign that you're in the room with us." The room went dead silent as we waited for something to happen. Earlier, we had all agreed that since it was so dark in the room, each of us would keep our hands above the table and in plain view. We wanted to make sure that if anything did happen, it would not be a prank. After an uneventful waiting period, which lasted several minutes, someone eventually broke the tense silence with a welcome joke.

For about a half hour, we took turns at telling jokes. Sometime after 11:00 p.m. Tony waved his hands in front of and around his face.

He announced that he was feeling something around his head, and it looked like he was trying to fend off an annoying but unseen bug. A moment later, his hands returned to the top of the table and conversation resumed. Almost twenty minutes later, I happened to glanced at Chris, who was intently staring at Tony's face. He was soon straining his eyes as if to see something through the darkness. He slowly leaned closer to Tony and eventually, in a calm voice, he asked, "What's on your forehead?"

Tony reached up to touch his forehead with his left hand. As he did, Chris leaned in even closer. He suddenly threw himself backward into his own chair. "It's blood!" he exclaimed.

As Tony turned to shoot me a questioning look, I could easily make out a rather large trail of blood creeping about two inches down his forehead. In the dim light, I made a closer inspection and found the blood was trailing from a few little scratches above his eyebrows. They actually looked like cat scratches, but I knew that none of the cats had been downstairs all night, let alone on the table amongst our little group.

Straining to look even harder, I noticed a good-sized gash above the other two scratches and very near his hairline. The third scratch was much worse than the others and a good deal deeper. It also looked like it would have caused a good deal of pain when it happened, but when we asked him about it, he reported he hadn't felt a thing. Strangely enough, the more severe-looking scratch did not bleed much, and the small amount of blood that had seeped out was already drying.

After a thorough discussion of the time before noticing the scratches, we each agreed that Tony could not have inflicted the injury upon himself. We all agreed that Tony hadn't left the table and no one had seen his hands go to his head except to swat at whatever had bothered him earlier; his hands had never made contact with his head. We further agreed that the horizontal motions of his hands simply did not correlate with the vertical injuries on his head.

I believe that whoever did the scratching was trying to respond to George's request to let us know they were in the room. I think the first attempt to do so produced the upper scratch. When that effort didn't bring the desired attention, the lower scratches were produced. One thing I can't explain is why some of the scratches oozed more blood.

Tony's curiosity got the best of him as we continued to talk about and examine the scratches. He eventually got up and went in the bathroom to look at them himself. While he was gone we talked, wondering who had been responsible for scratching Tony. Had it been Sallie, or the other spirit?

When Tony returned, the conversation strayed to other things. Yet in the back of our minds, George and I were still trying to think of what should be done next. George and I decided to ask Sallie some questions. "Sallie, did you scratch Tony's head? If you did, don't do anything else, okay?" We waited and nothing happened. With the knowledge that our requests had never before been answered in a timely manner, we gave it more time. About fifteen minutes went by. Nothing.

If Sallie was cooperating with us, her inaction at this point should have meant she did scratch Tony. Wanting a better confirmation, we asked, "Okay, Sallie, if you did scratch Tony, light your oil lamp like you did earlier." We waited a few minutes. I began to think she might be scared to admit to the harm she had done.

"Sallie, if you scratched Tony, light the lamp, but don't scratch him again or I'll be mad at you."

Again, we waited. Thirty minutes went by and nothing happened. Was this just a show of her stubborn side? Was she just too scared to admit to the action, or was the dirty deed not hers? At the end of the evening, we were no closer to understanding what or who had caused the scratches or the reason behind them.

"Sallie, would you do something for us to show that you're here." I quickly added, "But no more scratches, okay? Just do something different."

While we patiently waited for verification, boredom set back in and we returned to telling jokes. Much of the time we spent telling humorous childhood stories and embarrassing moments. Several times, we broke into fits of laughter.

It was during one of these times that everyone except Tony and George detected the sweet scent of perfume. Chris had smelled it first and just as he was about to say something about the aroma, I smelled it and then John did. I hadn't worn perfume for several weeks, and this night had been no exception. To confirm we smelled the same thing, I tried to describe the familiar scent to the others. It was mildly sweet and floral, soft and pleasing—a perfume I would wear. Then I recognized it. It was one of mine. It was an Avon brand called Pearls and Lace. I kept it up on my vanity in our bedroom. I went up to see if it was still there. It was. If someone had gone upstairs to get it and used it to fill the air, the bottle would have still been missing, and we were all able to attest to the fact that no one had been upstairs, at least within the previous half hour. If someone was playing a trick, where and how would they have been able to hide the smell until the right time? I shared with the others that Barbara had said this was Sallie's favorite perfume. I almost squealed with excitement, "Oh, isn't it neat that she brought that smell to us?" Chris and John agreed.

Something caught our attention about 1:00 a.m., shortly before we turned the lights back on. Chris and John announced that they were tired and going to head home. As they stood up to leave, I stood with them. I had only taken a step or two when I noticed George and Tony with their heads under the table, obviously looking for something. I thought that one of them had dropped something.

"What are you looking for?" I asked.

"A light or something reflected or something like that," said Tony.

"What do you mean?" I asked.

"A bright flash or light just flew past us and went under the table."

'What was it?' I questioned.

"We don't know," said Tony.

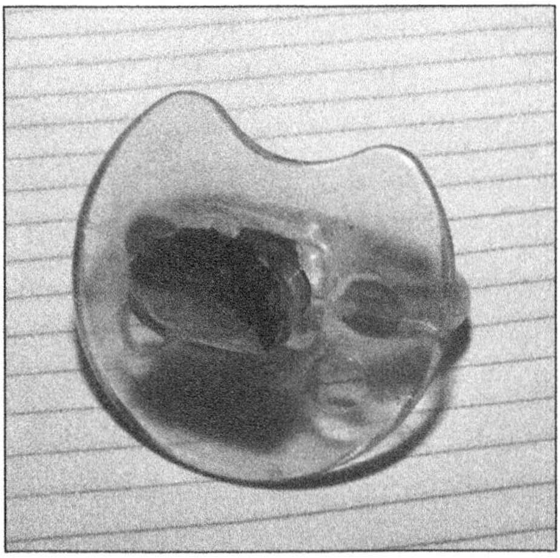

As I bent down to help them look for whatever it was, I realized it was too dark to find anything. I walked over to the switch for the overhead light, and by the time I had turned around, the two of them had gotten on their hands and knees. I too found myself down on all fours and soon discovered what had been the cause of the mysterious flash of light.

Under the table was one of Taylor's pacifiers, one specially designed with a thermometer inside it. There was a small disk-like sensor in the nipple of it that changed colors after you let a child suck on it. Depending on the color of that sensor, you could tell whether or not your baby had a fever. Actually, it was quite an ingenious little gadget, but it hadn't worked well with Taylor because he didn't care for the hard nipple.

Earlier that evening, the pacifier had been sitting on top of one of the stereo speakers just around the corner and out of view if you were sitting at the dining room table. I found it interesting that it flew not in a straight line to land under the table, but in an arc. It was also striking that no one had gone near the living room for at least forty-five minutes prior to catching sight of it in the air, nor would they have had the opportunity to pick it up and throw it across the room.

With the lights on, it was much easier to inspect the pacifier. We were rather amazed to see that it was badly melted at its tip. It was horribly bubbled and there was a nasty odor of burnt plastic. The brightness of the light emanating from it as it flew across the room and under the table had been rather unmistakable. It was still warm when we picked it up. According to what I had researched, when a spirit touches something, the item will briefly maintain the heat generated by the force put upon it.

We wondered if the pacifier had been intentionally set on fire by a spirit or if the heat and burning had been a side effect of a spirit interacting with it. It seemed perfectly clear that spirit was ready, willing, and able to communicate with us, but we also realized that we needed a better plan and a more logical approach if we expected to catch activity or receive reasonable answers to our questions. As eventful as the night had been, we had gathered no real information from the evening's activity and the unexpected responses we had apparently been given. Next time we would prepare better questions and perhaps get a video camera to monitor our immediate area.

## FIFTEEN

# REACHING BEYOND WHAT WE KNOW

Things remained quiet at the house for eighteen days. Then, while Tony was at work, something unexplainable happened in front of a co-worker.

Earlier that day, I'd spent several hours at the library thumbing through the card catalogue, diligently searching for any publications on ghosts, hauntings, and any other related topics. It was then that I realized how little material documented factual accounts of ongoing hauntings and determined that there was a distinct need for such public information. I also discovered, in my conversation with the librarian, that when new books on this and similar topics arrived, it was often hard to keep them on the shelves. Some are sought after so much that they simply don't see much shelf time between one borrower and the next; others just seem to disappear.

I had screened dozens of books, looking for the properties and specific differences between the activity of ghosts, spirits, residual hauntings, and poltergeists. Since each one was significantly different and handled in a variety of ways, I wanted to know how to categorize our experiences so we could learn how to deal with the occurrences and live with the situation. I also thought that if Tony read some of the books on his own instead of getting suggestions from me or the psychic, he might take things more seriously. That afternoon I returned home with almost a dozen books.

Before going to work that evening, Tony and I spent several hours reading excerpts from the references I had brought home. Occasionally, one of us would run across something especially interesting that seemed to parallel our own experiences and read it out loud to the other. Instead of shedding light on our situation, however, all the reading just left us more confused. Notable activity and significant behaviors did not suggest one specific situation but instead seemed to cross over into several of the categories; the activity we had been experiencing seemed to suggest residual spirit, interactive spirit, and poltergeist activity.

Tony left for work at 10:30 p.m. and took a couple of the library books with him. I continued to read as well. Preoccupied with the subject matter, I found myself reading into the wee hours of the morning. It was close to 4:00 a.m. when I finally went to bed. At the very same time, Tony and a co-worker experienced one of the strangest things they had ever witnessed.

The grain elevator where Tony worked was sizeable. It could be described as a couple dozen huge grain silos standing side by side and paired off in rows of twos. The silo-like enclosures are called bins, and each is approximately thirty feet in diameter. There are roughly 120 bins in all at the Atchison facility. About 120 feet above ground level and along the top of these bins is an enclosed hallway called a galley. It runs the length of the bins, approximately 2,640 feet or 900 yards long. At the far end of the galley, you turn the corner, walk a few more feet and open a heavy metal door to Tony's office. The room is the size of a good-sized kitchen. Across from the door on the opposite wall inside the room is a window that measures approximately three feet by six.

The window frame consists of welded steel bars and crossbeams, and the glass panes within them are each one-and-a-half by two feet.

Tony usually occupied this room alone. However, that night a co-worker stopped in and the two of them sat for a while talking about ghosts and a few of the experiences that Tony had witnessed at home. Suddenly and without any warning, an unusually strong gust of wind ripped open the heavy office door with extreme force. The wind rushed across the room towards the window with an intensity that blew out the window. The whole window, frame and all, went crashing to the ground below.

Tony and his co-worker sat there dumfounded by the force of the air and the power that had just ripped past them. There was nowhere that gust of wind could have reasonably come from. If it were a natural occurrence, its path would have started at the other end of the enclosed galley hallway, almost half a mile away. It would then have had to turn a corner, and still have enough speed and force to blast through a metal door and blow out the heavy window.

Of course, this was inconceivable. Ruling out that possibility however, left room for only one other. This was a paranormal incident. The experience did not sit well with either one of them and was the beginning of strange occurrences at work on the midnight shift. Word spread to the rest of the elevator workers, and soon not even the maintenance personnel would work in Tony's area of the facility.

## MARCH 1994

On March 3rd, one of Taylor's musical toys played continually throughout the day without anyone activating it. It was interesting to watch these occasional and innocent forms of communication become more frequent. Sallie was with us often throughout the day.

One night about 2:00 a.m., an extremely loud musical nursery rhyme awakened me from a sound sleep. I'm sure it seemed excessively loud because it was so abrupt in the dead silence of a peaceful night. It had come across the baby monitor I kept at my bedside. The other monitor stood on a shelf above the crib in the nursery where Taylor slept. I recognized the music as coming from an electronic top-like toy in the room. You only had to touch the toy to get it to work.

Figuring that it was Sallie being ornery, wanting acknowledgement or play-time, I scolded her for making so much noise and told her to stop before she woke the baby. The music did stop, but not necessarily because of my request. It was likely because it was the end of the tune. As I started to drift off to sleep, I was startled again by the same musical toy. I hollered, "Sallie, quit it!" This game continued for a few hours and I had been awakened no less than four times. About 4:00 a.m., the toy continued to play the same tune over and over. This was very odd because the toy had a bank of six different songs that it could play at random; normally I had never heard it play the same song more than twice in a row. If this kept up, the baby was sure to wake up through all the noise.

Maybe there was something wrong with Taylor and our house spirit was desperately trying to get my attention. Or, depending on where the toy was in the room, a blanket from the crib could have been hanging low enough to hit the toy. This might have happened repeatedly if Taylor's arm or leg was in motion while he slept. It also hit me that I might have left the nursery door open. Perhaps one of the cats had gotten to playing with it and was responsible for bumping the toy.

I got up to investigate, but when I got to the hallway, I saw that the door to the nursery was already closed. Thinking that I might have mistakenly shut one of the cats in the room, I reached to open the door. As I did, I noticed both of my cats sleeping at the other end of the hallway.

At this point, I had run out of logical explanations and just wanted to stop the toy from bellowing out another ballad. I quietly entered the room, carefully picked up the toy, holding it as if it were a land mine ready to blow at the slightest bump, and left the room. I quietly shut the door and gently placed the toy on the floor in the hallway. I wasn't about to put it in my room for fear it would continue to wake me. Although leaving it in the hall would have put it closer than before and surely louder if it would have gone off again, I did so as an experiment. I was testing to see whether the cats were able to set it off. The toy never made another sound that night.

On March 11, Tony had another terrifying encounter with an unnatural force. Early in the evening, after putting Taylor to bed, I went upstairs to do some sewing. Saint Patrick's Day was coming up, and since Taylor was going to ride in the parade with his grandfather (who was grand master of the parade for the year) I'd decided to make him a green outfit to wear. I had been working in the sewing room for about three hours. I had taken a few breaks to go downstairs and get a snack or a drink and at some point noticed that Tony had fallen asleep on the couch. It was therefore completely unexpected when he burst into the sewing room. I could see that he was upset or preoccupied and was breathing rather heavily. It was odd for him to just keep me company while I sewed, trying to make small talk, and it was odd how close to me he needed to be. Unable to figure out the reason for his strange behavior, I finally I asked him, "What is wrong?"

"She was downstairs with me." He paused, and then continued. "Jesus, Deb, she was right on top of me and wouldn't let me up."

I tried to console him and then asked him to tell me what exactly happened.

"I was sleeping on the couch, lying on my back, and I remember feeling a strong, cold breeze. Actually it was more like a wind, because it moved my hair."

As he spoke, he pointed to the top of his head. Tony used a lot of styling products on his hair and his hair was always stiff; I often joked that he someday would poke someone's eye out with it. As he continued to tell his story, he raised his hand to the top of his head and then moved his head toward me. He wanted me to feel his hair in order to verify how stiff it was. The breeze would have to have been very strong to move it at all.

After describing the brisk wind that had blown across his face, he said, "I tried to get up, but I couldn't move! It was as if someone was sitting on top of me and wouldn't let me up. In fact, I couldn't move any part of my body!" He described how terrified he'd felt and how he'd tried to scream, but because he was so scared, nothing came out. "I finally said, 'Sallie, let me up,' and almost immediately I felt a heaviness lift from my body."

I decided to call it a night and returned with him to the living room. We sat down close to each other and watched TV. My mind wandered often. It wasn't long before I was remembering an episode of *Unsolved Mysteries* we had watched just a few nights before. Although we didn't know it at the time, we realized it was the same episode my sister had called us about back in November. It had been about a female spirit who was haunting a young man and woman.

Early in the episode, the couple was shown lying in bed. The female entity had allegedly entered the body of the young woman and caused her get on top of the man. The woman had laughed in an unusual manner, and although she was much smaller than the man, she was able to keep him restrained. He was unable to dislodge her or get out from underneath her.

We were shocked by the similarity of the televised couple's experience to Tony's. We stared at each other.

He asked, "Do you think she learned that from watching TV, too?"

"Probably," I said. "Which means we'll have to be really careful about what we watch."

Humor being a large part of his personality and his only form of defense, he was compelled to jest. "She's a quick study, huh?" He meant to be funny, but somehow we couldn't laugh—we felt so cornered, defeated, and worried.

In one of my calls to Barbara updating her on how we were doing, I told her about this experience. I was concerned that Sallie might have learned this trick from watching the program with us, and I asked Barbara if she thought it was possible.

Her response was not one that I had anticipated or hoped for. "Yeah, sure," she said. My first thought was, "Oh, wonderful." We not only had to be careful about what kind of television we watched in front of our own child, but also our ghost. Since we really had no idea when she was around, that meant censorship had to be enforced morning, noon, and night. I wondered how Tony was going to take this intrusion.

On March 22, we got together with what I called the baby club—Samantha and Mark, Rodney and Jenny, and our three babies. There were two other individuals that came that night, too: Mark's cousin and his cousin's friend. I will call them Chad and Tom. They had heard of the ghostly happenings at our house and were apparently interested enough to tag along for the evening.

Everyone had arrived around dinner time, so we ordered pizzas and rented a few movies for the evening. As was usually the case, the conversation focused on Sallie stories, strange events, and photos. Although they were very polite, it was easy to tell that Chad and Tom were non-believers in the paranormal. They were however, very interested in seeing something with their own eyes, and indulged themselves for the evening.

Mark, Chad, and Tom eventually found their way upstairs and into the nursery while the rest of us remained downstairs. From there, we could hear them talking, and it seemed as though they were gently taunting Sallie. "Come on, do something if you're here."

Overhearing their pleas for activity and realizing no one was responding to them, I went up to tell them they should refrain from demanding a show because we didn't know how she would react if she got mad. For a while we stood there quietly, and feeling that she might perform for me (after all, Sallie told Barbara that she would "show off" for us if we wanted her to) I simply asked her to do something for us to show that she was there. I could tell she wasn't going to do anything; I could sense her reluctance to comply with our requests.

Wanting an experience for them as much as they did, I came up with an idea that I thought would work for all parties. I recalled one of the photos we had taken of the staircase, and that after viewing it Barbara told us that Sallie was protective of the private "family only" rooms upstairs. With this in mind, I wondered if I could force her into performing on the promise that we would all leave the upstairs.

"Alright Sallie, I know you really don't want us up here, and if you do something to show us that you are here, I promise we will leave." We stood in the doorway of the nursery waiting for a sign, but nothing happened. It took three more attempts to interest her in the arrangement. "You can move something or even throw something at us if you want. Or you can turn out the lights." We waited, and just when it seemed that she was not going to comply, something happened.

The guys had been standing at the doorway of the nursery looking into the room when suddenly the light in the hallway behind and above their heads went out for a good three to four seconds. Then it came back on. I recognized the questioning look in their faces and I volunteered that the light switch they were getting ready to ask about was on the wall several feet behind them.

Without saying a word, they looked at each other for support and a clue as to what they should do next and what they should believe. Without warning, Chad and Tom turned toward the stairs and all but trampled each other to get downstairs and away from the ghost they realized was in the area. It reminded me of two boulders tumbling down the same narrow space. As Mark had been witness to other experiences in the house, his fear level was low. The two of us stood there almost snickering at the sight and sound.

When the two of us joined everyone else downstairs, Chad and Tom tried to act like they had regained their composure. Both, however, were wide-eyed with anticipation and fear. Tom had been nervously pacing the floor and had eventually planted himself on the end of the couch nearest the door. I'm sure he felt that getting the seat closest to the door would give him a quick getaway, should something else happen. After one of the guys explained about the lights in the hallway going off and then on again, Samantha volunteered that the living room lights had done the same thing downstairs. Instead of showing fear though, she had simply said, "Hi, Sallie. Thank you."

Having had an experience of their own, Tom and Chad wanted to know more. The rest of us took turns talking. As we did, Chad reported that he was feeling a funny coldness around him as he sat there at the end of the couch. I got up from the other end and walked past him over to the front foyer just a few feet to the left of him. Feeling the same coldness as I stood at the bottom of the stairs, I was sure he had been feeling Sallie. I told him that she was likely standing her ground and not about to let anyone go back upstairs. Rather nervous that she was that close to him, he got up and moved into the dining room with the rest of us.

Twenty minutes later, Tony moved to where Chad had been sitting, and he also reported a distinct coldness across the left side of his face. A few minutes later, Tony got up and sat on the floor where Taylor and I were playing in the middle of the room. As he turned around, Samantha noticed a scratch on his face that went from the left side of his forehead down almost to his chin. It was on the same side of his face where he had felt cold. He reported that it didn't hurt at all. In fact, he hadn't even realized it was there until Samantha pointed it out. I guess the lack of pain, coupled with the thought that he may have inadvertently done it himself without realizing it, kept us from focusing on the possibility that it could have been paranormal. None of us were concerned or frightened by it.

The more I thought about it, the more obvious it seemed what had happened. In Sallie's eyes, Tony and I had allowed the guys to go up and poke fun at her. As a father figure, he should have protected her; any child would have found it humiliating. I believed that this was Sallie's way of letting us know she was unhappy with us.

Samantha and I supervised the playing babies from the couch and pursued our own conversation. The men had gathered at the dining room table, except for Tony, who was sitting on Taylor's little rocking horse, just a few feet away from the dining room table and behind the rocking chair in the living room. From the couch, we could only see Tony's neck and head above the rocking chair.

Suddenly, Samantha was pointing at something that was obviously shocking to her. Her eyes were wide, and she gaped as if she wanted to say something but couldn't. What I saw seemed to be a very narrow, two-foot flame shooting straight up from behind the rocking chair. It also seemed to be just in front of Tony. Just as I took notice of it, Tony jumped off the wooden horse. He stood there in shock.

One of the men handed him the closest thing they could find to put out the fire—a can of Pepsi. With the fire out, we realized it was one of the leather-like ears of the rocking horse. It had apparently turned into a torch. It was burnt black and crisp around the edge of one ear.

I hollered at Sallie for starting the fire and sent her to her room. I thought she must really be mad to start a fire like that because lately she had been so good about not doing so. Within minutes, we were all talking about what had happened and trying to explain it.

Since Tony had been sitting on the horse, he was concerned about being held responsible. He asked if he could use my lighter experimentally to try to light the other ear. "It's already ruined," he said, to forestall my objection. We were all curious to see if, and how, it would catch fire and burn. I knew we needed to rule out the possibility that Tony may have set it on fire, so I reluctantly gave my permission.

As Tony tried to light the other ear, we realized that the ears on the rocking horse were made of flame-resistant vinyl. Tony and the guys made every attempt to torch them, but they barely caught fire. We concluded that Tony could not have started the fire.

By 10:30, everyone except Mark and Samantha and their baby girl had left. We had been standing near the dining room table when Samantha asked who was still in the house. She said she heard footfalls in the room above us. We all stopped to listen, hearing what sounded like thumps on the floor. I suggested that it was the cats, but Samantha pointed out that they were both on the floor near our feet.

The noise upstairs continued. Apparently, Sallie wanted to make herself known again. I was thankful that it wasn't another fire. Was this her way of apologizing, of letting us know that she was still upstairs where I had told her to go as a punishment? Was this her way of asking to come back downstairs?

Mark and Samantha had been to the house often since Taylor's birth and it seemed that Sallie was comfortable with them. Maybe she even felt safe. Had she acted out because she was not familiar or comfortable with Tom and Chad? Had her fear of them made her act out by scratching and setting the fire?

On March 28th, Tony and I both noticed that Taylor's musical clown was playing itself at intervals over the course of the day. We each noticed it on separate occasions. At the end of the day, we concluded that the clown had played itself over half a dozen times.

Over the course of the next several months, we gained many new acquaintances, some of whom would invite themselves over or stop in without warning. We soon caught on that this was a way for others to challenge us and get a shot at their own paranormal experience as well. They were more inclined to give merit to our claims if we gave them the opportunity to see it for themselves. Allowing all sorts of people into our house had actually become our best attempt to defend ourselves.

Soon, though, we felt as scrutinized as a zoo exhibit, and although things sometimes happened while others were in the house, many times there was no activity at all. People often left without the proof they were hoping for and we felt this reflected on us personally. On one hand, Tony's worst fear was that people would not believe us, so for those who would judge us, we took seriously the burden of proof. On the other hand, we wanted our personal and private life back. The frustration of having so many family and friends distance themselves from us because they couldn't comprehend the situation was excruciating. Although we needed their support more than ever we eventually withdrew from friends, family, and social events. It was at this point that I realized we could no longer put the desire to prove our story ahead of our own life and happiness.

## TRIP OUT OF STATE: APRIL 1994

During the last days of March, I had arranged for a trip to my hometown of Buffalo, New York. We had been planning the Easter trip for several weeks, and to head off any negative activity, I had shared this information with Sallie. I also explained that in our absence, our neighbor Lisa would feed and take care of the animals.

On March 28, and several times throughout that day, we noticed Taylor's musical clown play music without anyone winding it up. Perhaps it was Sallie's way of letting us know she was around and happy. These were the only disturbances we noticed prior to leaving for New York.

We drove to New York a few days later and arrived in Buffalo early the next day. We stopped at my sister's business to pick up the key to her house and went on to the house to unpack and rest. We made several trips in and out, and on one of these trips I heard a noise from the basement door. It was open. I knew Karen would not have left it open with Kori being so young, so I closed it and continued unloading the car. Moments later, I again found it open.

Tony denied doing anything to the door, so I checked to be sure it was catching right, and shut it once again. Again I found it open and moving to and fro as if in a slight breeze. I told Tony what was happening and we both knew that Sallie had come with us. This was the only strange or unexplainable event we encountered while staying with my sister.

Six days later, we traveled to my father's house, eighty miles southwest of Buffalo. This was the first time my father had met my husband

and Taylor. Dad's fiancée Christine and her children were also at the house when we arrived. Matt and Tim were sixteen and seventeen, respectively, and her daughter Shelia was fifteen. About three years earlier, I had stayed briefly at Christine's house and gotten to know them rather well.

We talked, laughed, and shared photos while Christine cooked a special Easter dinner. Afterward, while we women cleaned up, Dad asked Tim to turn off the outside light. It was a tall lamp in the front yard which shed a lot of light on the surrounding area.

Twenty minutes later Dad was quite upset. "Tim, I thought I asked you to turn off the big outside light."

Tim defended himself and walked over to the switch to double check. "See, it's still flipped down," he reported. He then flipped it up, but nothing happened. When he flipped it down again, the light went off. Knowing how mad Dad would get if he had not followed his directions properly, Tim immediately restated his defense. "I know I turned it off because when I looked outside, it wasn't on." I exchanged a quick look with Tony before informing Dad that it could have been something that came with us—Sallie.

Dad looked at me, puzzled and skeptical. "She came with you?"

Tony quickly chimed in, "We're not sure, but we think so."

"How could she come with you?" Tim asked.

Although we certainly tried to explain things without sounding like freaks, it was a hard sell. The conversation made some folks curious and it made others uncomfortable. In an attempt to put everyone at ease, we pulled out some of the photos we had brought along for the trip.

I'm not sure if it was the late hour, the fact that Christine had worked a long day in the kitchen, or that the topic of conversation had upset her, but about ten minutes after the photos came out, she and her children left for their own home. We looked through all the pictures and talked about each one, then the topic of Sallie faded and we enjoyed a quiet evening before retiring to bed.

Around mid-afternoon the next day, we said our good-byes and left for the long drive home. We made even better time on the drive back and arrived in Kansas very early the next morning. Except for two hours of the drive, Taylor had slept the entire way. Knowing he would soon be awake with energy to spare, we dropped him off at Tony's parents' house before we got to our own.

We woke up late that afternoon and unpacked the car. Tony picked up Taylor while I stayed behind to unpack the cooler and suitcases. While I was doing so, our neighbor Lisa came over to welcome us back home and ask about the trip. We chatted a while and I thanked her for looking after our pets. Then in a whisper, as if someone might hear her, she said, "I wouldn't come over without Joe." She scrunched up her face and continued talking in the same whisper. "I was scared."

I remember laughing to myself. She reported that neither she nor her husband had noticed anything out of the ordinary.

The next day, while Taylor was sleeping in the nursery, Tony and I decided to give the car a much-needed cleaning inside and out. On one of Tony's trips into the house to get an item or two, he witnessed something strange in the front foyer. The railing that went along the right-hand side of the stairs was shaking somewhat violently. It had been loose and wobbly for a while, so the exaggerated movement was quite noticeable.

Several minutes later I entered the house, wondering what had been taking Tony so long. He told me what he had seen and together we tried to figure out what had happened. Nothing we came up with could explain how the railing could have rattled like that without someone shaking it.

On April 17, I received another phone call from Barbara in California. She had gotten my last letter and the Christmas photos I'd sent which showed what looked like two separate entities. During this conversation, she confirmed that there was another spirit in the house.

The spirit was an older person, a woman, someone close to Sallie, perhaps her mother, and she was trying to get Sallie to go with her. She felt that this woman usually wore a hat but sometimes she took it off. "She's about five-foot six or five-foot seven with light-colored hair, and she is very spirited," Barbara said.

Having gotten Barbara's definition of the different colors that spirits might give off in accordance with their emotional state, I asked her why the two spirits in the Christmas photos had presented themselves the way that they did. She had previously told me that murky colors were a sign of anger or protectiveness. I explained that we had been very festive through the holiday and had invited Sallie to join us in many holiday activities. I also expressed concern over this other spirit and questioned whether it was in any way a threat.

"I don't think so," she said. "I think the woman wants Sallie to go with her and Sallie doesn't want to go." She went on to affirm that the colors in the photos seemed to signify conflict, perhaps anger or frustration. She assured us that these emotions were not directed at us and were nothing to worry about. She did urge us to keep her informed. She also told us that if anything crazy started to happen or things started getting out of hand, we should call her right away and she would do what she could to help.

Before ending our phone call, I told her about our recent road trip to Buffalo and asked her if she knew whether Sallie had gone with us or stayed behind. "Both," she said. Before I could ask what she meant, she continued, "She went with you but she was bored and went back home to look after the house like you asked her to."

I found it interesting that she mentioned that I asked Sallie to look after the house—it was not information that I had volunteered to her in any conversation.

What she said made perfect sense and was likely why we had noticed relatively little strange activity. The two experiences we had while in New York surely could have been caused by Sallie, but they were playful things. She did not do anything bad and she didn't do anything to scare anyone.

While Barbara continued talking, my mind drifted. How was Sallie able to travel with us and then miraculously find her way back home again without guidance or a vehicle? How did she travel? How long did it take? Barbara graciously explained that spirits work in different ways from the living and before that statement could sink in and provoke more questions, we were saying goodbye. I sighed with some frustration but figured it was something that could wait until the next time we talked. Most importantly, we knew that Sallie could and did travel with us.

## QUIET TIME: MAY 1994

For more than a month after our return from New York, nothing happened except the incident Tony had witnessed the day after our homecoming. I don't want to discredit him or what he saw that day, but if I don't see a thing for myself, I tend not to believe it. At the very least, I wonder what else could have reasonably caused an event. With the house so quiet and inactive, I certainly did begin to question whether there had been any activity since we returned home.

Five weeks and two days after our return, I still had not seen any sign of Sallie's presence. This was the longest duration without activity we had had to date. Again, I was worried that she had left us; I actually began to feel a great loss, not knowing whether she was around. I realized how attached I had grown to her; it was more than I'd ever imagined possible. How crazy was that?

What really surprised me was the extent of the loss I felt. I was sad, angry, and depressed. In trying to accept the possibility that Sallie might not come back, I felt hurt and empty, as though I had lost a good friend. I displayed all the signs of emotional upheaval: I was withdrawn, cranky, rash, and irritable. In addition, I had no patience with the baby or Tony and I desperately wanted someone to blame for this loss.

Perhaps, though, Sallie was closer than I thought. Within a few days of my realizing what havoc my emotions were in, she gave us a small sign that she was still with us.

It was about ten o'clock in the evening when Tony and I saw the wooden balls on the ceiling fan swing in that familiar way. The behavior continued for about thirty minutes and it amazed me how content that sign made me feel. At the same time, I struggled with more questions. Why had she been so quiet since our return? Was she spending a lot of time somewhere else? Had her trip with us all but depleted her energy? Was she regenerating? Maybe she was just as exhausted from the trip as we were.

## SIXTEEN

# HAPPY BIRTHDAY

### JUNE 1994

By the first of June, Sallie was back and as active as ever. At 5:30 that evening, Tony was in the kitchen. Taylor stood at the baby gate in the doorway and seemed to be intently watching something in the dining room. Suddenly Tony heard the Mickey Mouse musical toy in the dining room start playing. No animal or person was anywhere near it. At 8:00 that night, with Taylor asleep in the nursery and Tony and me on the couch, the toy played itself off and on for about fifteen minutes. It happened again at 9:15 p.m., and again around 10:30 p.m.

This happened so often that I wondered if Sallie was trying to tell us something important—perhaps something was wrong with Taylor as he slept in the nursery. I scurried up the stairs to check on him, but he was perfectly fine.

June 2nd was another musically active day. At 7:30 a.m., I went to the kitchen to fix a bottle for Taylor and the Mickey Mouse toy sounded once more. It happened again about 2:00 p.m. Two minutes later, the toy phone in the living room played its own musical tune. The last tune of the day was played by the Mickey Mouse toy at 2:25 p.m.

On June 7th, the three of us and my in-laws were leaving the house. Tony and I had talked about moving to another house and his parents were anxious to help. Many times Tony's mom had voiced her fear that there was something evil in our house. She wanted us to move. Earlier that day she had called to tell me about a house she wanted us to look at. As I opened the car door, I remembered something I wanted to take with me and went back to the house. When I opened the front door, I heard voices. For a moment it alarmed me, but then I realized it was the TV—the same one I had turned off minutes earlier. "Okay, Sallie, if you want to watch TV, I'll leave it on for you." I quickly grabbed what I needed and headed back out to the car.

Taylor was almost a year old at this point and a week later his delight with the musical clown suddenly turned to fear. For him to look at it was one thing, but as soon as I would wind it up, he was terrified of it. I wondered, since we wound it up and set it nearby each night when we laid him down, if he was beginning to associate the clown with going to bed. A logical assessment, but I soon realized I was very wrong.

I had removed the clown from Taylor's bedtime ritual and kept it with his toys in the living room. A few days later, he found it and showed great joy in doing so. Thinking we had broken the association of the clown with bedtime, I wound it up for him to enjoy the music. To my surprise, his look of delight turned to total terror. He scurried over to me and crawled up into my lap, trembling as he held on tightly.

I tried a few more times to present the clown again in fun ways, but each time it was met with the same hysteria. I couldn't help thinking that no child should ever be this scared of a toy. I figured he just needed more time to forget the association he had made, and again found a place to hide it for a few days before I tried to reacquaint him with it. This time his reaction was even worse. Just the sight of it sent him into a frenzy. In fact, he wouldn't even look at it, often reaching out blindly to push it away. Finally, on June 17, I became more proactive. Taylor had already caught sight of the clown sitting on one of the built-in shelves in the living room and was in a major panic. I took him into the kitchen and we got a large paper bag. Although I felt Taylor, even as young as he was, should somehow be able to face his fears, I opened the bag and explained that we were going to send the clown away. I was sure that if he took part in sending it away, he would feel a lot better.

Taylor seemed to understand exactly what I had told him, and with that knowledge it didn't seem to bother him to pick up the clown and put it in the bag. I rolled up the top of the bag, we walked to the front door, and I put it outside. "Now you go away, clown," I said in a stern voice. "Go away." We shut the door, and that was the last time Taylor saw the musical clown until we moved.

For a long time I wondered why my wonderfully contented son had all of a sudden become so frightened of one of his favorite toys. Crazy ideas went through my head. Taylor had two musical clowns; he was still willing to sleep with the other one in his crib. None of the musical toys had ever frightened him before (or since). Could it be that Sallie or another spirit had used this particular clown to interact with Taylor? Had this spirit set out to play with him or had it intentionally wanted to scare him? If in play, had the playfulness become too rough?

If this toy was animated by a spirit, was it simply the animation of it that scared him or was it something it did specifically that frightened him so? Had it actually done scary things to my son? Thoughts of the latter really infuriated me. To think that my son might have been frightened to such an extent, in his own bed, by one of his own toys, filled me with rage. As difficult as it was, I tried my best to put it out of my mind. After all, the clown was gone and so, it seemed, was Taylor's fear.

Soon we faced an onset of new and strange disturbances. It all started on June 24th, in a very familiar way. Around 9:30 p.m., we put the baby down for the night and Tony and I sat on the couch to relax after a long day. Tony happened to look up once again and caught sight of the wooden ball on the ceiling fan. We spent about two hours watching it swing. I mentally took notes to see if there was any particular pattern it followed as it swung, but found none. It was after the first hour or so that I realized that the ball's movement was somewhat mesmerizing. It was like looking into the coals and embers of a burning fire and watching the flames dance. Time seemed to get away from us as we watched it.

About 1:00 a.m., Taylor woke up screaming the kind of scream that curdles your blood. I went to his room and tried to comfort him, surveying the area for any problems and rocking and bouncing him gently in my arms. When I thought he had fallen back to sleep, I tried to set him back in the crib. Each time, even before I took a step away, he would wake up screaming. This went on for almost an hour until finally I gave in. I carried him into our room. As soon as I put him down on the bed, he fell fast asleep and stayed that way until morning.

The next day, shortly after noon, I was upstairs in the master bedroom talking to Tony and sitting on the edge of the bed closest to the bedroom door. From there, I could see the upper portion of the stairway and a good section of the hallway. I had casually glanced up and saw what I could only describe as a tennis ball-sized lightning bug.

Unlike a lightning bug, however, its glow was steady. Even with the mid-afternoon sun shining through the window just behind it, I could plainly see its brightness. For a split second, it lingered motionless in the air approximately six feet above the ninth or tenth stair from the top of the landing. It then made a quick, spiraling motion, darted down the stairs, and vanished. The diameter of its corkscrew-like motion was about twelve inches at first, and as it descended the stairs, its diameter diminished until it became a straight tail of light. This wonderful display took place within an area of about three to four feet and ended within a matter of seconds. This wouldn't be the last time we saw this strange ball of light.

That afternoon, I put Taylor in his crib for a nap and closed the door as usual. He seemed to have slept fine. That night, however, he would not go to sleep in his room. Something had him so upset that each time I left the living room and started up the stairs he would turn around and cling to me with what seemed like the strength of ten men. At the time, I didn't think fear was the reason for his reaction; I simply thought it was his wanting to stay up, fighting the fact that it was time for bed.

After a few more attempts, I eventually rocked him to sleep and carried him upstairs to lay him in his bed. Several hours later, however, we were awakened by his panicked screams. It took me almost an hour to get him to sleep again. I really had not thought anything odd about his waking in the middle of the night; sometimes that just happens.

On the way back to bed, however I started to wonder if Sallie or the woman spirit was causing Taylor's distress. Coming to the realization that he might have been terrified by something in his room was an awful feeling. I didn't know what it was that was bothering him, but I had just laid him down in there. Alone. I swore to myself that if he woke again I would let him sleep with us in our bed.

Fact is, I had wanted to go scoop him up and bring him to our room. On the other hand, maybe I was just overreacting and being ridiculous. To combat my rising anxiety about the situation, I went to his room to check on him and then left the door open. On the way back to bed, I wondered again if it was Sallie messing with him in his room. I wanted to yell at her and tell her to stop it, but if it wasn't her, I didn't want to lay false blame.

Sallie knew the rules; I just couldn't see her intentionally disobeying them just to get attention. She knew there were other ways to do so. Maybe Sallie wasn't causing the problem. I concluded that it was the woman spirit causing the problem in Taylor's nursery.

Although I'm not really sure why I didn't just tell the woman to stop what she was doing, I did think that Sallie might be helpful. After thinking about the words I was going to use, I finally called out to her.

"Sallie, do you think you could help me? I need you to watch over and protect Taylor. He's really tired and needs to get some sleep. Can you make sure no one wakes him or scares him tonight? It would be a really big help to us and Taylor, too." I waited a minute, as if expecting a response, and then thanked her. Taylor did not wake again that night and even slept in the next morning. It was June 26th, Taylor's first birthday.

Tony and I had gotten up early and were anxiously waiting for him to wake up. We had spent several days planning his first birthday celebration. The house was decorated with streamers and balloons, and his gifts filled a small plastic pool in the dining room.

While Tony and I sat on the couch, we noticed one of my cats run into the living room by way of the stairs. As if being chased by something, she had come down at race car speed. Suddenly she turned and hissed, as if to give final warning to whatever was chasing her. But there was nothing there. For about forty-five minutes, we watched her bolt back and forth through the few rooms downstairs, hissing sharply at something unseen behind her.

Taylor finally woke up around 10:00 a.m. Tony got him dressed and brought him downstairs. Taylor opened gifts and we took pictures, then played for hours. About 4:00 p.m., we started greeting family and friends as they joined us to celebrate.

By 8:30, almost forty family members and friends had come and gone and we were sitting with two other couples who also had one-year-olds. The babies had been playing on the floor when one of them let out a howl. It was as if someone had reached out and pinched her. She had always been a quiet and contented baby and I had never heard a peep out of her before then. I was overcome with a sinking feeling that Sallie had done something to Michelle in an act of protection and possessiveness toward Taylor's new toys.

Throughout the day, we video-recorded some of the visitors and events with a borrowed camera. In 1994, EVP (Electronic Voice Phenomena) was not widely known as a tool for seeking proof of spirit activity. In more recent years, it has become a significant tool and we have had the original recording analyzed by EVP analyst Renae Leiker.

The tape was more than ten years old, and although it was difficult, she was able to pull out some interesting audio.

Two of the most remarkable clips were captured while most of the children were together, opening the gift bags we had prepared for them. The voices that were caught in the audio recording sounded like children saying "Rabbit's foot" and "That's all she gets." It suggests that spirit children were not only aware of our activity and surroundings, but watching and commenting on the activity they were seeing in the room. I found this amazing.

The next day was rather quiet. We spent most of it playing with Taylor and helping him explore his new toys. At 9:05 p.m., Taylor looked up and whirled around as if to watch something speed through the air above him. Ten minutes later, as Tony lay face up on the floor, he saw a flash of light in the corner of the room near the ceiling. He described it as a whirling ball of very bright light just like the one I had seen in the stairwell only days earlier.

After that, almost three days passed without activity. Instead of worrying about Sallie's lack of activity or fearing that she would leave us forever, I came to realize that she would always be back. She was comfortable in our house and with our family. In fact, it seemed that we were her family.

About 10:00 in the evening of that third day, when Tony went up to the nursery to check on our son as he slept, he witnessed something alarming. Tony tucked the blanket around Taylor and almost immediately, it was ripped off the baby and tossed across the crib. Thinking he must have caught the blanket on his watch as his arm retreated from the crib, he replaced the blanket on the baby. Again the cover was thrown across the crib. Aggravated, but seeing no real threat, Tony quietly whispered, "Now quit that," and for the third time, spread the blanket across Taylor's little body and tucked it under him. This time it did stay put.

## JULY 1994

Throughout the day of July 6th, Tony and I had a multitude of troubles with the portable phone. While we were using the phone, it would cut out or switch to a different frequency. After the first few times this happened, we discovered that pushing the little on/off button would allow us to hear the person on the other end again.

This problem did not occur with every phone call that day, while we were in any particular room, or talking to any specific person. The weather that day was clear and calm, and there were no incoming storms for the area—we felt confident that we could rule out weather as contributing to the problem. Ruling out logical reasons, however, didn't often give us answers. In fact, it most often left us with more questions.

At this point, we'd had knowledge of our ghost for about a year and were discussing our experiences and their effect on our lives. We both agreed that the level of activity had lessened and almost as if Sallie was comfortable with life and her role in our home. On occasion, though, she enjoyed reminding us of her presence by interacting with us.

Physical activity that we could see was not the only way she got our attention. Even though they could not speak of it, Taylor and the animals seemed to be able to detect unseen activity, something Tony and I could not do.

We did not feel that our little family was in any danger, but Taylor's reactions were like an early warning system, as he often looked off in a direction where there seemed to be nothing visible. He would give a big smile or wave as if to say hello. There were also times when we observed him squirm and giggle joyously, just like he was being playfully tickled.

The most noticeable thing we observed was the way he would often whip his head around in order to watch something whiz past the area just above or near his head. Watching where his eyes had been focused, it was easy to determine that he had not followed the path of a bug or beam of light. Many times, we would watch him track something across the room, or his dedicated focus on something that was interesting enough to keep his interest for several minutes. Most times however, we were unable to figure out what it was.

For several days, things were back to normal. Normal meant no activity, even though activity was quickly becoming the norm. Then, on July 9th, we were faced with a few new and interesting activities. That morning, around 8:45, Tony stretched out on the bed in the master bedroom. He had gotten home about an hour earlier, and he had finally unwound enough to attempt sleep.

While he slept, I spent some time in the nursery with the baby in hope that it might lessen the aversion he had developed to that room. We played for quite a while and witnessed some interesting activity with one of the electronic toys. It was a sound-activated toy that hung from the inside of the crib with a feature that automatically began to record a thirty-second clip of the voices or sounds in the room. It would then play back what it had recorded. Its purpose was to reinforce the activity of a baby's babble through the child hearing its own recorded voice.

We had been sitting on the floor for quite some time when I heard a strange, loud, almost screeching static noise coming from the crib. It startled me at first, then I realized it was one of the birthday gifts that had recently been installed on the wall of the crib. I found it odd that the toy would have been sensitive enough to pick up our quiet play from where we sat on the floor several feet across the room.

The unit seemed to have recorded and played back some other form of energy or noise, something that was close to it. Had it been Sallie? Had it been the woman? It certainly didn't sound like a human voice and I wondered if it was something more menacing. The sound had been somewhat loud and ominous, and it was the first time I wondered if any of our experiences could indicate a demonic presence. Was it a warning of sorts?

Fifteen minutes later, the phone rang. I jumped over the baby gate at the top of the stairs and ran to the first floor to answer it. After a short conversation, I hung up the phone. On my way back up the stairs, I could see Taylor waiting on the other side of the baby gate. Then, just before I reached the top of the stairs, I heard a strange yet faint groaning sound come from the bedroom where Tony was supposedly sleeping.

Thinking it was probably the clock radio, which he often left on in order to drown out the daytime noises, I ignored it and stepped over the baby gate to pick up Taylor. A moment later, I distinctly heard the sound again. This time, I recognized it as a distorted version of Tony's voice calling out my name.

"De-e-e-e-e-b!"

"What?" I called back, but there was no answer.

This happened several more times, and each time I became a little more aggravated that he wouldn't reply. After the fourth or fifth time, I concluded that he was probably dreaming and I was simply overhearing him talk in his sleep. So again, I ignored it. A few seconds later, he called out yet again. I put the baby down and yelled, "What?"

There was still no answer. Finding his repeated calls a bit odd, I decided to go see what he wanted. Still very aggravated with his lack of replies, I abruptly opened the door.

"WHAT?"

When the door was opened enough that I could see him, I found him on the far side of the bed with his arms stretched out from his sides, palms and body laid flat on the bed; his head was lifted and a look of terror was apparent in every line of his face. I looked at him quizzically, trying to understand why he looked the way he did. The fear did not leave his face and my annoyance quickly switched to concern and compassion. I asked him what was wrong. Instead of speaking, he gasped deeply for air as if he hadn't taken a breath for several minutes. What he described next was baffling.

Apparently he had fallen asleep and for some reason had woken up, which was not unusual, since he had an awful time trying to sleep during daylight hours.

"It started out as the specks of dust against the light from the window. I thought it was dust from the vent in the wall near the end of the bed. That is, until I realized it had not been cool enough in the room for the heater to come on.

"I felt the water bed mattress start to gently roll and wave. Within a few seconds, it became violent, as if someone was standing on the bed and jumping up and down. Soon the motion was causing the pillows near my head to bounce several inches into the air and my body began to flop uncontrollably.

"The formation of dust particles near the foot of the bed began to get darker and denser. I think I was mesmerized by this formation, and before I realized, it had taken the shape of a woman's upper torso, her arms folded in front of her and across her abdomen.

"This thing started to move closer to me and as it did, I could make out more details, like dark hair and a bitchy look, like the store owner's wife on *Little House on the Prairie*. I was getting pretty scared and I don't know why I didn't try to get up and leave. As she got closer, I could see she was dressed all in black with a high collar adorned with a brooch. At that point, the water in the baffle of the mattress was frantically sloshing and it got so violent that I was barely able to move away and toward the other side if the bed. My heart pounded like crazy and I thought it would burst out of my chest at any minute. I tried to call for you, but nothing would come out.

"And then, in an instant, she was in front of me. The bedroom door slammed shut, the drawer from the night stand flung itself open and closed repeatedly, and the top of the highboy spun around. It was like being in a sci-fi movie and I could not scream.

"The woman's hand suddenly lunged for my face and I heard a voice say, 'I'm gonna…' There was more that was said but I couldn't make it out. I remember her hand was covered in a long black lace glove and just as it was inches from my face. I saw a black bird on her finger. I struggled to crawl out of bed and over to the door, and I don't know if I was just too scared to work the knob properly or what, but I couldn't get the door open. Then, suddenly, everything that was moving stopped and she was gone.

"I tried to scream several times but couldn't; it was like nothing would come out. I don't remember anything more; I don't know how I got back on the bed except that maybe when everything stopped I got back up on the bed. I don't know, maybe I blacked out or something. Then you opened the door."

I had noticed nothing out of the ordinary except for how oddly Tony was splayed out on the bed and the look on his face. I didn't see anything moving in the room.

He went on to describe how the voice seemed to be one among many, that it had come at him quickly and then seemed to pass him, and before he grasped what was happening, the voice was out of range and completely inaudible. He reported other, indistinct sounds along with the voice, but nothing he could describe in any detail. He reflected on this experience for days, and later described the sounds as "a lot of muffled voices, deep in a tunnel, and far away." It had definitely been one of his most frightening experiences.

That afternoon, I was on the phone near the kitchen sink when the phone cut off. I hit the on button and within a second or so the party I was speaking to was once again audible. In fact, he had kept talking and apparently had been unaware that there had been any interruption at all.

On the 13th, just after 3:00 p.m., we were distracted yet again. I was upstairs with the baby and picking out clothes for the evening. Tony had just come home from work, and on his way up the stairs he noticed that one of the pictures hanging on the stairway wall was turned upside down but hanging perfectly straight. That morning, as Taylor and I were coming up those stairs, I remembered stopping to show him each of the pictures and explain who was in them. I knew for a fact that the photos had been right-side up at the time.

Many of the photos were of my family, who lived a good distance away, and that morning I had tried to familiarize Taylor with them so he wouldn't think them total strangers. As we got almost to the top of the stairs, I noticed that Taylor was craning his little head to look at something down the stairs and behind us. I figured he had taken a particular interest in one of the pictures and didn't give it much more thought. Thinking back, I wondered if he had been able to see interesting activity around the pictures.

By 3:30, Taylor and I were taking a quick bath while Tony stood at the sink, shaving. The bathroom door had only been slightly ajar, and because of a lull in the conversation, it was very quiet in the room. It was then that I heard a distinct moaning sound coming from the hallway. Wondering if Tony heard it, too, I asked, "What was that? Did you hear it?"

His reaction was sort of funny. He had been standing there, quietly shaving, and because he did not react to the sound, I thought he had not heard it, but he quickly turned around to me and said, "Yeah! You tell me what it was and we'll both know." He paused and then continued, "I didn't think you heard it."

He told me that when he heard it, his first thought was that his paranoid mind was playing tricks on him. I guess my theories about his lack of sleep and his mind playing tricks on him had started to make sense to him, so he simply ignored it and wasn't going to mention it. I could see the intense relief in his face when he realized I had heard it, too. I asked him what he thought it sounded like, not wanting to give away the sound I had heard.

"A moaning sound," he said.

"Where did it come from?" I asked.

"The hallway," he replied.

We both just sort of looked at each other with eyebrows high and eyes wide. Without saying another word, we knew that we had both heard the same thing.

Two days later, at about 5:00 p.m., the baby and I were in the nursery playing. I had been talking into the sound-activated toy to show Taylor how it worked, hoping to pique his interest in it. On playbacks, we heard not only my voice and his voice, but also the clanking of the toys we had been playing with. We also heard a loud humming sound that I know we had not generated during the thirty-second recording. My mind quickly tuned in to the world around us. The neighborhood outside was quiet—no one was mowing or drilling or sawing and there was no sound anywhere in the rest of the house.

That night around 8:10, Tony took the baby upstairs to lay him down for the night. Taylor's fear had dissipated somewhat over the previous nights, and he had been falling asleep on his own and in his own room without a problem. That night, however, when Tony entered the nursery, he had felt a certain foreboding presence. As he got closer to the crib, Taylor stared wide-eyed at the mobile above it.

Tony could tell by the look on Taylor's face and the little whimpering noises he made that the baby was aware of something in the room, too. Trying not to give in to his own panic, Tony laid the baby down. As he did, he felt as if something had just taken his breath away. At the same time, Taylor stood up with a fearful look and reached for him. It was apparent that he did not want to be left alone that night. Without any further hesitation, Tony scooped him up and returned to the living room where I was sitting on the couch.

"You're gonna be mad at me, I know, but I just couldn't leave him in there."

With his eyes still wide with uncertainty and his face very pale, he explained what he and Taylor had just experienced. I knew something must be very wrong. Feeling that one of the spirits had somehow been scaring Taylor with the mobile above his bed, I dismantled it and mounted it on the cradle across the room.

About twenty minutes later, I took Taylor to his room and put him to bed without a problem. Was it simply because I had been the one to take him up to bed that he went without a fuss? Or was it that he was finally tired enough to make no fuss about going to bed? Maybe it was the fact that the mobile was no longer above the crib? Since Taylor couldn't talk yet, it was impossible to understand the reasons for his reaction.

## SEVENTEEN

# THE INDUSTRY

Barbara had lived in California for a number of years and along with her work in the field, she regularly lectured at various universities to an audience of not only students, but also faculty, journalists, scientists, skeptics, news media, and more. By mid-June, and with our consent, she had incorporated our experiences and photographs into her presentations and elaborated on their uniqueness.

She worked hard at keeping us anonymous, referring to us only as a young Midwestern couple. Her lectures were so compelling and information so intriguing that interest in our case began to grow. She often had people pulling her aside afterward, seeking more information. At one point, she was approached by field representatives from both *Unsolved Mysteries* and *Sightings*; they wanted a closer look and asked Barbara how to contact us. She took their contact information and vowed that she would pass it on to us. She called us that night.

During our conversation, she warned us of the repercussions of going public. Once we did, we could never go back. She went on to say that if we allowed this, we should go with the show with the smaller crew, because they would invade our space and our lives. Either way, it was possible that we would never be free of the media attention. Knowing how judgmental our little town could be, she felt this was something we would want to consider when making our decision. I had never thought that any television show would be interested enough in our experiences to promote it nationally and it was rather overwhelming. I knew it would be even more so for Tony. I told Barbara that we'd discuss it and get back to her.

I talked to Tony about the conversation with Barbara and explained the positive aspects of allowing the team into our home. Hopefully, they would shed some light on the activity we had been experiencing, and possibly offer some answers. If our case was so unique, it might help others understand paranormal events.

Tony and I were on opposing sides. I embraced sharing our story with others, and taking a scientific approach to finding answers. Tony feared prying eyes and alienation from friends and family. He worried about his family's good name, disliked being photographed, and loathed the idea of seeing himself on TV. His worst fear was that we would be seen as fakes and that no one would believe us.

After a week of discussing our concerns, and more often arguing about them, I finally got Tony's okay to move forward and speak to one of the television representatives. He made it clear that he would prefer the smaller of the two shows. And before we committed to anything, he wanted our photos authenticated to rule out foul play. That night, Barbara called to let us know that a personal acquaintance from *Sightings* had just contacted her.

A few days later, I was talking to the representative, asking lots of questions and voicing our apprehension. Forty-five minutes into the call, I was feeling good about how they proposed to handle each of our concerns. I was rather excited and hoped Tony would feel the same, but this was not the case. We argued for several more days. He finally conceded, but insisted that his identity be disguised from the public.

Arrangements were made to analyze the photos, releases were drafted, and contracts faxed. Tony's concerns with going public grew, as did his fears of scrutiny by family and co-workers. As the day grew near for the crew to arrive, the tension between us grew. We argued more than ever before. Twice we reached the point of not speaking to each other for days.

Additional stress was caused by the fact that we had not yet heard anything regarding our photos. Then, on Friday, July 16, 1994, we received the call. The show's visual effects specialist, Edison Williams, reported that the photos were authentic. They seemed to contain genuine anomalities that he could not recreate with the tools he had. Although this was good news and settled some of our nervousness, Tony was still convinced that the show's goal was to debunk us and make us out to be frauds on national television. The crew was to arrive the next weekend.

## *SIGHTINGS'* FIRST VISIT

The *Sightings* crew arrived Saturday for a two-day stay to document our story. In order to minimize the damage of going public, they agreed that the identity of our town and our address would not be revealed and that any video of Tony was to be blurred. (The crew made every attempt to do this, but everyone who saw the show recognized him.)

To our surprise, there were only three crew members and minimal equipment. After about thirty minutes, they were ready to begin. The plan was to interview me first. Tony sat in the living room in the rocking chair with the baby, watching the interview on a monitor. A few minutes into the interview, we were interrupted by the neighbors and had to stop taping. It was about this time that Tony said, "Deb, I don't think she likes everyone here." I asked him what he meant and he suggested we come into the living room. The soundman was the first to see what concerned Tony. "Oh my God!" he exclaimed. "How did that happen?"

Tony was just as astonished and had no idea how to answer. Knowing he was now the focus of the camera, he fumbled for words. He described a very cold feeling around his arm just before he saw the scratches. I was the last one to enter the room and when I did, I saw that Tony had three bloody scratches across his left triceps, about four to five inches long. The last time I had looked, he had been holding the baby in that arm.

The crew instructed us about how the director wanted to present this and we sort of re-enacted what had just taken place. The cameraman quickly disconnected the camera, turned around, and zoomed in on Tony, who was now holding the baby in his right arm and presenting his left arm for all to see. The crew continued to film as I dabbed at the blood on his arm.

Sounding very worried about what might happen next, Tony said, "She doesn't like everybody here, Deb."

I remember standing there, experiencing a whole range of emotions. On one hand, I was glad that something happened while the crew was there. On the other, I was somewhat dumbfounded and in disbelief. Was our little spirit excited? Did she want to be the center of attention? If not, what was the provocation for the attack? What could we possibly have done to make her angry? I wondered what else was in store for us if we continued.

We all agreed that it might be best to curtail further taping until Barbara got there. After all, she was the person who had attained some form of communication with this spirit.

While we waited for her arrival, we talked about our experiences, giving the crew a better understanding of our situation. We were all standing in the living room. Craig was standing close to Tony when he became aware of a distinct coldness near him. The coldness seemed to come and go, and he was elated to feel the swirls of cool air around his hand. Soon the rest of us were holding our hands out toward the area where Craig and Tony had been feeling the temperature change.

This was certainly a new experience for me and Tony, and we were as astonished by it as everyone else. We all took turns trying to put our hands in, out, above, and below this area, amazed that no matter where our hand was in this field, the sensation was the same. It was as if we were putting our hand in front of an air-conditioning vent. We were able to determine that the cold spot was concentrated in an area equivalent to the size and shape of a four-inch pole running from somewhere above our heads and down to the floor.

When it moved, we found it again, and then we began to notice slight electrical charges associated with the cold air. We watched the hairs on our arms stand up, reinforcing the idea that there were electrical charges in the air. The more we interacted with this cold spot, the more excited and charged the energy seemed to become. Then we started hearing the small snaps of electrical discharges. A few of the crew members claimed to feel electrical shocks on their legs. We heard the continued sounds of snapping electrical shocks. This phenomenon lasted ten to fifteen minutes before it dissipated.

The time passed quickly and before we knew it, Barbara had arrived. The cameras had been set to roll as soon as she knocked on the front door. When she entered, we greeted her warmly. She was taken aback by the scratches on Tony's arm and abruptly grabbed it and asked, "What is this? Who did this?" We explained what had happened and asked if she could help us understand why it had happened.

"Yeah, I feel her. She's right here." She spoke to Sallie out loud and psychically. "Hi, Sallie. What's going on?"

Barbara paused.

"She's excited," she reported. As if to confirm what the spirit was telling her, Barbara said, "Yes, lots of excitement." She then turned her attention to the adults in the room, "She's upset." Channeling Sallie, she added, "I like it, but it's scary."

At that point, I could imagine that the unfamiliar people and strange equipment could quite easily frighten a little girl. Having Barbara as a liaison, we felt more confident that we could provide Sallie with a better understanding of what was taking place. We could assure her that no one was in danger and that no one meant any harm.

After my interview, the crew wired Tony and had him sit in a chair in front of the bay windows in the dining room. To honor our request for his anonymity, the crew created a silhouette of Tony against the window. During his interview, Tony seemed distracted and soon lost his train of thought. He began to speak again, but then had to stop because he wanted to relay something to everyone in the room. He had been feeling that strange cold sensation around his midsection.

Suddenly he reacted as if his breath had been taken away. "She's right here with me," he said. "I just felt her. That cold just went right through my stomach." Feeling compelled to validate the sensations he was feeling, he lifted his shirt to reveal his midsection. To our shock, we saw scratches straight down the center of his stomach.

The camera zoomed in and George shrieked, "Oh my God! Look, look!" All you could hear from Tony was deep shaky breaths as he realized he'd been attacked again. He pointed out the welts that were forming before his eyes and the camera zoomed in on them. Tony fumbled for the words to try to explain what he felt was happening. "She tends to do this because I upset her, and I think she wants to be noticed today."

After the initial shock of a second set of scratches wore off, Tony finished his interview with no further interruptions. The rest of the day consisted of several more interviews with other individuals. During her interview, Barbara told of her first encounter and the things she was able to sense about the little spirit. Relatives, friends, and neighbors spoke of their experiences and things they had seen and felt.

Shortly after 11:00 p.m., we said good night to the assortment of people that we had encountered throughout the day, put the baby to bed, and then grabbed something to eat before sitting on the couch, exhausted from the day's events. The day had become a blur, a whirlwind of activity and experiences.

The anxiety of doing the interviews and the taping had been overwhelming. The constant activity of setting cameras and listening to interviews, the visitors, the scratching attacks, cold spots, and the retelling of stories that sent chills down our spines had taken its toll on us. We sat there quite drained for the longest time, not knowing what to say to each other. Most of the activity that had taken place that day was new to us and it was difficult to absorb.

As I sat on the couch, I felt coldness around my legs. I assumed it was Sallie but didn't want to mention it for fear that the information might make Tony nervous or anxious about another attack. I did check my own legs for the emergence of scratches, but nothing appeared. I couldn't help but worry about Tony. His concepts of death, the afterlife, and the possibility of spirits interacting with the living had been severely shaken.

The next day brought even more excitement. *Sightings* had invited investigator Howard to bring in his own equipment and evaluate the house and the surrounding area. Among his tools, those that were most helpful were the digital temperature gauge (sensitive to even the slightest variation in temperatures) and an electromagnetic field (EMF) detector.

He walked around the house inside and out, and reported finding no abnormal EMF readings, which could have accounted for some, if not all, of the activity and experiences described to him from the previous day.

The second day was structured and handled very much like the first. Although it was a very sticky day, the hottest month of the year, and the house had been overrun with a multitude of warm bodies and equipment, both air conditioning units had to be turned off for most of the day for sound purposes.

While standing in the living room, we began to feel a significant change in the room temperature. Howard turned on his equipment and, rather perplexed by the drastic fluctuation, announced each tenth of a degree of temperature change and the fact that the temperature should have gotten warmer given the crowding and close proximity of everyone in the room.

Later in the day, we were once again given the opportunity to experience the distinct "pole" of cold air that most of us had felt the day before. This time it felt significantly more defined in size and colder than the previous day. Howard was experiencing it for the first time and seemed amazed at the experience. He was intrigued by the fact that even if one person held their hand above another's, it did not diminish the cold felt by either person. Before long, the electrical charges were also being heard and felt again.

Later, having filmed or interviewed in almost every room of the house, everyone but the crew members sat around the dining room table recapping the experiences of the previous forty-eight hours and speculating about what they represented. Tony had stepped into the kitchen to get drinks for everyone but instead came back and whispered something in my ear. I quietly got up and followed him into the kitchen. I looked at the small glass Coke bottle on the windowsill. The bottle held a small rose that Tony had picked for me the day before and the flower looked very strange.

The edges of each petal were charred black, as was later documented on camera by the crew. Howard examined the flower with a magnifying glass and reported that each petal was singed almost all the way around its outer edge and down toward the base of the rose itself. In his face, I could see the struggle to make sense of what he was seeing.

"This is impossible." There was a long pause. "It's as if each petal was individually burned and then the rose reassembled." He shook his head in amazement. "This can't be duplicated."

At some point that afternoon, we took Howard up to the nursery and showed him the corner and items we had designated as Sallie's. Readings on his equipment of the items and the area showed nothing abnormal. Five or ten minutes later, I was showing him a toy that had often turned itself on and emitted a horrible static-like sound. Although I didn't know about EVP at the time, I knew in my heart that the noise the toy had made was significant.

Any interest in the toy quickly faded when I noticed a sudden burst of cool, fresh air fly past my face. Everyone was able to feel the environmental change. Howard, once again excited and armed with his equipment, was able to verify each degree of the temperature drop over the course of about ten minutes.

The entire day had revolved around discussions of experiences past and present. Barbara, Tony, and I talked of some of the things we had experienced during her first visit, especially the lights turning off and on again. The crew spent quite a while reviewing our home video from that day, trying to figure out if anyone could have been responsible for the activity. They found nothing that stood out. We also reviewed photos and raw footage, for the sake of bringing Howard up to speed on the activities of the previous day.

There was no doubt that Howard was very intrigued with the presentation of such compelling evidence. Coupled with his own experiences in the house, it was certainly more than he anticipated on this investigation. Little did he know that he would experience even more before he left that day.

Before he left late that afternoon, the crew took the opportunity to film Howard examining Tony's stomach one last time. Tony had his shirt pulled up to reveal his abdomen, all the while feeling ridiculous as people and cameras zoomed in on his midsection. Howard was viewing the scratches through his magnifying glass. As he reported his thoughts for the sake of the camera, he suddenly stated with surprise, "Look, one's starting to bleed!"As he continued to examine Tony's stomach for a few seconds longer he then said, "Look! It's a nice dark one, too."

Some thought that one of the original scratches had begun bleeding again; however, the view through the magnifying glass showed it was a new red welt taking shape. It began about the same height as the others and ran the length of what was already there. The camera continued to roll for about nine minutes while this scratch formed. This raw footage ended up being touted as a groundbreaking video, the first known paranormal activity actually caught on camera.

Howard tried to process the events occurring before his eyes.

"You raised your shirt, I put the magnifying glass to your stomach to look at the scratches, and one just started to bleed!" Still staring in total amazement he said, "This is the most profound thing I have ever witnessed!" Then looking at the crew, he added, "And you have it on tape."

Several weeks later, that same raw footage would be reviewed and examined by world-renowned parapsychologist Kerry, lead investigator on the cases that inspired the movies *The Entity* and *Poltergeist*. After extensively examining the field-tape, he gave it merit as an intriguing phenomenon and called it frightening. He seemed especially excited by the fact that the camera had not pulled away from the scratches for the entire nine minutes, but cautioned further study and investigation of the phenomenon.

By 7:00 Saturday night, everyone had packed up and was heading home. The house was finally quiet and we were alone. Tony and I sat on the floor of the nursery with our son, trying to reconnect with him after two days of the constant hustle and bustle of cameras, cables, and strangers taking over our regular schedule and routine.

We had not been there long before I felt a distinct coldness seemingly snuggle up to my entire right side. An odd sort of delight crept over me. I found it interesting that after the noise and activity of the last two days had finally ended, Sallie still seemed able to make her presence known to me. Even so, I was not quite sure what to think about it. Was it for reassurance, or comfort? Did she feel like a part of our family? Was she tired or just enamored with the fact that she had finally been recognized? The simple act of snuggling seemed to solidify my maternal bond with this precious, lost little spirit.

Before leaving the next day, Barbara returned to catch up with us privately and without the cameras. She was curious about how our "coming out" on TV was being received and how we were coping. Although some friends and family were upset by our public actions, most did not say anything at all.

It felt strange to see ourselves on television as we watched the airing of the *Sightings* segment. Then it sunk in. How many others had seen us, too? We worried about family and friends seeing us and wondered what they would think of us. Had we embarrassed ourselves and the rest of our family?

We began to see ourselves as we had viewed and ridiculed so many others. We wondered if we had made a mistake by going public. Tony's experiences with his co-workers the next day seemed to confirm this. Although the show tried to disguise him, everyone who knew Tony had easily recognized him, and it seemed that his worst fears were realized. Watching the television show made everyone aware of our experiences, and that knowledge wasn't well received by Tony.

I explained to Barbara that co-workers on Tony's midnight shift refused to work near him and that someone had written "Devil Boy" in the dust on our car. People would stare and point at us in the local stores, and we received taunting phone calls at all hours of the day and night. Even the local college students ridiculed us as they drove past the house, yelling out ghostly sounds.

Some people seemed genuinely interested, though, and it felt good to talk to them. Tony and I often laughed at how many of these people seemed to "just be in the neighborhood." Most of them had never given us the time of day prior to our television appearance.

Barbara asked if things had been any better in the house since her last visit. She was curious about the fires and Taylor's interrupted sleep. After quietly conversing with Sallie, she told us that Sallie was happy with how things had been. Sallie liked her toys and her doll, but she still wanted to play with the baby.

I asked Barbara about the scratches Tony had recently gotten. We'd never really pictured a little seven-year-old girl being responsible for them, and Barbara confirmed our suspicion. Sallie was actually upset by them and the fact that she was being blamed for them. We wondered who else would be responsible for them and asked Barbara to ask Sallie.

It took Barbara quite a while to get any sort of answer, because Sallie didn't know either. Barbara struggled for several minutes to get more from her and was finally told that it was a woman who Sallie didn't know. She also told us that this woman hadn't been in the house when we moved in; she had been attached to another physical person who had come into our house. Apparently, she liked it at our house and decided to stay. Sallie said she wasn't nice, and that she did a lot of things that Sallie got blamed for.

At this point, I told Sallie that we knew a lot of the things that had been happening weren't her fault. I tried to tell her that we knew she was trying to be a good girl, and we were proud of her. We assured her that she was still welcome to stay with us and that we loved her.

With all that said and done, Barbara's curiosity was satisfied. She felt we had been doing well with the situation, but reiterated that we needed to be strong about the rules and that perhaps doing so might help drive this older woman spirit out of the house. She again extended an invitation to call her anytime, gave us each a hug, and said her goodbyes. Although we did not know it at the time, it would be the last time we would ever see her—Barbara passed away several months later.

In the days that followed the television crew's visit, there was no spirit activity. Although we took solace in the temporary quiet, we knew that Sallie would always be back.

## *SIGHTINGS'* SECOND VISIT

By the end of the week, *Sightings* called, requesting a return visit. Apparently, the experiences of the crew on the previous visit had set off quite a buzz in the production office and the show's host, a skeptic by nature, was very interested as well. They had lined up another paranormal investigator and wanted to come back the following week.

This caught us off guard. We had not known them to revisit a haunted location in any of the shows we had watched, and the host had *never* joined the field crew on location or become part of what was presented to the audience. In a way, this made us a little nervous. Was our haunting so unusual that it warranted this special interest? Or did someone feel there was fraud involved and intend to uncover it?

I reminded myself what I knew of the televised show. They had never aired a show where the case was proven fraudulent; it was not their style and I didn't think they would change their format. This must mean that there was a significant interest in response to the field experiences of the crew and our own story.

We spent two days talking, weighing the pros and cons. Tony agreed to allow them back. In a way, he felt compelled to prove that there was no fraud to anyone who questioned our integrity or the honesty of our claims. The next visit was scheduled for Saturday, August 6th.

As the sixth of August approached, Tony became more agitated. His mind whirled with thoughts that he was going to be the sole focus of the visit. He feared that skeptics disguised as people who wanted to help would try to prove he was a fake on national TV.

He knew the crew and those they brought were hoping to see him attacked and get it on film. He worried about what they would say or think if nothing did happen. He dwelled on what this would do to his and his family's reputation. He was afraid of embarrassing himself and his family.

Four days before the crew arrived, we spent most of the day arguing about the impending visit. No matter how hard I tried to convince him that he was being paranoid, he stood firm on his view. He got so angry that he left the house.

The moment he walked out the door, the baby monitor registered an extremely loud and continuous static that lasted for almost thirty seconds. I went up to the nursery where Taylor was sleeping to see if there was anything in the room that would cause such a noise. There was nothing. Had this been Sallie's way of acknowledging the fear and unrest between Tony and me? Had she gotten upset by our arguing, like any young child would when his or her parents argue?

Looking back, I have concluded that the static I heard *was* a form of communication, but one I could not understand. I think Sallie was trying with all her energy to add something to the argument. We will never know who the last word supported: Tony or me.

Tony calmed down enough to return a short time later and we resumed our discussion. This time the conversation was much better, but again the horrible static from the baby monitor rang through the house. Again I checked upstairs where Taylor had been sleeping, but found him fast asleep. Nothing in the room was out of the ordinary.

Returning to the living room, I told Tony about the same noise I'd heard on the monitor earlier that day. I felt that Sallie didn't want to see us mad at each other again and when she saw the discussion escalate, she tried to divert our attention to something else. Of course, there was no proof for this, just my intuition.

Tony usually got home from work shortly after 7:00 a.m. and although he crawled into bed about 8:00, he was usually back up by 10:00 because he didn't want to miss out on any time with the baby and me. Although I had known him to need very little sleep, the weekends were the worst and I grew concerned that the lack of sleep would catch up with him. I eventually mandated that he stay in bed till at least noon. Whether or not he actually slept wasn't the issue; I just wanted to be sure he had an opportunity to get the rest he needed. I found out later that he would set his alarm for noon, and make himself get up.

I felt he wasn't taking the lack of sleep and the possible side effects seriously. We had often discussed the fact that hallucinations were a side effect of sleep deprivation and a real concern, given our situation. We needed to know for sure that what he was seeing and hearing was actually happening and not something his mind was making up.

On one of these sleepless mornings, he saw the top of our highboy spin a little clockwise and outward on its lower base. He remembers sitting up to turn off the alarm, which had not gone off yet, and trying to focus his sleepy eyes on the dresser as he approached it. Within a few steps, he realized that the upper portion was indeed off-center. He realized he had not been dreaming or hallucinating.

I saw it differently and felt the side effects of too little sleep had created hallucinations that would explain many of his claims. I questioned it so much that it made him question his own mind and sanity. It is also one of the reasons he did not bring other things to my attention while we lived there.

It was Saturday morning and the TV crew was to arrive later that morning. Knowing they would need additional room, I moved some things out if the way. One of the items was Sallie's oil lamp, which I had temporarily moved to the buffet table. I had also taken the opportunity to remind Sallie about the TV people coming back to the house.

Tony was very anxious and decided to take a drive to help relax a bit. While he was gone, I headed to the kitchen for coffee and was startled when I noticed a small flame in the oil lamp on the buffet table. Only seconds earlier, I had stood in front of the table tucking a few last-minute things into the drawer and the lamp was unlit. It seemed that Sallie was just as anxious as we were.

It was close to noon before the crew arrived. They set up their equipment and attached wireless microphones to me and Tony. Technical gear and empty equipment cases were lying everywhere.

It was comforting to have the same crew as before. The only addition was Tim White, the host of *Sightings*. Tim was excited to talk with us. As the audio person wired me, Tim talked to Tony and then talked to me while Tony was getting wired. Tim was very concerned about the scratches that Tony had received during the last taping and asked to see them. For the most part, the ones on his torso were healing nicely, but the ones on his triceps had caused scarring.

Tim was captivated by the details of our experiences and eager to find the underlying cause. We sensed that he didn't really believe our claims and that he thought the mystery would be solved during his visit. He took a logical approach and took advantage of every opportunity to clarify facts and have us reiterate our experiences. I appreciated his healthy skepticism in playing devil's advocate and the respectful way in which he approached us.

Going into any type of unusual or unknown situation (let alone a paranormal one), it is necessary to have an open mind so you can see all elements and possibilities, even if they take you beyond your comfort zone. The more unreasonable the claim, the longer it should take to influence you and the harder you should have to work at believing it.

Throughout the day, I watched Tim's reactions, and I could see how often he struggled with his logical self. It was like I could hear his thoughts and see the process by which he drew his conclusions. His mind was being pulled in two different directions; to believe or not to believe.

Shortly after Tim arrived, a knock at the door revealed ghost investigator Al, who had been invited to the taping by *Sightings*. From the moment he walked in, his skepticism was apparent. When we took him on a tour of the house, he had an explanation for every activity and experience we had claimed.

For instance, he said that fishing wire could have been used to move the bears and that a hair dryer could easily have produced the effect of the wax dripping on the taper candles. They were all ingenious explanations, but ones we had already thought of and tried to duplicate ourselves.

Part of me wanted to scream, and I could tell that Tony was getting frustrated with what seemed to be accusatory remarks and insinuations of trickery on our part. Why would we subject ourselves to such scrutiny and take the chance of being revealed as frauds on national television?

For the sake of the camera and the audience, I wish Al had taken the time to re-create the effect on the candle. It is truly amazing how easy it is for skeptics to explain away phenomena that they have never experienced or tried to reproduce. As the day stretched on, Tony and I felt increasingly insulted by his comments. He was curt, dismissive, and condescending in almost every conversation he had with us and we found it hard to remain congenial.

He pulled each of us aside separately and said that he felt the other was responsible for generating the poltergeist-like activity in our house. He suggested that one of us had been molested as a child and the trauma had triggered a strong emotion that energized the poltergeist. He recommended that we seek professional help from a psychologist to get through the emotions that were wreaking havoc on our lives. It wasn't until our conversation the next day that we realized he had said the exact same thing to each of us.

This infuriated me, because he had not spent enough time with either one of us to have made such an assessment, and it seemed he was attempting to create a division between us. I felt it was irresponsible and unprofessional.

Throughout the day, we continued to migrate through the house, often feeling the distinct cold spots that had attracted so much attention. During each occurrence, Tim and the rest of the crew tried to find a plausible explanation for it. At one point, we were exploring a temperature fluctuation and electricity in the living room. Everyone was holding out their hands trying to detect where it was and where it was going. Meanwhile, Tony was nearby holding Taylor in his arms.

Suddenly he reached his arm out straight. I thought he was pointing to something or feeling something significant around him. Everyone else did, too. In fact, Tim held out his hand in the area around Tony's hand. Feeling nothing distinct, he withdrew it. Realizing that no one had picked up on what he was trying to show them, Tony calmly said, "Look at my arm."

We saw two scratches, one running almost the entire length of his upper forearm. Tim suggested that Tony sit on the couch behind him. George dabbed at the blood, and Tim noted Tony's apparent shortness of breath. Tim was obviously concerned for him and his safety.

Some time later, we had come up from the basement and were standing in the kitchen. The cold spots had returned and everyone was aware of them. Tony stood by the pantry door quietly watching as everyone followed the cold spots around the room. Then someone pointed out that Tony had huge welts forming across his forehead. Tim seemed very shocked by these, because they seemed to become deeper and more pronounced before our eyes.

Toward the end of the day, Tim asked me if it would be possible for Al to stay overnight for continued observations. When I relayed the request to Tony, he accused me of agreeing to it behind his back and told me, "Absolutely not! This was not part of the agreement we made when we said they could come back!"

I agreed. We were completely worn out by the day's events and the constant physical and emotional activity. We didn't feel that Al had shown compassion, been supportive, or offered relevant evidence to help us understand the situation or our experiences, and we weren't interested in spending the rest of the evening entertaining him and defending ourselves.

Al left a short time later, but Tim had done one last interview with him that Tony and I did not know about until it aired on national television a few weeks later. It didn't sit well with us, to say the least. Although Rauber spoke of the intense fear he sensed from Tony, that secret interview caught us off guard. Tony and I had never been told about the suggestions or comments that he made.

Had Rauber mentioned the need for a document of our experiences as they happened, I could have let him read my journal entries. Had he brought up the concern that putting toys in the nursery was encouraging the little spirit, I could have told him that we were instructed to do so in order to take her focus off fires, electrical appliances, and my infant son. Since we had given her things of her own, she had pretty much left the baby alone. (A week after his departure, we received a letter from Rauber explaining how dissatisfied he was with how the television show had treated him. The show had not allowed him to do an investigation in his own manner. He had nothing good to say about the experience and we guessed this explained the tension during his visit.)

We both felt drained by the end of *Sightings*' second visit. We were pleasantly surprised by their early departure and looked forward to having Sunday to ourselves. I can remember Tony asking, "We are done now, right? No more cameras, no more questions, no more people tramping through the house, right?"

I agreed. There was simply no reason for them to come back, and we didn't need the stress of more strangers interrupting the normalcy in our home.

EIGHTEEN

# PETER JAMES

## *SIGHTINGS'* THIRD VISIT

Several weeks later, just after the airing of *Sightings'* second visit, the phone rang around 11:00 a.m. Apparently, after the experience of Tim White and the crew, there was concern that there was something very real and worrisome about our situation. Although their experiences had primed them with a desire for more information, presenting concern for our family and its safety was an ideal approach to gain re-entry to our home, and that is exactly what happened.

I was hesitant, since nothing positive had come from their last visit. We were assured that the psychic they wanted to bring in was very good and would be very helpful. His name was Peter James and I was already vaguely aware of his paranormal involvement. I began to think that bringing him in might finally get us the answers we were looking for and I became excited.

I reluctantly relayed the information to Tony and his response was worse than I'd anticipated. To avoid further conflict, I dropped the subject and decided it wasn't something we had to do. This didn't go smoothly either, as Tony convinced himself that I was angry with him for not wanting to participate. The arguing continued all the next day. I didn't care if the *Sightings* crew ever came back.

I was finally able to reassure Tony of my sincere lack of interest in bringing the *Sightings* team back. Living with the spirit in our house had been going well, and if we came up against something we couldn't handle, we could look for further help at that time. This seemed to change the energy in the house to a lighter, more normal environment and our personal interaction was much better than the three previous days.

Tony went to work at three that afternoon and soon after that, our doorbell rang. I opened the door to a dark-haired woman about my age. She introduced herself as Colleen and apologized for the intrusion. Colleen explained that she had lived in the house for about eight months and had moved out only a few months prior to our moving in. During that time there were a few things that now seemed a bit strange to her, and seeing us on the television show the night before had brought several of those things to the forefront of her memory.

For one thing, her daughter had played with an imaginary friend called Sallie. She had never given much thought to her daughter's imaginary friend, because many children at that age have one. When they moved from the house her daughter's friend simply wasn't mentioned anymore, leaving her to think her daughter had grown out of the phase of needing a playmate.

It had certainly been an interesting conversation and before she left, I asked if she would mind sharing her story with the *Sightings* people. I couldn't wait for Tony to get home to share our conversation and my excitement over what I considered validation.

Up to this point, we'd only had Barbara's word about this little spirit, and since psychic impressions are often not well received, I felt this would offer more support to our story. Knowing they would like Colleen convinced Tony to allow *Sightings* to come back one more time.

Nothing happened for almost six weeks after the television crew left and I grew concerned. What would happen if the crew came and nothing happened? Would they think it was all a hoax? At the end of the last aired segment of our story, they informed viewers that they would keep them posted on the case. How would they present us if there was no activity?

The more I thought about the lack of activity, the more I began to theorize causes. Perhaps the entity was still in the house but her energy had been exhausted after such extensive interaction and commotion. Was she re-energizing?

It has been theorized that spirits draw from the many energies around them, including the energy that people generate or emit. The more people there are in an area, the more energy is available for spirit consumption. This could explain the distinct inactivity we were experiencing between the visits of the television crew, who were certainly anxious and highly charged with emotional energy when they came. Could those personal energies be responsible, in part, for the increase in activity during their visits? During *Sightings'* first visit, the emotional energy was compounded by the anxiety that Tony and I felt about being interviewed on camera for a national show. Had these emotions contributed to the spirit energy and its use against Tony?

In addition to the emotional energy present during each visit, there were large cameras, batteries and chargers that were in the house at any given time. This certainly could have lent itself to a higher concentration of available energy for the spirit world. The intensity and increased occurrences of the activity during each filming session would seem to support this theory.

I remember *Sightings'* third visit very well. Not only did we get to work with a fascinating individual who made a tremendous impact on our paranormal life experience, we also got two more independent confirmations of a force that had been in the house much longer than us.

Peter James arrived fairly early, and I watched him get out of the car that had brought him. He had been given nothing but very basic information on the case. The camera was rolling as he drove up and after being greeted by the field director, Peter stood in front of the house and studied the windows of the second floor. In his eyes I saw an intent interest.

As he pointed up to the window of the master bedroom, he whispered something to George. We later learned that he had seen the face of a little girl in the window and he was confused because he had been told that a young couple with a baby boy resided in the house. As he entered the house, there seemed to be a calming, angelic air about him, soothing and almost immediately comforting.

He was gracious and courteous, and asked if he could walk around a little to get familiar with his surroundings. He did not seem to need to take in his surroundings visually; instead, he walked with his head down, twisting it back and forth ever so slightly as if he was trying to hear something. Although his eyes seemed to shift from side to side, it was apparent that he was not looking further than a few inches or so in front of him. This behavior impressed me. He seemed to survey his surroundings, gathering important details to do a cold read of our setting.

Also as he walked around, he made short sounds, as if he was trying to sound out a word. "S, S, S, Sa, Sa." Working his way back to the front door and the stairwell to the upstairs, he suddenly stopped and pointed to the top. "There's a little girl standing right there." As we and the camera moved in to get a closer look, he put his hand up to stop us as if moving closer would startle or scare away the little girl. The camera got closer and he went on. "Right at the top of the stairs."

In a firm but friendly voice, he said "Hello, hello." Then he pointed again and whispered, "Look." The camera got close enough to see the stairwell and landing.

"Hello, can you speak to me? Sallie, is that your name?" Peter mounted the stairs. "Okay, okay," he said as he slowly ascended into her space.

I was standing just behind the cameraman. I heard Peter very clearly and when he asked if her name was Sallie, I was overjoyed. Within only a few minutes, he had been able to detect the little spirit in our house and put a name to her. I felt it was one more validation for our claims and us. Additionally, I was pleased that Sallie was comfortable enough to have already allowed him to get close.

A short time later, we had a knock at the front door. Apparently, *Sightings* had arranged for the previous tenant to tell of her experiences. Colleen had agreed to a short on-camera interview but, like Tony, had wanted to remain anonymous. They set her up as a silhouette on the couch and we listened as she spoke.

She told them that she and her three children had lived in the house prior to us. She described how her five-year-old daughter had played with an imaginary friend named Sallie, and that they often played in the walk-in closet of the master bedroom. She recalled many occasions on which she would scold her daughter for leaving toys out or making a terrible mess, but her daughter denied doing so, saying, "I didn't do it, Sallie did." Other times her daughter would do things out of character and then report, "Sallie told me to do it." With an air of regret, Colleen told of the times she punished her daughter for lying about those situations. Only now did she realize that her daughter had probably been telling the truth.

After her interview, the crew followed Peter in an attempt to get his impressions of paranormal experiences as they happened. Tony and I felt comfortable walking with Peter in the house, because it seemed there was a very real connection and he was able to communicate with the spirits. He had an "in" to the other side, so perhaps, we thought, there would be no more attacks on Tony. This, however, was not the case.

While in the hallway outside the master bedroom, Peter reported a strong level of resistance; he said that whatever was in the room didn't want him to enter. To show the spirit he was not intimidated and was ready to stand his ground, he said, "Hello, hello." With the rest of us standing just a few feet behind him, he stepped a foot or so into the room and in a demanding voice said, "Speak to me!" Tony and

I had been standing in the doorway of the room and although I was not aware of it, Tony felt a distinct rush of fresh cold air fly past and through him right after Peter's command; seemingly in reaction to it.

Tony was clearly nervous at this point, and he paced the hallway outside the room. With our previous experiences in mind, I knew there was something very wrong. A moment later Tony complained of a stinging on his lower back and stepped away to the area at the top of the stairs.

At the time Peter had no idea that Tony was sometimes physically attacked when the spirit wanted to make its presence known. So when the visibly distressed Tony backed away from the area, Peter tried to assure him that he shouldn't be frightened. Peter told Tony, "You're in control here." Tony and I, however, knew differently.

I asked Tony to lift his shirt and found the letters "M" and "C"—each about four to five inches high—carved into his lower back. The cameraman documented these scratches and as he did so, we all heard electrical snaps sounding all around us. Peter felt one of them on the area of his wrist.

Aware that there was significance in the activity and likely fear on the part of the spirit, Peter firmly said, "Hello. Easy!" He paused for a moment. "I'm not afraid of you!"

He stood just outside the doorway for a minute and then reentered the room. He then resumed his attempt to communicate further and asked the spirit not to harm Tony.

He mentally asked who was in the room, but reported that all this particular spirit would give him was the letter "B." Possibly the spirit was uncomfortable with the questions, because Tony was attacked again. This time, the back of his shirt was set on fire.

At first it seemed to smolder, and this is what caught the eye of one of the crew members standing behind Tony. The shirt then burst into flame and several of us began to smack at it to put it out. Tony seemed to have been completely unaware of what was happening. When the flame was finally put out, inspection showed that Tony's skin was not affected, only the shirt.

Tony changed shirts to make the burnt one available for closer inspection. Each person was given the opportunity to look at the shirt. The manner in which it burned seemed normal and everyone agreed that there was no smell of a flammable substance on the shirt to have ignited it so inexplicably. The experience baffled the team. One of the crew members had been standing behind us to get the best camera shot of all of us, and had not seen Tony's hand or anything else that could have been responsible for the incident.

Peter reported that at least three individuals had actually died in the house and there was a medical feeling attached to at least one of them. According to the crew's research and ours, this was likely Charles C. Finney, who moved out of the house in 1906. He was the son of Michael C. Finney (MC?), who died in the house in 1871. James Finney died there in 1900, and Kate Finney in 1918.

Peter also seemed to speak directly to Sallie. She told him she had a pain in her lung and a pain in her foot or ankle. In relation to this young spirit, we looked at a preliminary list I had put together with possibilities for who she was.

My research from earlier in the year allowed Peter to home in on one little girl in particular. The television crew jumped on this and suggested that it correlated to their own research. At this point, the crew shifted the filming to the cemetery and the next show's segment showed Peter standing at Plot One, Fourth Row West, suggesting that this was Sallie's final resting place and that she had died of pneumonia.

We had no reason to believe otherwise until later research revealed the following according to *The Atchison Daily Globe* dated February 23, 1905:

> **Sallie I. Hall,** colored, wife of Will Hall, who works at the Wolters brick yard, died this morning and the funeral will occur Sunday at 2:00 p.m., from the Sixth Street Baptist church. Mrs.

> Hall was only thirty-four years of age, but had given birth to fourteen children within the past sixteen years. All had died at birth but three girls and a boy, who survive their mother. The oldest is sixteen and the youngest is two. A baby was born a week ago. Think of the suffering, think of the tragedy crowded into one brief life! Every year there has been a birth and a death at the house, and this year there have been four deaths: an uncle at Christmas, a sister of Will Hall a few weeks ago, the baby a week ago, and now the mother. The family lives in the alley east of second street and adjoining Mound.

More recently, however, there was additional confusion when I was contacted via email by a researcher from the *Sightings* show. She reported that although she didn't have the records available, she did remember the following:

> I found an entry in one of the logs in 1905 of a Sallie (she was 5 or 6) that died along with her mother in an accident. I believe they were riding in something that tipped over. It did not say if they died in your home but the accident was in an area just behind your home on a road that is still dirt. At the time I was also able to confirm the grave location that Peter James took us to, even though it was illegible. I was able to confirm that it was a child's grave—she was named Sallie and she was 5.

In typical TV fashion and if my memory is correct, when Peter says he found the grave he's not actually at the grave, I'm not certain of this but it is possible. Visually, it wasn't a good spot, so they may have faked it and moved him.

This researcher also reported that the information found was given to those in charge of the story. I wonder why it wasn't included in one of the show's segments, but the editors often said they had had a difficult job editing our story because there was so much to work with and they hated to cut out any of it just to make it fit into the show.

I regret that we were not with Peter and the crew at the time they were at the graveyard, because we have no way to confirm or further research this information.

The Hall family mentioned in the obituary lived on Mound Street just around the corner from the Sallie house. We have speculated that perhaps this family had worked for the doctor's family in various capacities. It was thought that the doctor and Mrs. Hall may have had an association beyond business. This was portrayed in the made-for-TV movie *The Heartland Ghost*, made by Paramount several years later.

## NINETEEN

# THE ALL-NIGHTER

### *SIGHTINGS'* FOURTH VISIT

*Sightings'* fourth visit began much like the others. I was told that no story the show had done had generated more email and interest than ours and this time they wanted to bring in a ton of equipment to monitor the house and its activity for a twenty-four-hour period.

This, of course, was a very hard sell for me to pitch to Tony and we passed the days arguing over our concerns, fears, and wishes. Tony wanted to be done with it all. He wanted to go back to some normalcy and not have family and friends question him because of what they saw on television. I simply wanted more answers—real answers. After days of heated discussions, fits of rage, and periods of not speaking, Tony agreed to let the crew come back.

We were told that every available monitoring piece of electronic equipment used in paranormal investigating was going to be used. Our kitchen was turned into a virtual electronic studio able to monitor everything. There was a thermal camera to measure heat changes, an oscilloscope to monitor voltage signals, and closed circuit surveillance cameras to monitor all areas of the house. These cameras were placed strategically in areas where we and the crew had reported activity, namely the nursery, the top of the stairs, and the living/dining area.

The team had counted on Tony and me going to bed at some point that night and for the sake of our privacy did not place cameras in our bedroom. However, there was a frequency counter placed at the top of the stairs to measure the number of cycles in an electric signal during a preset time interval. Multiple cameras from different vantage points were set up on tripods downstairs to gain the best overall view of an entire area. Mobile hand-held cameras were also ready to go.

For this event,Tony wanted to be sure there was no reason for anyone to believe that he might be causing any of the physical injuries himself. He removed all jewelry and suggested that someone constantly be near him to monitor his actions and whereabouts. The crew agreed to this, and as it happened he spent most of his day in a chair in the living room.

By his side for most of the investigation was world-renowned parapsychologist Kerry Gaynor. He arrived mid-afternoon, and right away seemed genuinely concerned for the safety of Tony and our family. For most of the night, he sat on the end of the couch right beside Tony.

For his experience and professional understanding of paranormal situations, Kerry had been consulted for several months about this case and his interviews had been aired during segments of our story. He had already been shown the footage of the initial scratches that erupted on Tony's stomach and mentioned that it was "exciting that the camera didn't pull away for nine minutes." At the end of his initial interview, he reported that he felt there was possibly more than one thing going on in the house. He felt that along with the playful activity that had been reported, there was some potentially more dangerous activity as well. Knowing that he had some knowledge of our experiences and of other malicious haunts, we welcomed his presence and input.

Tony was asked often if he wanted something to eat or drink and someone would bring him what he wanted. If he went to the bathroom, he removed his shirt and the crew took notes on the marks already existing on his body. When he returned, they went through the same ritual to detect any additional marks. There were never any new or questionable marks reported during these inspections and new injuries didn't show up for close to twenty or thirty minutes afterwards.

When new marks were discovered, they were thoroughly inspected for authenticity and trickery. The scratches were all genuine and there was no magical powder hiding a scratch or waiting to be acted upon in order to bleed on demand, as was later suggested by a fanatical skeptic. I was actually very impressed by the diligence of the team members to ensure that there was no foul play. Although a bit uncomfortable at times, Tony and I welcomed these inspections so that rumors of trickery could be ruled out once and for all.

While the team set up equipment and rearranged our home to suit their needs, Kerry worked with us to gain a more thorough understanding of our experiences and concerns. He had us each fill out a lengthy questionnaire while he talked to the other one. This questionnaire delved into our religious beliefs, our personal traumas, our family life, and our medical and mental status. It also asked about possible past paranormal events, our feelings and thoughts during the ongoing experiences, and specific paranormal events that had taken place to date.

During Kerry's stay, he witnessed eleven separate attacks on Tony while he sat in the chair next to him. Some of them were pretty brutal, and except for the cold air that seemed to signify something was near, Tony felt nothing. Each successive attack frustrated Kerry more than the last, because no matter how closely he observed Tony, he was unable to detect when they happened or a reason for them.

After nightfall, Kerry requested that the investigation continue under low-level light. I'm not sure why, because we had reported that it didn't have to be dark or night time for activity to occur. As we sat without any activity occurring, Kerry suggested that Tony make a verbal request to Sallie. I know this was difficult for him, especially on camera, but he did make an attempt. He asked Sallie if she was there and if so, would she please make her presence known. This she seemed to do, but not as everyone expected.

It was not done via an attack on Tony's person, and nothing moved or flew through the air. In fact, no one recognized it until the crew was back at the studio going over the raw footage. What was very apparent on the review was a low-pitched groaning sound. I can remember getting a call from them right after they discovered it in the edit room at the studio back in California. They were extremely excited to share with us that they had seemingly captured an anomalous sound. As we spoke, the audio in question was being sent to an expert to further analyze it. For almost a week we waited for results.

Rick Wilson, president of Digisonics, was a forensic audio specialist who had worked with the CIA and FBI. He had also worked on black box recordings with the FAA. His findings ruled out any electronic, mechanical, or human sounds. The frequency of the sound was too low to have been produced by a human body. Rick ruled out any natural reason for the sound, but suggested it might be magnetic. He was unsure how this would have been introduced into the audio in question and because he was not experienced in the paranormal had no way to say for sure that it was a ghost.

The sound file was then taken to Sarah Estep, who is often referred to as the mother of Electronic Voice Phenomena. At the time, she had taped and studied recordings from numerous haunted locations for over eighteen years. She reported that in all her years, she had never heard anything quite like the sound captured in our home. She referred to it as an "energy sound, perhaps put out by the other side." She found it quite interesting that the sound came right after Tony asked the spirit to make its presence know.

We recorded the show when it aired, and watched that particular segment of the audio and video several times. One thing I noticed was something I had seen many times before. When Tony asked Sallie to do something for him, Taylor looked up at the ceiling and seemed to track something flying back and forth above his head in the darkened room. We had witnessed the baby doing this many times, and felt it was a sign that he could see what we could not.

In reviewing the footage, it was determined that there may have been some sort of activity or reaction upon one of two oil lamps that were being used to illuminate the room. Any draft in the room should have had no effect on the short wick within the glass chimney of the lamp. However, there was a distinct flicker and movement of the flame within the one sitting between Tony and Kerry. Soon Tony felt the familiar cold presence in front of him and his midsection.

Kerry bent down to look at Tony's stomach, and as he stood up, said, "Yeah, we have a new scratch!" Viewing it with in better light, he went on, "Yeah, we have fresh blood. This wasn't here two minutes ago!" This type of thing continued several more times through the night.

I tried my best to make things as normal as possible for Taylor and took him upstairs to the nursery to play for a while. At the top of the stairs, the team had placed a frequency counter, and when I went past it, the digital readout jumped from 399 to 575 MHz. This happened several more times through the early morning hours of the all-night vigil.

The closed-circuit camera recording the hallway and stairwell from the top of the stairs distinctly displayed interference and then returned to normal, all while no-one was in the vicinity. Likewise, several times throughout the night the camera in the nursery was overcome with a fuzzy sort of interference and drifted so badly at times that it would completely lose the signal before returning to normal. It was explained to us that being on a closed circuit, the cameras were unaffected by interference from nearby appliances or wiring.

Although we had planned on going to bed that night as usual, it was a little nerve-racking to know that virtual strangers were monitoring our house from within. Tony, not being the night owl that I am, gave in and went to bed about 2:00 a.m. I, on the other hand, was incredibly interested in what the equipment might pick up and didn't want to miss anything.

I watched the monitors with the skeleton crew of television staff that remained through the night, and talked about the experiences in the house. We tried to come up with ways to get activity or gauge a reaction. One of our ideas was to leave a few shiny objects as gifts on the living room coffee table. We then sprinkled the table with baby powder, so that we could detect any movement of the items that might occur.

Throughout the rest of the night, however, our attention was focused on the activity that took place with the oscilloscope and cameras at the top of the stairs. By morning, after the rest of the team had returned to the house, we had all but forgotten about checking the coffee table and the items we had left there. When we finally remembered to check the table, we noticed that one of the items had slid slightly in the powder. We were unable to confirm that this discovery was paranormal, though, because others had been in the house and may have moved it themselves.

Morning had come with no more significant activity, and after the final interviews were done everyone went home. I remember Kerry's interview; the things he said were a little startling. He claimed that in his twenty years of experience and the 850 cases he'd been involved in, he had never come across anything quite like the activity in our house. He spoke of the fourteen straight hours he had just spent in the house and that some of the attacks on Tony were quite frightening. He referred to our case and the experience as "interesting, exciting, and potentially dangerous."

TWENTY

# THE CLEANSING

The night after the television crew left, we were approached by an individual who felt she had some insight into our experiences and wanted to help us through a shaman-led cleansing. She explained that she had a shaman guide on the other side, one that she had worked with for years and that he had never led her astray. She was more or less a vehicle for him to work through.

She seemed sincere in her desire to help us rid our house of the negativity that had become a part of our life. She had already gained input from this guide that told her there were things in the house that didn't belong. Her offer to help seemed to come at an opportune time, since Tony looked like a scratching post after the previous nights. It seemed like each time the television crew, came the attacks were more frequent and more severe.

We agreed to let her do the cleansing, and she announced that she would have to prepare. She would return to her hotel room for a few hours and come back after dinner. She alerted us to the fact that she would be dressed in traditional Native American garb.

Although we talked with her for quite some time and she seemed very sincere, we really had very little idea what to expect. A few hours later, she returned, beautifully dressed from head to toe in a white leather dress adorned with beads, turquoise, silver, and feathers. I remember heading to the front door when the doorbell signaled her arrival. When I saw her, I turned to Tony, who was standing close by with an "Oh my God, what did we get ourselves into?" expression on his face.

She looked absolutely out of place, and I wondered how many of the neighbors saw her and what they thought of her. She looked like she was dressed in an elaborate Halloween costume, exquisite as it was.

Once in the house, she told us that she had made her own dress, as was traditional, and that everything that adorned it had significance. She went on to explain more details of what she was going to do. She mentioned that the house might become quite active as she was going to ask the spirit, or spirits, to move on. The house already felt very heavy and somewhat menacing, but I'm not too sure this wasn't simply my mind playing tricks on me. I was getting rather apprehensive about what we were going to do.

Since we had already put the baby down in the nursery for the night and didn't want to wake or move him, we decided that we would stay in the upstairs hallway to be on the lookout for any activity that might be near him. This also seemed to be a good location because there had been a lot of activity in and around the area at the top of the stairs.

We watched as she smudged the house, burning sage to balance the energy and soften the spirits. She did this from front to back and top to bottom. We then set up an analog recorder, lit a candle to set on the floor in the center of the hallway, turned out all the lights in the house, and took our places, sitting cross-legged around the candle. Our instructions were to join hands and not break the circle, no matter what. Our shaman-led medium said a few prayers and told us to follow her lead.

For some of the time she meditated. At other times she enlisted our help by asking us to join her in saying the Lord's Prayer. At one point, she was able to sense an older gentleman. He had apparently been in the house for quite some time, unbeknownst to us. She described him as a perfect gentleman. She also became aware of a woman hiding from us, and from her. She told us that these two needed to go, to cross over and into the light.

Before long, she described a seemingly frightened young girl in a corner of the nursery. I knew this was Sallie, and felt bad that she was so scared. The medium asked if we wanted Sallie to go with the others.

I was unsure how to answer this. On one hand, I felt that there was probably a better place waiting for Sallie on the other side. On the other hand, I didn't want to make her leave, since she had seemed so needy and so comfortable with our family. I also felt obligated to her in some way. I had often wondered if Taylor had been prone to SIDS and if Sallie woke him in the middle of the night to remind him to breathe. If this was the case, I owed her Taylor's life—how could I just throw her out of our house?

When I voiced this dilemma, we were given the option to let her stay for now. If we ever wanted her to go, she could be removed another time. Tony and I agreed to let her stay, and the medium and I invited her into our circle. Strangely enough, I soon felt the cool sense of her energy and presence in my lap.

Then there were more prayers asking the gods for protection, light, and guidance. The medium asked us to help visualize each room filled with white light. She started in the kitchen, and as if she was talking to someone in a trance, she calmly and slowly guided us from room to room. Visualize a light in the center of the room: God's light. Visualize the light getting bigger and brighter...visualize the warmth of the light... visualize the warm bright light filling the room from top to bottom... visualize the light going into the corners and out the windows and doors.

We visualized this same light in the dining room, living room, and in the hallway coming up the stairs. The process took about six to eight minutes for each room. We filled the nursery, the bathroom, and then the utility room at the back of the house. Somewhere in between filling the rooms with light, the medium helped the man cross over. He didn't understand why he had to go, but he went just the same. Filling the upstairs hall with light seemed to be more of a challenge. Even more of a challenge was the female figure; she was stubborn and refused to leave.

We spent quite a while working on the hallway and trying to move the light into the master bedroom. All the while, the medium seemed to be having a turbulent time convincing and then demanding that this woman spirit leave the house. I can remember not being able to see very well at this point, because the candle had burned down close to the level of the wax and there was very little flame left. We could not break the circle to pour out any of the wax and make the flame burn brighter.

While the medium worked through her shaman guide to cross the female over, Tony began making slight, painful sounds. I suddenly felt his hand grip mine tightly. It was very apparent that he was being attacked in some way. The medium confirmed this, and shared with us that the stubborn female was angry and taking it out on Tony. She told him to be strong. We again started to fill the room with light.

For me, this was tough to do. I am not sure if it was simply the energy of the spirit in the room with us that wasn't allowing us to do what we intended, or that I was so distracted and concerned by Tony's intermittent spasms of pain. He was holding my hand so tightly that it felt lifeless and cold.

We worked on filling the hall and master bedroom with light for almost thirty minutes. Several times, the medium asked Tony if we needed to stop. She had become gravely aware of the pain and attacks he was enduring as he described a burning sensation across the top of his shoulders. Each time however, his reply was, "No, I'm okay. Keep going."

He was focused on completing the task we had all set out to do. He wanted it to be done, once and for all. He knew the female spirit was

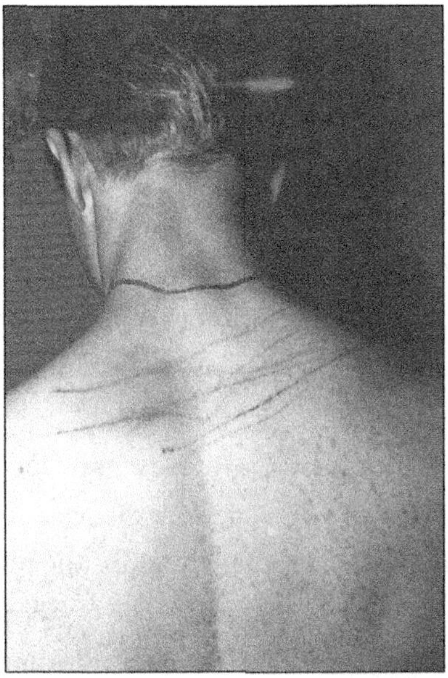

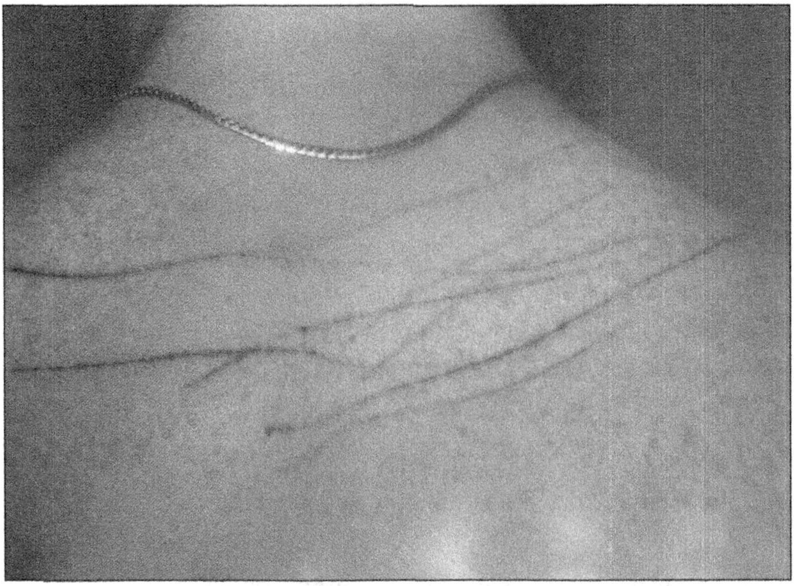

angry, and leaving the job undone would only allow her to come back at him or our family with a vengeance.

As the medium continued her attempts to convince the female to leave, telling her that she had people waiting for her, the female started to give in and get closer to the light. She would then get scared or angry and back away, thinking we were trying to trick her. We would repeat the prayers we had said so many times that evening and work at filling the two rooms with white light. This ebb and flow took place several more times.

Eventually, it seemed that the female gave in. We said a closing prayer and thanked God and his angels for the help, strength, and protection they had given us. We sat quietly, hands still entwined, waiting, listening, and feeling for a sense of change. The candle was almost entirely extinguished and the recorder had stopped recording almost forty-five minutes before.

Tony reported that the attacks on his back had stopped; that although the burning continued, he wasn't getting hit anymore. He and the medium also reported feeling a lighter sense in and about the house. After several more minutes, we loosened our grip on each other, and stretched out our cramped legs to stand up. By then it was rather late; the whole process had taken almost two hours.

We turned on the light to inspect Tony's shoulders, which were covered with eight distinct and fairly deep scratches, some of which were twelve inches or more in length. We tended to his wounds and checked on the baby before moving to the living room downstairs. There we sat for a short time and discussed what might be expected over the next few days. The medium warned that there might be residual energy flying around for awhile, but that after a few days, it would dissipate. Then we could be sure our job had been completed successfully. The medium left us with some instructions on smudging in order to maintain the calm energy in the house, gave us her business card in case we needed to call her, and said another prayer for us and our protection before she left. All was well, we thought.

## TWENTY-ONE

# TONY'S PERSPECTIVE

*Because Tony's experiences and perceptions of the activity we encountered during our stay were so different from my own, it is necessary to be aware of this and fitting to hear about it from his perspective.*

Honestly, that house scared the hell out of me. At one point, I truly thought I was going to need an exorcist. I constantly feared for myself and my family's safety. I was worried that if the spirit got tired of messing with me, it would go after someone else, perhaps even Taylor. After all, he would not be able to tell us if something was wrong or was harming him. I worried every moment of the day for his safety.

After several months of activity, my mother and I tried to tell Debra about our concerns, but she had such a different view on it and a strong desire to experience it that she never really listened. Every time I brought it up to her, we argued about the difference between her perspective on the situation and mine. She would say things like, "How could we just leave this little girl without helping her?"

I was also very insecure at that point of my life, and although it seems silly for me to admit it, I allowed myself to be led by Debra's choices. She is a headstrong woman who focused on logical arguments, and if she did not want to leave the house, nothing I could say would change her mind. Each time I voiced my concerns, her reasons for staying would override my pleas to leave. She simply did not take me seriously. Finally, I just gave up trying to get through to her and decided to live with the experiences, quickly realizing that my days in that house were going to be long and lonely.

We really did not have the money to move. We had incurred expenses when we moved into that house and soon there were more expenses to make it our home: curtains, blinds, wallpaper, and a washer and dryer, among other things. The daily expenses of living in such an old, poorly insulated house added to the difficulties.

My experiences continued to get worse and became more threatening. I remember thinking of cases such as the one that had occurred in Amityville where the situation and claims were similar to what I was going through. It scared me that so many of these situations ended in the killing of innocent family members. In the years prior to living in that house, I wondered how anything like that could happen, how no one could notice there was a problem before it escalated to such a devastating level. As the weeks and months passed, however, I felt the evil wrap around my every thought and emotion. I began to understand how someone could be driven to unwanted actions. I prayed to God every day not to let that happen to me.

While living in that house, I struggled terribly with many emotions and insecurities. Realizing that Debra didn't have any fear of the paranormal activity around us, I felt like less of a man for being so fearful. Certainly I was the man of the house, the strength of the family who shouldn't show fear when others did not. With this in mind, I put up a strong front and hid my emotions from everyone.

There were a lot of internal conflicts and discussions with myself that made me wonder what was wrong with me. Although these conflicts pushed me toward just leaving my family and walking away from them, something kept me focused on their safety and my responsibilities.

Keeping it together was not easy since I questioned my own sanity and state of mind nearly every day. It was very difficult to understand what was happening to me and around me. It wasn't something I could casually talk about with a co-worker, or sit down with a family member and ask their opinion. The mere mention of the word "paranormal" was taboo in this part of the country. If people were interested in the topic, they hid it. I knew my experiences weren't run-of-the-mill, and I shuddered to think what people would think of me if I shared them.

The only person I could talk to was Deb. She was very biased in her views and fascinated with the possibilities of the experience. The bigger problem seemed to be that while I told her there was something evil in the house, her own experiences presented something innocent. She saw no problems, wasn't afraid, and there were times that I just couldn't understand why she wasn't more concerned. If the roles had been reversed, I would have gotten her out of the house as soon as I could.

The experience with the television show brought mixed feelings, too. Although we argued horribly every time the *Sightings* team came into our house, deep down I really hoped they would bring us answers. Somewhere along the way, I also wanted someone to realize that some terrible thing was in our house and help us to live in peace again. However each time they came, the activity escalated. I dreaded the focus on me and the focus on the scratches that would appear on my body. I felt like a science experiment and a freak.

There were times that we would go without any activity at all, often a few weeks or a month or more. Although this was a relief, it threw me back onto the emotional roller coaster that happened each day. I would again begin thinking that there had been something wrong with me all along. I was exhausted and hallucinations seemed to be the only reasonable explanation for my experiences. On the other hand, I knew there was something in our home. Debra was very aware of the paranormal activity and had experienced it herself. I just couldn't understand how and why our experiences could be so different.

Almost from the beginning, Tony's experiences were very different from mine. Was it the fact that he and I viewed our situation from two very different perspectives? My perspective was from a lifetime interest in and desire to know more about ghosts and the paranormal and his perspective was from childhood fears, borne in the closet the night he saw the white ghastly face and bony hands peering out from behind the door. I had often felt that his religious upbringing and Catholic schooling played a huge role in how he interpreted his experiences. While I saw non-threatening activity, he saw the possibility of demons and their trickery.

Several years after moving out of the house, I began to realize he had not shared with me many of the things he had encountered there. Looking back, my reaction to any experience had been logical, but often without considering other paranormal possibilities. I know there were many occasions when I must have seemed skeptical of his personal experiences. Over the years, there have been many times where I have been disappointed in myself for not believing some of the events that Tony had witnessed and experienced. It is the worst aspect of having lived in that house and it is also my deepest regret.

Working nights and attempting to sleep during the day was never easy for Tony. He never got a full night's rest. I knew that getting only a few hours of sleep a night could lead to hallucinations; I often told him that his tired mind and body might be contributing to the things he felt, saw, or heard. I ultimately chalked it up to his imagination running away with crazy thoughts and blowing things out of proportion. Not that I thought he was making things up, because I knew he truly believed what he was experiencing was real.

My attempts to dismiss his experiences as mere hallucinations seemed like a reasonable explanation. This led Tony to doubt himself and his experiences. It wasn't long before he stopped sharing his concerns with me. He didn't want me, or others, to think he was losing his mind or had some other kind of psychological problem.

He must have felt very alone, living through experiences that he couldn't control or understand. In the years since leaving the house and continuing to investigate it, I have realized the distinct negativity and demonic nature of what was there and the danger that existed. Tony knew in his heart that there was something bad in the house, but didn't know how to protect himself or his family from it. His only hope was that it would not escalate or harm his wife and child. His prayers and belief in God's grace was the only thing that kept him from losing his mind.

As the years have passed, I have learned about many events and experiences that Tony endured without my support, assistance, or understanding. Hearing the details of these tormenting events makes me feel worse for not being there for him. I continue to realize how agonizing his life must have been.

One of the first things he remembers telling me was the scratching he could hear in the walls. For him it seemed to be constant—something trying to get through the walls and make itself heard throughout the day. I do not remember the sounds at all and I probably chalked it up to squirrels or something else more plausible. He never brought it up again, even though the sounds occurred more often and became more distinct as time went on.

I do remember the nights he heard what sounded like running up and down the stairs. We just assumed that it was one or both of our cats playing. Of course, this theory was comforting to the both of us until the night that Tony stepped out into the hall to investigate and discovered it was definitely not our pets. It was something unseen, perhaps a ghost.

As noted earlier, Tony had the hardest time getting enough sleep in the house. I often thought the sounds and voices he heard were the side effects of a lack of sleep. It was only a few months after we moved in that he began hearing strange conversations, even though the voices seemed distant and unclear. As the days and months passed, these sounds got louder and it was easy to determine that they were indeed voices.

For a while, he asked if I heard them too, but I never did. I'm sure this was daunting and made him question his sanity even more. Eventually, he stopped asking me about them, fearing that I would think he was hearing voices that were not there. Over the years, he mentioned that it often sounded as if many people were talking or whispering to each other. They often seemed to be talking at the same time or over each other and in the same room with him.

Although he was often able to detect several distinct and separate conversations, he was never able to make much out of the snippets of words or phrases. These voices seemed audible to him only for a few seconds before disappearing completely. There was no way to replay it or for him to determine what he actually heard.

Although he often heard the voices throughout the day and in different rooms, he usually heard them as he was drifting off to sleep. His focus was not on things around him, and certainly not on deciphering the strange voices. On the edge of sleep, it was very difficult to react or respond. This made it even harder to determine what he was hearing.

As weeks turn into months, the voices seemed to gather strength and remained inaudible, except for a few specific words. Sometimes they did become a little clearer to him. He slept even less since he knew he might hear the voices and tended to lay awake, listening for them.

Just before moving from the house, he reported that the room sounded like it was constantly full of people talking. Once, he heard a phrase spoken by a woman who was manifesting in front of his eyes at the end of the bed. She said, 'I'm gonna get..." and then faded out. The combination of these ominous words with a black gloved hand reaching toward him seemed a definite threat and this certainly concerned him.

## FULL AND PARTIAL APPARITIONS

Tony was now seeing full-bodied apparitions that (except for the little girl in the kitchen) scared him even more. Since they always seemed to look like me, he found them even more disturbing. I think he really did want to see the experiences as I did—innocent and, for the most part, not harmful. However, something told him what was going on was not benign. The more he reflected on the events, the more he was sure there was a demonic force in the house. Even though this force presented itself as a little girl and then as a woman who looked like me, he was sure it wasn't innocent.

I wasn't aware that Tony thought these apparitions were demonic, but I did believe he saw them and I was excited. I was intrigued by the idea that there might be more than one spirit in the house and I was thrilled with the opportunity to communicate with them.

One day he called me at work shortly after 11:00 a.m. He had been trying to sleep when he saw something odd near the foot of the bed. This was the second time he had seen it. Weeks earlier, he had experienced a similar situation that had started out as non-threatening but ended traumatically.

Eventually, I became aware of the terror that Tony was experiencing and the toll it took on him. He became distant and very distracted as he struggled to understand, accept, and deal with the situation. Although I did not pick up on this for quite a while, I soon realized that he was not himself for days afterward, which was excruciating to watch. At one point, we had agreed that I would be more open to believing him and understanding what he was going through if he let me know when these experiences were happening.

I also thought being close to the activity might actually deflect some of it, since it seemed very little of the events were witnessed by more than one person. In fact, when any of us attempted to get involved in the activity, it often stopped dead in its tracks. So the second time Tony saw the telltale signs of a spirit apparition forming near the end of the bed and heard the familiar female voice whispering, he called me at work.

Whispering to me as if it were a big secret, he described how the many voices seemed louder than before. As we continued talking, he described what the dust-like particles floating and forming in front of the window and near the foot of the bed looked like. After three or four minutes of telling what he was seeing and hearing, the activity seemed to come to a halt. We hung up and I finished work. When I arrived home shortly after 5:00 p.m., Tony reported that no more activity had occurred after our conversation.

Tony always got the brunt of the extreme activity and we thought it interesting that the activity stopped when we spoke on the phone. It gave us hope that we could thwart the malicious spirit by standing against it together.

Later that evening as he got ready for work, he seemed very tired. When I asked him about it, he said that he had not gotten any sleep that morning. He was afraid that something might happen while he slept. He was even afraid to close his eyes while he washed his hair. He felt like an easy target, a sitting duck with an ambush waiting to happen. This fear was always on his mind so he was often distressed before going to sleep.

## HAND PRINTS

Tony's fears about things happening while he slept was not unfounded. Several months before the *Sightings* group began investigating our experiences, Tony was attacked in a different way. Originally, he had thought it was a dream. The only odd thing about this dream was that he never saw a face and just assumed it was me.

At one point, however, he told me that incidents were happening more frequently and while he was awake. As I listened to his description of the events, I was shocked. He told me about the pressure he would feel on his upper thighs and the feeling of cold hands moving up his legs.

A few nights after he told me about this, I felt him violently shaking me out of a sound sleep to tell me it was happening again. As he lay next to me, he could feel pressure on his lower body. He could not see anything there, but he also could not move his legs. Realizing that something seemed to be on top of him, I sat up and forcefully yelled at whoever or whatever it was to get off of him. I know I yelled loudly several times and later wondered what the neighbors thought. Within a minute or so, Tony reported that the pressure was finally gone.

Upon inspection of his legs and thighs, we found red marks shaped like handprints on his upper and inner thighs. The red marks then morphed into bruises. I wondered how this happened and doubted that something paranormal had been responsible for such an act. I could tell from the location of the handprints that Tony could not have made them himself. They pointed upward in such a way that it would have been impossible for him to fake. We came to realize that he was being attacked while he slept. In the morning, the bruising was completely gone.

I wondered how many times this had occurred, leaving no telltale signs of physical harm or damage to validate his experiences. It was horrifying to think that someone was messing with him and that he hadn't realized it. I wondered how long it would have continued if he had not been honest with me.

After I realized the nature of some of his experiences, I finally began to understand that Tony was going through more than I had been willing to admit, and perhaps more than he had actually let on. I knew I needed to be more supportive and not only listen to him more, but actually hear him. A united front against whatever was affecting him seemed to be our only defense. Of course, it was easier to decide that than to actually accomplish it.

## POSSESSION

As Tony and I bonded as a force against whatever was in the house, it stepped up its efforts and began working from within Tony. Sometimes I didn't recognize it for what it was. For instance, I generally attributed his changing moods to a lack of sleep. I didn't consider that there could be evil spirits in our own home, and I was not aware of all the signs I needed to look for.

I didn't recognize the first sign as it was happening. Several weeks later, I realized that specific event mimicked a possession. At the time, I dismissed it completely and didn't think about it until after we had moved out of the house. Now I wonder if some influence had been clouding my thoughts.

This event took place in the living room on a weekend afternoon. We had spent a leisurely morning playing with Taylor. He was now upstairs taking a nap while we relaxed on the couch. I was sitting at the far end of the couch while Tony stretched out lengthwise, his feet within a few feet of my hand. I don't remember what we were watching, though the television was on.

Tony had fallen asleep as he often did on the weekends after his tormented attempts to sleep during the week. It was probably easier to fall asleep when someone else was in the house.

Without warning, Tony sat up. He then stared me straight in the face and, in a strange voice, said, "He's mine!" Confused by this behavior, I looked at him dumbfounded and waited for him to say something more. He remained motionless for several moments, but said nothing. Then, he simply lay back down and remained quiet for quite some time.

I tried to figure out exactly what was so weird about what had just happened. Certainly the manner in which he sat up and the sound of his voice struck me as odd. While his voice did sound like him, it was cold and disconnected, even mechanical.

Since I thought he was just talking in his sleep, I wondered what he might have been dreaming about. Who was he talking about? Perhaps he had been dreaming about someone wanting to take Taylor, and his reply was, "he's mine!" This explanation suited me just fine. Perhaps because I didn't want to think about other implications, perhaps I wasn't being allowed to think about them.

Weeks later, I thought how strange this was and how strange he sounded. The way he moved and spoke just didn't seem like him at all. What if it wasn't Tony who spoke to me? Was the word "him" actually referring to Tony and not the baby? What if something in him was challenging me and claiming Tony for itself? Was it the same woman Tony had seen so many times? Had she been trying to gain his affection? Had she been the one attacking him in the bedroom when he slept?

I remember asking Tony his opinion. He simply said, "I don't know what to think." We never discussed it again, which makes me wonder why I didn't pursue it further. Maybe I didn't have enough information and had put it on the back burner until something else triggered thoughts that made me reconsider it? Had I been influenced to ignore what my gut was telling me? All I know is that it wasn't like me not to explore this theory further. It didn't come back to me until years later.

## DEAD CAT

I now believe the event was the beginning of the turbulent feelings Tony had toward me. As he later described it, he'd been having very angry and harmful feelings toward me on a daily basis. He described having hateful thoughts when he saw me. He remembers how hard he fought the desire to hurt me. To this day he wonders what stopped him from actually doing so.

One day, he called me at work and told me he had trouble sleeping that morning. After some general conversation, he mentioned how uneasy he felt and he suggested it might be time for us to move because he felt that someone was going to get badly hurt. "And I think it's going to be you," he said. He described that I was the focus of anger and rage coming from the spirits in the house. We hung up the phone and I was distracted for the rest of the day, trying to make sense of his words.

It just did not make sense. I had not been the one physically attacked and I was not having trouble sleeping. I didn't hear the voices or fear the dark. Tony seemed to be the focus of the spirits in our home, not me. Once again, I did not heed the warning and I chalked it up to his growing paranoia and lack of sleep.

His feelings of aggression continued to grow. He became argumentative, short on patience, and his temper flared often. Unaware of its depth or origin, I blamed this on a lack of sleep, and the anger on our arguments each time *Sightings* came back to the house. I'm not even sure how aware Tony was of what was going on, since he found himself confounded by his actions and thoughts.

One of these instances had to do with what I assume was a neighborhood cat. There had been two significant and horrifying experiences in the house concerning cats and these experiences were very different. One was the unfortunate incident with the cat in the dryer described in chapter 10. The second I didn't find out about until we moved from the house.

Tony had gotten home just before I awoke. We both went about the morning as usual—I got ready and left for work while Tony tried to unwind before going to sleep. Years later, he described this day and he sat on the couch downstairs with terrible thoughts about me.

He remembers getting a bowl of cereal shortly after I left. As he turned to put the milk away, he saw a cat drinking out of the bowl. He did not recognize the cat and had no idea how it had gotten into the house. Seeing the cat drinking from his bowl completely infuriated him. He took a few steps closer, angrily pulled the French knife from the countertop holder next to the stove, and stabbed the cat.

He remembers being very proud of the act. Knowing how much of a cat lover I was, he was excited about leaving it there for me to see when I returned home. Without a care in the world, he then went into the living room and sat on the couch, his feelings turning more hateful and wretched. "I'll just stab her, too," he thought.

His thoughts continued to reinforce his mood: "I can't stand the way she looks at me. It's her fault we're here. I can't stand her nagging. I can't stand looking at her." Eventually, he made detailed plans to kill me upon my return. "If she walks by me, I'm just gonna slit her throat." He remained in this state all morning with the dead cat in the kitchen.

At some point in the early afternoon, he went up stairs to dress for the day and eventually left the house to pick up Taylor, who was staying with Tony's parents. He returned a few hours later feeling more like himself. He cleaned up the dead cat so I wouldn't see it and thought, "Oh, God. What was I thinking?"

## OVER THE RAILING

Two days after he killed the cat and planned my demise, there was another attempt to do bodily harm to me. Tony reports the following:

"I wasn't thinking about anything in particular, just going about my day. I had just gotten out of bed and was going to head downstairs. As I approached the doorway, I was suddenly struck from behind with great force. It felt like someone had run up behind me and shoved me as hard as they could. My feet left the floor, I was airborne, and flung towards the upstairs railing, which was about three feet in front of me. My upper thighs hit the railing and my knees, legs, and feet inadvertently knocked out three of the rungs below it. It scared the crap out of me and to this day, I don't know what stopped me from going over the top of the railing and going headfirst down the stairs.

"Startled and nervous, I made my way down the stairs, holding the railing as I did so. When I reached the living room, I sat on the couch, afraid to move, for the rest of the day. I flinched at every sound I heard.

"I called Debra at work, hoping the comfort of a familiar voice would relieve the feeling of being alone. Although I didn't tell her my most recent experience, I did tell her that I had a feeling that I just couldn't shake, a feeling that someone was going to get hurt, and that I thought it was going to be her. Then I told her that we really needed to get out of the house. Her reply was that we would talk about it when she got home, and I feared that my words, once again, fell on deaf ears.

"I remained in the living room until she arrived home later that day. I told her about the threatening event I had experienced that morning. I realized that this time she had taken my concern seriously. Perhaps there was something in my voice when I called her, or perhaps it was something I said. Whatever it was, it motivated her."

I remember Tony's phone call and that I was distracted by it. I knew that something was very wrong. Tony had never been so adamant about moving. I knew there was more to this than just a call out of the blue to suggest a move. I couldn't wait to talk to him and find out what had led to the desire to move.

When he told me about the morning's experience, I was immediately concerned. If there was that much force or energy acting against us, what else would Tony or anyone else suffer? I wondered why he was pushed with such force, and what stopped him from falling over the railing. I couldn't help but think it must have been some sort of angelic protection or intervention that saved him from a tragic accident. If this was truly the case, I didn't think we should take it for granted.

Over the previous six months, Tony had done a few things in a desperate attempt to help himself and understand what he was going through. He had started talking on a weekly basis with a priest at the St. Benedict Abbey that was located on the north end of town. Although he left each session feeling much better, within days he was again feeling oppressed and unlike himself. The anger, hateful feelings, and thoughts all crept back in.

Through these weekly and sometimes bi-weekly sessions, Tony told the priest much of what went on, but held back some of the more personal things. He chose not to share information about the scratches, voices, noises in the walls, his mood swings, hatred for me, and the fear that he felt for his family.

Shortly before we finally moved, the priest had planned a trip to the house in order to better understand what Tony had described to him. He also talked of blessing the house, but before this took place, the priest died suddenly. We'll never know if the timing of his death had anything to do with what was going on at our house.

Shortly after he began seeing the priest, Tony began to share some of his more grueling experiences with me. In turn, I realized that much of what he was experiencing was not just in his head. Although I had not known many of the details, I had witnessed the changes in his personality and some of the activity myself. I knew things had been changing, but couldn't put my finger on exactly what it was or why it was happening. As he continued sharing some of his experiences, it became easier to understand why I noticed changes in him.

I also realized that he was not in control of these changes. While I considered that he might be acting as an agent of a poltergeist, I dismissed this thought because that typically takes place with young adolescents and Tony was twenty-nine years old. Additionally, I had seen the bruising and the looks of terror on his face. I felt his heart pounding, heard the fear in his voice, and witnessed the unnatural mood swings.

Eventually I realized there was something more to our haunting than anyone had originally thought or understood. Tony and I agreed that I would try to help him as best I could. I would listen more and give more credence to his personal experiences. It was about this time that I became very uncomfortable with the spirit and activity in our home, and I became more concerned for his safety as well as that of our family.

After months of extra support from the priest and me, he no longer felt so isolated and alone. Not only did his love for me seem to win out over the horrible thoughts being put into his head, he also realized that leaving the house washed away some of the emotions he had felt while in the house. We spent a great deal of time at his mom and dad's house and on outdoor excursions with Taylor. Although we didn't fully understand what we were up against, Tony and I tried to thwart the activity and oppression that seemed to focus on him.

Was something lashing out at him even harder because we made it more difficult for it to control Tony's thoughts and emotions? Looking back and knowing what we know now, there was something more than just benign spirits at work in that house. It seemed that our united front raised the stakes and Tony became even more of a target.

The little prankster and child-like activity dwindled and almost disappeared completely until *Sightings* returned. And although there were non-threatening parlor tricks on each successive visit, more malicious activity also became prominent. The scratches were significantly more numerous during each visit and whoever or whatever facilitated the unnatural activity seemed to take pleasure in baffling the investigative team.

What took place after the team left was more focused on creating havoc in Tony's mind and physical condition. Over several prior months, I definitely noticed the lack of sleep, the inability to eat, and the fear and anger Tony displayed did not reflect the man I loved and had married. There were the complaints of feeling sick as well as several emergency room visits. Tony would feel pain in his chest and arm, along with other life-threatening symptoms. The battery of tests done during and after each visit ultimately revealed nothing wrong with him. None of it made sense and for some reason, I was finally able to see that it was simply adding to Tony's torment.

Not only were we dealing with unknown and unwanted changes in our life and relationship, we were also trying to understand the more treacherous paranormal activity that had seeped into our home. The medical bills were piling up and Tony missed a lot of work putting our finances in a precarious place. There was also the concern that something might be medically wrong with him, which weighed heavily on us.

After the incident where Tony was pushed toward the railing, I realized it was the last straw and that the situation was very grave. Tony and our family were in danger and I agreed with him—it was time to leave the house.

The next day, we got a list of rental houses and that evening, we began looking at them. Tony's mom did everything in her power to help us and within two weeks, we were packed and ready to go. We moved to a house only a few blocks away on October 31, 1994.

We informed Kerry Gaynor of our move and asked if he believed that the activity would stop. He did not give us the resounding yes we had expected. Instead, he explained that there were different types of hauntings. There were location hauntings and people hauntings. He went on to say that in a location haunting, the activity was generally localized to the dwelling or land. In the case of a person being haunted, we might never actually be free of the entity that affected Tony and our lives.

"Time will tell," he said. "It might take a couple of weeks, or it might take a couple of months before we know for sure." We thought we were done with the activity, but in early January 1995, we got our answer and it was certainly not the one we had hoped for.

# EPILOGUE

Over the course of a little more than a year and a half, we experienced enough to begin drawing conclusions about who or what we were dealing with. Sadly, they were based mostly on the events that I and others had witnessed rather than Tony's experiences which at the time seemed unlikely due to the sleep deprivation factor.

I had gone several months feeling that Sallie had grown warm and friendly to us, and I talked to her every evening as if she were in the room with me. I could swear there were times that I would feel or smell her presence. One night I even felt a cold presence, which I assumed was her, lay down next to me and cuddle close just as a frightened child in search for comfort would do. I felt that was a sign of her acceptance—I was a step-parent finally being acknowledged. There were also times in which I felt especially in tune with her, as if through telepathy she was telling me her thoughts and feelings.

In contrast, it was very easy to see that Sallie was not fond of my mother-in-law. Perhaps it was jealousy or what Sallie perceived as her overbearing nature when it came to the baby. The activity surrounding events when my mother-in-law was around was just too coincidental and seemed to clearly signal Sallie's displeasure.

There was a very human quality to my relationship with the spirit in the house. Most times when I made a request, Sallie seemed to make an effort to comply. She stopped acting up when my mother-in-law was visiting, she stopped waking the baby, and she lit fires in the lamp when excited or needing to make her presence known. These and other instances suggested that Sallie was capable of understanding and compliance, suggesting an intelligent spirit and real-time interaction with the surrounding area.

Barbara Connor told us during her first visit that Sallie "would gladly show off for us if we wanted her to" and just as a proud parent would, we tried asking for this a few times. More often than not, we would get what we asked for, but sometimes, in desperation for compliance, I would entice her participation as if trading favors: "I will let you play with my pearls if you turn out the lights." Like most young children, however, she only did these things when she felt like it.

More often than not, her antics were completely unsolicited but within the "comfort zone" of the witnesses. I do believe she enjoyed showing off, especially since her activity would steer the conversation in her direction. When it strayed, she would make her presence known again, as if to say "Hey, don't forget about me." I noticed this reaction to be reliable and the timing and level of activity suggested that she thrived on the attention.

Quite often, the activity in the house and around us was subtle; things could go unnoticed for hours and sometimes even days or weeks. Some things, I'm sure, went unnoticed completely. Often we would run across something out of the ordinary and not be able to determine when it had taken place. We began to question each other almost daily. "Did you put this here? Why did you move this? When did you do this?" It was an attempt to narrow down the time frame of the event, to associate it with other known activity, and perhaps even to correlate it to the moods or emotions that we had experienced or inflicted upon Sallie.

So much of my time and efforts went into trying to understand Sallie that I didn't see the possibility of something other than a human spirit being responsible for the activity and events in the house. I was too excited about communicating with spirits to be concerned with what sort of spirit or energy I was dealing with, and my motherly instincts to coddle a seven-year-old were primed with the birth of our newborn. Honestly, I don't think I was able to see much beyond what I wanted to see.

I also observed that when the activity we had attributed to Sallie would cease for short four- to ten-day durations, we initially wondered if she was gone for good, but soon realized that she would always resurface. We wondered where she went and why she became so inactive. It was also during these quiet periods that we would catch ourselves wondering why our minds were perceiving the things it did; were we both going mad or making things up? This emotional teeter-totter continuously forced us to re-process the available information, in order to realize the reality around us. This happened on a regular basis.

I don't understand why I questioned our experiences so deeply. Why was paranormal activity and interaction so hard to accept? I had looked for it all my life. Perhaps in not finding it sooner, I had begun to disbelieve the possibility existed.

Then there came the realization that what we were dealing with might not be an innocent little girl. By the end of our first year, we had realized from the Christmas photos that there were two distinct entities in our house. This was a significant time period, because this is the first time I honestly began considering some of the experiences Tony had shared with me acknowledging and that there might be more than a little girl in the house with us.

I took a giant step back, re-evaluated our situation through a broader perspective, and began to listen more to what Tony would tell me. As I did, I also tried to understand why our experiences were so significantly different. There had to be a reason.

Not only had Tony seen and heard another woman, two independent psychics were aware of another presence in the house. Coupled with the very nature of the harm that was coming to Tony, it seemed reasonable to assume that a spirit had some sort of vendetta against Tony. Maybe it was what he resembled or represented in the eyes of his spirit opponent. We even considered the idea that Tony was a reincarnation of this woman's husband, lost love, or even a foe. It was simply theory, however—none of which we have ever been able to corroborate with historical facts or evidence.

What did not make sense was why Tony was being enticed by this female and then attacked with physical injuries and force. Why would she do him harm if he was the object of her desire? Was it a fatal attraction thing, in which his denying her advances and her need to be acknowledged made her angry? Maybe it was a case of, "If I can't have him, no one will." Or was it more sinister than that? Did it simply want to ruin the bond that Tony and I shared or ruin him by influencing him to kill me? Actions and events seem to have suggested just that. Realistically, though, even this type of influence seemed to be too much and too powerful to be coming from a human spirit with a grudge.

From a slightly more sinister perspective, if the entity wanted us to stay in the house for a specific reason, and its first attempt was to entice us with the innocent Sallie, it didn't make sense for it to work so hard to remove me from the picture. I seemed to be an unwitting advocate in its goal of winning Tony over. Why, then, did it work so hard to wear him down? Why did it make so many attempts to tear our relationship apart? It simply didn't make sense, and was more reminiscent of demons and the way they work. I was won over easily; very accepting of what the entity originally presented to us. It was not able to convince Tony that what was in the house was good or innocent.

We often look back and wonder if the female entity actually entered with her own objectives. Then again, it may have been something more sinister from the beginning. We seemed to willingly accept the presence of a demon who encouraged us to open ourselves up to treachery and to the possibility of a terrible demise.

It really seemed, though, that something didn't want us (particularly Tony) in that house. After all, my murder at his hand would have taken both of us out of the picture. Why would a spirit work so hard to drive him crazy but offer me positive experiences? Was I a sacrificial lamb, something to add to Tony's confusion by challenging his thoughts and beliefs? Had I been so blind to the motives of the spirit(s) that I had grossly misjudged their actions and allowed myself to be easily manipulated?

Once we realized there was more than one entity in the house, the level of activity changed. It became more vicious and less playful. Was this because our concerns were focused more on impending dangers rather than on Sallie, or that we had stopped accepting the idea that she had been responsible for all the experiences and activity? Had whatever appeared as the little girl finally realized the game was up? Recent research supports the idea that there never was a Sallie. So "Sallie" could very well have been the demon in its earliest manifestation.

They say that hindsight is wonderful, but in this case, we still don't have the answers or enough of an understanding of the situation to have chosen a different path. The only thing we know for sure is that there was a significant negative presence in that house, one that lashed out at Tony for reasons unknown. It was one that created danger, infiltrating the mind and thoughts of its victims. As the years have passed and others have experienced the diabolical aspects, I have come to understand more of the events that Tony experienced and the forces that existed unseen around us.

I worried that we wouldn't make it through such turbulent times and wouldn't end up growing old together as we had planned. I feared that we might not be able to raise Taylor in an unbroken home. I prayed that against all odds we would somehow come out of our situation and remain the family we had hoped to be: a family filled with love, devotion, and each other.

What if the goal of the entity was even more sinister than we had ever thought? Over the years, my mind has reflected on the day Tony sat straight up on the couch, looked me in the eye, and said, "He's mine!" Had this been the first sign of something working its way into Tony? Had there been a demonic force, quietly but effectively manipulating him to make him defenseless?

Since our departure from that house, I wonder what would have happened had we stayed just a few weeks or months longer. I have no doubt that something else was talking to me that day on the couch. Was it a warning of what was to come? Was someone about to get hurt? Would it have been me or Tony?

I wondered if Tony's resilience was more than this negative force anticipated. Had this been the reason it became so angry, so violent against him? When he was shoved toward the railing and somehow managed not to go over it, I can't help but wonder if some angelic force or spirit had intervened on our behalf. Was it an act of God, a guardian angel of sorts, who had knowledge of the evil and harmful intentions against us? If so, had these supportive spirits been trying from the start to tell us something? Or did they try to scare us out of the house in order to help us avoid possible torment?

We have to entertain the idea that our experiences were much more than a mere haunting, that there were not only human spirits in the house, but something negative or demonic. Did the negative force have a specific use for the human spirits? Is that why they were there? Was it possible that they were trapped or being used against their will?

Whatever it was, it worked hard to make Tony miserable and to wear him down. Ultimately, it made him extremely vulnerable. It also worked at putting a wedge between us. By midsummer 1994, it became apparent that this had been going on for the better part of our residency. At the time, things were getting worse. Much worse. It became quite clear that the safety of our family was at stake.

Tony and I left that house and for years were deeply concerned about ever going near it again. After several years, paranormal groups began investigating the house. They would often call to speak with us in order to gain an understanding of our experiences. They invited us to take part as they investigated the house. Tony declined, but I looked at these invitations as an opportunity to learn more. This level of participation led to Tony's concern that my going back to the house would stir up activity. He worried that one day I would bring something home, and the trouble would start all over again.

My involvement and that of others led to a renewed interest, which led to more reading and more research. We found no historical records supporting the idea that our spirit was that of a little girl. Had we been better researchers in the years we lived in the house, would we have heeded this information as the warning it should have been?

We also realized that demonic entities thrive on causing chaos, ruining relationships, and breaking down the bonds of friendship, love, and trust. This ultimately leaves people feeling alone, helpless, and forsaken. Who would ever think they, or someone they knew, would come up against a demon? Well, the more I knew about the signs of an encounter with a negative entity, the more certain I was that that was exactly what we were dealing with.

As I began to think about specific events, this theory began to seem more likely. My interest had been renewed, and I eventually returned to the house as a guest of other investigative groups to gain more knowledge of the entity that existed there. Over the course of time, I learned much. After approximately ten years of avoiding the house, Tony also gained an interest in confronting what had once been his greatest fear.

Today, we have no doubt that there was, and is, a demonic force in that house. This force knows how to play on fears, anxieties, and desires and it is utterly amazing that through all of this, Tony and I did not divorce. Those twenty months had been, and remain, the most confusing times of our life. All I can figure is that Tony's prayers, and the support from his God-fearing mother, kept him grounded enough to make it through each day. Additionally, the strength in the love we share for one another had reinforced a certain resilience against anything that attempted to come between us.

Over the years, Tony has told many people that he is torn regarding the spirits he encountered there. On one hand, he felt there might have been human spirits in the house. On the other, he also knows that demons appear to us as what they want us to see. All along, he felt this had been the case. First, it appeared as an innocent and harmless little girl, then it progressively tried other things to gain our acceptance. Now he believes that it was all just bait, a way for him to voluntarily allow "it" in and to welcome it.

Our experiences certainly didn't end when we moved from that house. However, each subsequent visit allowed us a more detailed understanding of the role it would play in our lives. Ironically, each visit also allowed us to be unknowingly manipulated by the entities that reside there. It once again baited us into trusting what we saw and heard. It played on our desire for answers and left us vulnerable.

As my fingers hit the keys on my computer to finally bring this book to reality, I am thankful that when all this started, I kept a journal. It's strange how we can forget things that seem to be so significantly cemented in our minds.

In the months after leaving the house, we began to live a normal life again. It was quiet and untainted by paranormal activity. Our relationship and marriage began to repair itself and we realized how thankful we were that we got out of the house when we did. We took solace in what we perceived as a new beginning. This solitude, however, did not last long.

Thanks to his strong belief in God and the support and guidance of prayers, Tony continues to win the ongoing battles he experiences in relation to that house. It is something that will always be a significant part of our lives.

## TO WRITE TO THE AUTHOR

If you wish to contact the author or would like more information about this book, please write to the author in care of Llewellyn Worldwide Ltd. and we will forward your request. Both the author and publisher appreciate hearing from you and learning of your enjoyment of this book and how it has helped you. Llewellyn Worldwide Ltd. cannot guarantee that every letter written to the author can be answered, but all will be forwarded. Please write to:


Debra Pickman
% Llewellyn Worldwide
2143 Wooddale Drive
Woodbury, MN 55125-2989


Please enclose a self-addressed stamped envelope for reply, or $1.00 to cover costs. If outside the U.S.A., enclose an international postal reply coupon.

Many of Llewellyn's authors have websites with additional information and resources. For more information, please visit our website at http://www.llewellyn.com.

# The Uninvited

## *The True Story of the Union Screaming House*

STEVEN LACHANCE WITH LAURA LONG-HELBIG

Steven LaChance was forever transformed by the paranormal attacks that drove him and his family from their home in Union, Missouri. When another family falls victim to the same dark entity, Steven returns to the dreaded house to offer aid and find healing.

Paranormal investigators, psychics, and priests are consulted, but no relief is found. The demon's presence—screams, growls, putrid odors, invisible shoves, bites, and other physical violations—only grow worse. LaChance chronicles how this supernatural predator infects those around it. But the one who suffers most is the current homeowner, Helen. When the entity takes possession and urges Helen toward murder and madness, LaChance must engage in a hair-raising battle for her soul.

*The Uninvited* is a true and terrifying tale of extreme haunting, demon possession, and an epic struggle between good and evil.

**978-0-7387-1357-1, 264 pp., 6 x 9** **$17.99**

---

To order, call 1-877-NEW-WRLD

Prices subject to change without notice

Order at Llewellyn.com 24 hours a day, 7 days a week!

# Don't Call Them Ghosts

*The Spirit Children of Fontaine Manse—A True Story*

KATHLEEN MCCONNELL

A true ghost story that will give you chills and warm your heart.

In 1971, the author and her family moved into a historic home known as the Fontaine Manse. Two days after moving in, she and her husband had an extraordinary experience that left them with no doubt that unseen residents occupied the house, too.

This is the true story of how Kathleen McConnell came to know and care for the spirit children who lived in the attic of the mansion—Angel Girl, Buddy, and Baby. From playing ball with Kathleen, to saving her son Duncan from drowning, the spirit children became part of the McConnell family in ways big and small. Finally, a heart-wrenching dilemma triggered an unexpected and dramatic resolution to the spirit children's plight.

*Don't Call Them Ghosts* is an inspiring story of the transcendent and lasting power of a mother's love.

**978-0-7387-0533-0, 264 pp., 6 x 9** **$13.95**